# Every Recorc

## A vinyl handbook

By

## Steve Carr

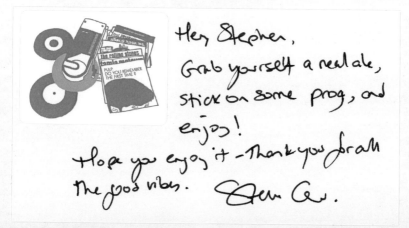

Hey Stephen,
Grab yourself a real ale,
stick on some prog, and
enjoy!
Hope you enjoy it - Thank you for all
the good vibes. Steve C.

Every Record Tells A Story – A Vinyl Handbook

First paperback edition printed 2020 in the United Kingdom

A catalogue record for this book is available from the British Library.

ISBN: 978-1-913663-38-4

Published by i40 Publishing

For more copies of this book, please email: i40publishing.gmail.com

Printed in Great Britain by Biddles Books Ltd, Kings Lynn, Norfolk

Cover design by Ruby Hartley

## About the Author

Steve Carr has been writing about music since 2012 on his blog *Every Record Tells A Story*, which has been read by over a million people. He appeared in the BBC4 Documentary *Pop Charts Britannia: 60 years of the Pop Charts* in which he demonstrated the long-lost skill of taping songs from the Top 40 onto cassette. His writing has appeared in publications including *Classic Rock* and *Record Collector*.

Almost exclusively a heavy rock fan in his teens, Steve now spends his days unlearning everything he thought he knew about music.

When not writing about music Steve works in London; his actual day job is providing advice to businesses. He lives in Leigh-on-Sea, on the Thames estuary with his wife, two children and two Burmese cats named Ziggy and Genie.

# WELCOME TO *EVERY RECORD TELLS A STORY'S* VINYL HANDBOOK

This is a guide to help make the most of your LPs, turntable and music collection.

Inside we will look at a selection of records and hear the stories behind them ...

We will discover why the Flaming Lips aren't stoned quite as often as you might think ...

... what links Black Sabbath to Gypsy jazz and talcum powder ...

... and the link between Gwyneth Paltrow and Brian Eno that isn't Coldplay.

Also, we will learn:

Why Bernie Taupin's mum is a tidying sort of hero ...

... why Chris de Burgh may have held a grudge against Nick Drake ...

... and why, despite what Journey may have you believe, there is no such place as South Detroit ...

... all while deciding whether to buy these records on vinyl or CD, what to look out for when buying second hand, and why it all matters ... or doesn't matter.

Because every record tells a story, doesn't it?

# Acknowledgements

When you start writing a music blog, you don't really know whether anyone is interested. It is therefore tremendously inspiring when writers stumble across your blog and take an interest. I would like to thank Push, Pete Paphides, Dave Reynolds, and Scott Rowley, all of whom provided encouragement, support, kind words and general good vibes early on.

Thank you also to Martin Colyer, Graham Jones, Daryl Easlea, Dave Collins, Ian Pile, Tim Elsenburg and Jana Carpenter of Sweet Billy Pilgrim, and Mike Ladano, all of whom I am sure share a great many features, the main one being that they are all very good people.

Thank you to Chris Marrable, Chris White, Jason Webster, Mark Salter, Eric Jenkins and Russ Harper for their entertaining friendship in general, especially when buying records and attending various gigs and festivals.

The UK's record shops continue to provide a bounty of treasure, and my collection is particularly indebted to Bob at Leigh Records, Paul at Carmel Records, Sandra and Pete at Five's in Leigh-on-Sea, Rough Trade East and West, and the many vendors at the Southend and Spitalfields Record Fairs. I have also been fortunate enough to find gems at the following record shops on my travels, all of which I would heartily recommend, and without whose help my record collection would be smaller and my house roomier:

- 101 Collectors Records, Farnham,
- Latimore Records, Seville,
- Rat Records, Camberwell,
- Flashback Records, Islington,
- Rob's Records, Nottingham,
- Henry's Records, Burton on Trent,
- Alan's Records, East Finchley,
- Discovery Records, Barnstaple
- Record Detective Shop, Palmers Green,
- Big Apple Records, Nottingham,
- Uptown Records, Spalding,
- Collectors Records Centre, Kingston Upon Thames
- Ben's Collectors Records, Guildford,
- Grey and Pink, Chester
- Reckless Records, Berwick St, London
- Vinyl Resting Place, Manchester
- Vinyl Guru, Newcastle
- Bulldog Music, Bletchley

- Rock Bottom Records, Whitstable
- Holt Vinyl Vault, Norfolk
- Sound Machine, Reading
- Vinylos and Discos Eternos, both in Lima, Peru.

Thank you to the cocktail bar at Hawksmoor for their mixing skills.

Thank you to John and Steve at i40 for their enthusiasm and belief.

And finally to Sarah, Logan and Rosie, who almost uncomplainingly put up with far more records and record players being in the house than they believe is strictly necessary. Without their encouragement and support my record collection would be twice the size.

# FOREWORD

As many other people would have done, I first encountered Steve Carr on *Pop Charts Britannia*, a 2012 BBC documentary about the history of the pop charts. It just so happened that I was *also* interviewed for the same documentary. Within ten minutes, it had become apparent that Steve and I had both been asked to participate for broadly similar reasons. He and I were there to talk about the spell that the weekly hit parade would cast on a certain sort of teenager, with their drive to collate, catalogue and immortalise the comings and goings of that week's hit parade.

Steve recorded Radio 1's weekly chart rundown every Sunday on his C90 cassettes. I was there by virtue of my short-lived home-made magazine Pop Scene, written on chip paper from my parents' fish and chip shop. It was pretty clear that had we been to the same school, Steve and I would have been friends. Or rivals. Or both. I recognised that much in Steve. I hastened to his blog Every Record Tells A Story, and once again, a sense of *deja vu* descended upon me: the enthusiastic levity of someone who conforms to the *Smash Hits* way of looking at pop. In other words, to implicitly recognise that the deeper your love of records and the people, the more license it gives you to relax into a perpetual state of equanimity and, sometimes, even arrant whimsy when discussing them.

Steve might not have even consciously realised it, but he's the product of the age of the high street record shop – a far cry from the modern era in which record shops survive by catering to the niche tastes of collectors. He's like most record collectors. He doesn't purport to be all-knowing. His guide to the first six Rolling Stones albums (featured here) was written out of a desire to find out if those early albums were actually any good. In doing so, he saved me the bother of having to do the same. By making them funny and companiable, he did what he does so well, turning an ostensibly dry research project into a pub chat you were delighted you overheard.

He's a great storyteller too: his accounts of the creation of classic albums such as Neil Young's *Tonight's The Night*, Pulp's *Different Class* and Jimi Hendrix Experience's *Are*

*You Experienced* immediately hasten you to the records they bring to life and reawaken them in the process. His theorem of 'Record Collector's Logic' is so uncomfortably true, it made me want to lie on the pavement like one of those people in the video to 'Just' by Radiohead. And he can introduce vital elements of jeopardy and suspense to the business of amassing the back catalogues of canonical artists: being challenged to buy the back catalogue of the Beatles and the 70s output of David Bowie for a pre-agreed budget otherwise have to incur Mariah Carey or Westlife-related forfeits.

Out here in the real world, these are the sorts of conversations actual music fans have between themselves. Sometimes, us music critics forget that. But, even though his writing has turned me on to hitherto unfamiliar masterpieces such as B.B. King's *Indianola Mississippi Seeds* and *Clube da Esquina* by Milton Nascimento, Steve isn't a music critic. Every Record Tells A Story is what he does when he isn't doing his "real" job. He wears his knowledge lightly. Which is what all experts should aspire to do. He once gave me a copy of Junior Parker's *The Outside Man*. I once gave him a copy of the Smithereens' *Especially For You*. I was a fan before I became a friend. And now that I'm a friend, I'm even more of a fan. I think you'll feel the same after you've read this book.

Pete Paphides, December 2019

# INTRODUCTION

*EVERY RECORD TELLS A STORY* is a music and vinyl blog that came into being at the beginning of 2012, just as the first green shoots of a resurgence of interest in vinyl and records began.

Sales of LPs had been steady (but low) for more than a decade, since the compact disc began its slightly bland creep into our homes, to be followed more invisibly, and with less interesting packaging, by the download. In the UK it took until 2011 for the vinyl format to connect with people again, evidenced by an uptick in sales of 44% year-on-year, albeit just 337,000 units. Yet this impressive increase in sales was modest compared to what happened next: by 2017 the BPI reported 4.1 million vinyl albums sold in the UK, truly a remarkable recovery in popularity for a format believed to be, if not dead, then certainly pining for the fjords just a decade before.

I rediscovered vinyl in 2011, part of that group of people who had been crying out for an excuse to reconnect with the format. A regular buyer of vinyl in the eighties, and CDs in the nineties, I had sold my cobweb-attracting record player in 2003, having become convinced the future of music was the iPod. Jack White had been telling me (and everyone else who was listening) "Your turntable's not dead" for some time, but it wasn't until 2011 I finally believed him.

I wanted to write about music, so started a blog, as was the fashion in 2012 for people who liked music and had too much time on their hands. I wrote about buying records again, and one or two things connected with the small readership, and *Every Record Tells A Story* morphed into a site that best reflected its title – telling stories about finding records and about the talented people that made them.

Early on, the BBC provided a confidence boost – they found something I wrote and asked me to appear in a BBC4 documentary about the pop charts. Both *the Guardian* newspaper and *Classic Rock* magazine saw something else, the former reprinting a piece about legendary heavy metal record shop Shades, and the latter publishing a piece about sexism in heavy rock music, and then about the ethics of Spotify.

I reviewed a gig in *Record Collector* magazine and before I knew what was happening, it had all escalated and I was a quasipart-time music writer and Radio 4 were on the phone asking me my opinion about the cultural significance of moving release dates from Monday to Friday (my hot take: no-one ever listened to 'Stairway To Heaven' and said "Great song, but I wish it had been released on a Tuesday.")

A few of my friends were swept along by the tide of interest in vinyl at the same time and together we muddled through the various challenges that we met along the way. Questions such as "Why is *that* copy of the LP £5, and *this* copy £100?" (answer: *that* one is scratched and is a repressing, and *this* one is near mint and an original copy) and, perhaps more importantly, "Which one is the better buy?" Or questions like "What's wrong with a cheaply purchased, suitcase-style record player?" (everything, apparently). And "Is anti-skating something to do with Tonya Harding?" (it isn't. It's far more complicated and less entertaining).

This book collects some of those real-time explorations. The idea is threefold:

Firstly, it is to share and present solutions to vinyl-related issues that 'vinyl-heads' may come up against at various times in their vinyl-lives;

Secondly, it is to share the stories behind some great records, in the hope the reader may seek out or re-acquaint themselves with these LPs and songs. (For example, did you know the story behind ELO's *No Answer* LP? Apparently, a US record company executive told his secretary to call the band's manager, Don Arden, to ask the title. She couldn't get through and left a note to say she had phoned - but no answer. ELO's first album was therefore called *No Answer* in the USA, much to the bemusement of the band):

Thirdly, and perhaps most importantly, it is to do what *Every Record Tells A Story* set out to do seven years ago, and that is simply to entertain. There is precious little plumbing-depths-of-the-soul on display here, and that's just the way I like it.

What follows is a collection of stories and articles - some published over the last seven years, others being new material to bring it all together. Expect to read about what happens when record buying combines with a competitive nature, interspersed with a series of stories about some of the records I have bought over the years.

I hope you enjoy it.

# CONTENTS

# 1

## LET'S START

So, you find yourself with a record player. Unless you are very odd, or perhaps a little too busy, before long you will want to build a collection of records to play on it.

It's tempting to buy online, because buying new records online is easy, and you don't have to go outside in the rain and cold, or talk to anyone about quite why you would want to buy a complete set of LPs by Peter Frampton. If you have the budget, it's a straightforward way to buy lots of new records. But part of the enjoyment of collecting records is finding bargains. Unearthing music for less than the price you would have to pay to Amazon is much more fun. You also find other things along the way. And who wouldn't like to get to know their local record shop owner just a little bit better?

The following story records a maiden voyage of discovery buying Beatles records. It touches upon why some records cost more than others, and why new isn't always the way to go. It all began when the Beatles reissued their albums in a nice, shiny box set for a large amount of money. Was there a way, I wondered, to build a record collection that didn't involve spending quite so much money? And what were the pros and cons of doing so?

Without wishing to spoil the ending, the pros so vastly outweighed the cons that it sparked off the basis of everything that followed. Collecting the Beatles' records had so many nuances that a collector could devote an entire collection to just the Fabs without getting bored. They might well bore their friends and family, however, so further exploration outside the Beatles' oeuvre was warranted.

Prices have risen a little since writing this, but the same principles apply ...

# THE BEATLES BET

# PART 1

The announcement made on the 27th September 2012 that the Beatles were to re-release all their albums on vinyl on the 12th November of that year in a deluxe box set got people of a certain age (me) slightly excited at the thought of getting those re-mastered records in 180g vinyl, all shiny and new.

The problem was – when I looked up the set on Amazon when they announced the launch – the price was £445. That's right. Four hundred and forty-five English pounds. During a recession. We're all darting about diving in bins, or foraging for mushrooms to feed our families and rummaging through charity shops to find an old pair of winter boots and here come Ringo and Macca seeking another few hundred notes. It's almost the cost of a ticket to see the Rolling Stones.

I was telling my friend Chris about this problem on the day of the announcement. "There's always the option of not buying it, of course …" he helpfully suggested.

"That seems somewhat dull, and not really entering into the spirit of the thing," I countered. "It's probably cheaper to buy the originals though …"

"No chance," said Chris with a knowledgeable air. "Some of those records fetch hundreds on eBay. You've got as much chance of saving money buying the originals as I have of enjoying Mariah Carey's next record". The words sprung forth from his lips, as if thrown like a gauntlet at my feet.

"You're on."

"What?"

"You're on. I bet that I can buy the LPs in that Beatles Albums Box Set for less than it costs on Amazon."

We did a quick bit of maths. Fourteen albums divided by £445 was less than £30 each. Surely that was possible?

"And the loser has to buy a Mariah Carey album and listen to it. A lot. At least ten times." The stakes were getting higher. The consequences of losing were becoming pretty dire.

We shook hands, and agreed the fine print. I had until we saw each other again (the 20th of October) to complete the task – just a few weeks. No stealing or borrowing records. And no bootlegs or knock-offs. They had to be original releases.

"There's a book as well. You need to get the book".

"But it's exclusive to the box set! I can't get the book!"

"Then you need to find an acceptable replacement. You have to factor that in, otherwise it's not the same".

The rules were starting to get more strict. "The records have to be in decent condition too. No jumps. And they have to have a cover".

So there it was, **The Challenge**: Buy all the Beatles' records on vinyl for less money than the cost of these re-issues. I raced home and flicked through a copy of the *2012 Record Collector's Rare Record Price Guide* to see if my impetuous bet stood a chance. How much do vinyl Beatles records cost? I didn't want to listen to any more Carey than I had to. Sadly, it didn't make for good reading. Here's a brief run-down of the 2012 value of the original first pressings of Beatles records in mint condition:

- A first pressing in stereo of the Beatles' first album *Please Please Me* in mint condition was worth … £3,500. A mono copy was £750.
- *With The Beatles* was £120 in mono, although a later 1965 pressing was £50.
- *A Hard Day's Night* was £80 in mono and £140 in stereo for a first pressing. *Beatles For Sale* was almost the same: £80 mono and £150 stereo.
- *Help!*: £80 mono £120 stereo
- *Rubber Soul:* £150 mono £200 stereo
- *Revolver:* £100 (mono or stereo)
- *Sgt. Pepper's Lonely Hearts Club Band:* £130 (mono or stereo)
- *The Beatles* (also known as *The White Album*): these were originally individually stamped with a unique number. Numbers below 1,000 were £1200. Below 10,000 were £700. Other copies were £250 for mono and £200 for stereo.
- *Yellow Submarine* would set a buyer back £80 for a stereo copy.
- *Abbey Road* was £50.
- Finally, *Let it Be* could cost £300 for a mint box set.

A full set of the Beatles records might therefore set me back at least £2,000!

It looked like I might have a bit of catching up with Mariah Carey to do ... unless I could come up with a devious plan. It was the sort of knotty problem that Sherlock Holmes would nip off to an opium den to think through. On the basis that my opium stocks were running low, I made do with a cup of Earl Grey. The plan was this:

1.  Charity Shops
2.  eBay
3.  My local used record store
4.  Record Fairs
5.  Er, that's it.

## PART 2: Buying Records in Charity Shops:

Having struck a bet with my friend Chris to buy the Beatles records on vinyl for less money than the box set costs, I started to plan my campaign with his parting words still ringing in my ears: "You'll never do it! Mariah is waiting!"

I shuddered at the thought.

I started by trawling through some charity shops. With autumn drawing in it wasn't the time of year for boot sales, and frankly I have better things to do with my time than get up at six am on a Sunday morning to trawl through row upon row of broken Power Rangers, John Grisham novels, baby clothes, and Other Things That Aren't Valuable Enough To Sell On eBay, whilst elbowing other crate-diggers out of the way to get hold of any potential undiscovered bargains. Charity shops were the low-cost option, and didn't require an early start. If I could find something for a pound, that might give me leeway for some of the more expensive records.

That was all very good in theory of course. And to be fair, charity shops are good for records. They have loads of them. If you ever want a record, that's where to go. So long as you're a big fan of Max Bygraves, big band music, Peter Frampton or *Now!* Compilations from the eighties or want to buy no small number of Billy Joel and Linda Ronstadt albums. As I surveyed the detritus in the shop I couldn't help but reflect that these records seemed to possess an air of gloom about them. They were dog-eared and sat in these crates of sadness probably destined never to be played again. It was like a Greek tragedy, or like *Romeo And Juliet* – or perhaps more like *Toy Story 2* – you know, the one where the toys get sad because they'll never be played with again.

One shop – my local Dr Barnado's - was especially galling as they had what appeared to be a complete set of Elton John's records. If only I had bet on Elton! As I came out of my fifth Phil Collins and Shalamar-infested charity shop my spirits were lower than that of a worm that had decided to make an early start, only to bump into a bird of a similar mind.

Just as I was going to give up I found a bric-a-brac shop. Miraculously, David Bowie's *Low*, his *Stage* double album and the Jam's *Sound Affects* were all on sale for a pound each. They might not be the Beatles, but they were in perfect condition: bargain. "Have you anything by the Beatles?" I enquired, more in hope than expectation. "Oh yes!" said the shopkeeper. My hopes rose like an iceberg from the sea. What did he have? As the shopkeeper went out back to look for whatever it was he had I began to dream: perhaps he had a full set – all for a pound each? Maybe he's just a nice bloke who doesn't realise the value of the things ...

"Here it is," he said, and triumphantly held up a 1,000-piece jigsaw puzzle of *The Yellow Submarine* from the seventies. It was lovely, and came with a poster, but it wasn't a record. And he wanted thirty quid for it ... he was no mug.

It started to look like the chances of finding a complete set of the Beatles records in charity shops might be a lifetime's work rather than that of a few weeks.

Time for a change of tack. Time to try eBay...

## PART 3: Buying Records on eBay

A week had passed since my foray into the charity shops but I wasn't worried. Undoubtedly the laziest way to win the bet would be to buy everything on eBay – assuming the price was right. This – clearly – was going to be the way forward for me. I'm not averse to a bit of laziness...

Of course, there are a few drawbacks when buying records online – in particular you place faith on the seller wrapping the things up in a decent bit of packaging so the records don't break, scratch or warp. A non-refunded breakage would eat into my budget to catastrophic effect. Catastrophic in that I would have to listen to Mariah Carey – and if that isn't a catastrophe then I don't know what is...

My first trawl for *Please Please Me* wasn't encouraging. I looked under "recently completed" transactions to see what the going rate was. Top of the list was a mono record that sold for £560. Nightmare. There was another in stereo that sold for a bargain £1,800.

Very soon however, by reading the descriptions of all the different records I started to learn a bit more about the insular world of record collecting. The one that cost £560 had a black and gold Parlophone label – a first pressing and very rare. The stereo one really was a bargain compared with the £3,500 valuation in the *Rare Record Price Guide*. A bit further down on the listings was one described as a "fifth pressing" which was £24 including p&p. That sounded a bit more on-budget.

## Record Pressings – A quick guide (without trying to be too dull):

The difference between a £560 record and one that costs £25 comes down to condition ("mint" is worth twice as much as something described as "VG+" with a few minor flaws, which in turn is worth double something described as "VG" which may have more serious scratches or creases.) It also comes down to the pressing. Like with books, first pressings are valued by collectors as there may be fewer records made – especially for a debut album – and collectors believe the sound is better on some early pressings due to the thickness of 1960s vinyl and the freshness of the stamper (the metal mould that presses out the imprint on the wax) used to press the records which inevitably must suffer from slight wear and tear after printing many thousands of copies of a record.

The way to find out if your record is a first pressing is to read the etchings on the disc itself (between the grooves and the label) – there's a series of letters and numbers on each side that is unique to each pressing. You then have to look up the number on-line or in the *Record Price* guide book. Sometimes, the song-writing credits change – this happened with some Led Zeppelin records and also on *With The Beatles*.

The second pressing from 1963 has a further clue on the label: the track 'Money' is credited on the label to "Jobete" in first pressings and corrected to "Dominion, Belinda" in later pressings. Third pressings had the text "The Gramophone Co. Ltd" on them which is absent on first and second pressings. The disparity in price was across the board: copies of *Sgt. Pepper's Lonely Hearts Club Band* had sold for £280 and £25 dependent upon pressing.

I did a quick search on all the Beatles records and worked out that if I was lucky I could spend £330 and get the set. Even if I got carried away and over-bid on a couple, I still had a decent amount of headroom in my budget of £445. The book remained a problem, but I would worry about that later.

Some of the records were more of a problem than others. There weren't any *Past Masters* on sale and *the White Album* was around £60 without all the postcards. Anything that had a poster and postcard set intact was creeping up to £100 or more, which was on budget still, but the thought of spending £100 on a record rather filled me with horror. Knowing my kids, they'd use the discs as frisbees and the nice white sleeve as the world's most expensive colouring pad. One copy of *the*

*White Album*, with a low number on the sleeve (they were all individually numbered with the first four going to the boys themselves) went for £400.

A *Let It Be* box set (with book) had sold for £125. I had budgeted £20. Perhaps the book might be good, but that's a lot to pay for a book…

Then the phone rang. It was the friend I had the bet with: Chris. He sounded rather chirpy. "Have you looked on Amazon lately?" he asked with extraordinary amusement in his voice. "They do have some bargains on there, you know".

He hung up the phone. I instantly knew what had happened. My stomach dropped as I looked on the site. Amazon had reduced the price: *the Beatles Box Set* on vinyl was now £299. I had bet I could find the originals for less than the Amazon price. But that was when the price was £445. Buying solely on eBay was no longer an option. £60 alone would be spent on postage at an average of £4 a record. That only left £240 to buy fifteen records – that was just £15 each. *The White Album* alone cost £60-£100!

Time to talk to an expert: Bob at Leigh Records – my local used record store.

## PART 4: Abbey Road's Misaligned Apples and Sgt. Pepper's Red Wavy Lines

With the 20th October deadline fast approaching I popped across to my friendly local second-hand record store – Leigh Records – where I knew Bob, the owner, would be able to give me some advice. How exactly do you buy The Beatles on vinyl? Is it important just to buy first pressings? Or does it not really make much difference?

I asked Bob if he thought it was possible to buy a complete set of first pressing Beatles records for less than £300.

"You can – but they won't be in great condition" was his view: "If you buy the ones with the silver box around the Parlophone label from the '70s and '80s you could though – maybe that would be your best bet"

Bob showed me a great copy of *The White Album* – number twenty thousand and something. He wanted £350 for it. I felt like I was Hugh Grant in that scene in *Four Weddings And A Funeral* when he buys a wedding present in an expensive art gallery.

"Do you have anything for around forty?" I ventured… Bob had just the thing. A number up near three hundred thousand, but an original gatefold sleeve, opening at the top and with the black inner sleeves. Discs in very good condition. An early pressing. One problem: no photos.

"What about a rare *Abbey Road*?" suggested Bob. "This one has a misaligned Apple logo on the back cover". Looking at my slightly baffled look, Bob explained that some pressings of *Abbey Road* were rarer than others because of a printer error on the reverse of the cover. It might set me back £25, rather than £20 (or £60 mint rather than £50), but it was a genuine collector's item.

Bob also had a new copy of Let It Be (Naked), complete with a 7" single. I much prefer this version of Let It Be, so that was an easy decision – and it was an original! Another £25, but I had three tricky albums in the bag. The photos? I found a set on eBay which admittedly had Sellotape marks on the corners, but were clearly authentic and were £15: a lot for photos, but now The White Album was complete and potentially worth more than what I paid.

That was £105 for the three records. With D-Day approaching, I felt slightly better about the bet. Bob had plenty of stock, but not everything, and I couldn't quite get under budget. All that was standing between me and the dog-whistle pitched shrieking of Mariah Carey was a couple of bargains, but they didn't seem to be coming my way.

## PART 5: Southend Record Fair

My hopes were pinned therefore on the local monthly record fair at the local school which took place on the 14th October – less than a week before the deadline. Bribing the kids with Haribo and the threat of playing Mariah to them, I took them along and began rummaging through one of a huge number of boxes of records all priced at £2 each. My hopes weren't high, but miracle of miracles, within five minutes I found a copy of *Help!* The record looked a little worse for wear, and there was no inner sleeve, but the cover was clean enough and for £2 I wasn't going to argue.

Flushed with excitement, I looked through another dozen crates, but to no avail. Four records, £107 – and my first genuinely cheap Beatles record. I moved on to some other tables. One guy had a small selection, but inside was a copy of *Sgt. Pepper's Lonely Hearts Club Band*, complete with gatefold sleeve and cut-out Sgt. Pepper mask. And, (I discovered later) even better, it had an inner sleeve with red wavy lines – a bit of a rarity.

The record wasn't perfect by a long way – it had a few visible scratches on the surface, but they didn't look too bad. I haggled and got the price down from £20 to £10 because of the scratches. This was going well. (It turned out that this was a first pressing – and no jumps.)

Another stall had a half-price sale. I noticed two copies of John Lennon's *Imagine* – one with the original inner sleeve and one complete with poster. The more expensive one (an earlier pressing but with no poster) was £5. This was promising. I asked if I could have the poster from the other one, and the vendor agreed. Result! It was in perfect condition too.

Even better – there were copies of *Revolver* (£4 – reduced from £8), *Rubber Soul* (£3), *With The Beatles* (£2.50), *A Hard Day's Night* (£2.50) and the *'Blue'* and *'Red'* albums. The latter were £2 each and are 'best-of' double LPs – which I first owned on cassette – the first Beatles albums I ever owned. Not part of the box set, but for £2 each – why not?

I couldn't believe my luck. I know it is obvious really – that is to say where better to buy old records than at an actual record fair? But to have found six of the albums for just £24 in less than an hour – plus two 'best-of's for another £4 and a lovely pristine copy of *Imagine* for £5. Maybe, just maybe there was hope ...

What's more, I noticed a very clean copy of David Bowie's *Aladdin Sane* – and it had an insert inside where you could apply to join David's fan club. I paid £3. When I looked it up in the *Rare Record Price Guide*, it told me it was worth £70 with the insert – as they are quite rare. Although I am sceptical about that price[1], it was a nice bonus – and it is a great album.

To take stock: I had nine albums and had paid £129. Well on-budget. The remaining records were:

- *Yellow Submarine*
- *Please, Please Me*
- *Past Masters 1 & 2*
- *Magical Mystery Tour (LP version)*
- *Beatles for Sale*

The only trouble? eBay had no *Past Masters* and Bob didn't have it either. He did have a couple of the others though – and Spitalfields Record Fair was on Friday – the 19th October. It was cutting it fine, but it is a huge record fair in London and I fancied my chances of finding a copy of *Past Masters* there.

---

[1] 2019 note: I sold this copy in 2017 after finding a slightly cleaner copy also with the fan club insert for £5. It fetched over £50 on eBay.

# Part 6: Spitalfields Record Fair

The record fair at Spitalfields Market in London is a twice monthly event which attracts ~~nerds and obsessives~~ record collectors from miles around on the first and third Friday of each month. With over forty different stall-holders it is an Aladdin's cave of ~~old tat~~ rare and valuable vinyl.

As I sped around the fair seeking out the remaining five LPs I asked a few record traders if they thought that the 2012 re-released Beatles albums would affect the market for second-hand Beatles records. They thought not. "They're always re-releasing the Beatles on vinyl!" was the first thing they all said. One continued, "It's a collector's mentality – it's the same music but people always want the first pressing. As long as that continues, I don't think these new releases will affect prices for the originals".

Within a few minutes I found a nice copy of *Beatles For Sale* which was just £6. That made ten Beatles LPs for £135.

The nice thing about the record fair (as was the case in Southend) was that I also found a couple of other bargains whilst looking around. A stall selling books had Neil Young's biography *Shaky* for just £2 (sadly not the story of the Welsh Elvis: Shakin' Stevens) and *Diary of a Rock n Roll Star* by Ian Hunter for £5 – a classic paperback for a good price in great condition. I also found *Our Band Could Be Your Life* – the classic alternative rock bio for just £1.

But more importantly, there was also a glut of Beatles vinyl. Oh yes! Looking around the stalls I found:

- *Yellow Submarine* for £30
- *Please, Please Me* for £15 for a '70s copy (but £60 minimum for an earlier pressing).
- *Magical Mystery Tour* for £20 with an Apple label.

Bob at Leigh Records had a couple of these in better condition, so I could pop back to him, but I had everything sewn up: except for *Past Masters*. Suspecting I had missed it, I began asking around, but no-one seemed to have a copy. This was beginning to be a serious problem – tomorrow was deadline day.

Finally a stall-holder finally said he did have one! I breathed a sigh of relief – victory was within my grasp! Until he said "But not here I'm afraid. I can bring it along next time though. In two weeks".

"Aaaaaaaaaarrrrrrgggghhhhhhhhhh!" I screamed inwardly and smiled weakly, with the air of a condemned man about to have to listen to a Mariah Carey LP.

"Out of interest, how much would it cost?" I asked, torturing myself. The stall-holder twisted the knife.

"About thirty quid…" I would have been on budget … That was it then: I had failed the challenge.

With Chris coming over the following evening, I made a call, through slightly gritted teeth. So near and yet so far.

"Chris – you've won. But only just. You **can** buy a complete set of Beatles records for under £300 – no problem. I have all but one record and have spent £200. But the last one – *Past Masters* – is hard to get hold of, and even though it's only £30, I haven't got it. You can go out and buy your Mariah Carey CD to torture me with".

"Or perhaps just take it out of your CD collection" I added bitterly. Chris whooped with glee. I suspect he punched the air in triumph. And no little relief.

## PART 7

The day came for Chris to present me formally with a Mariah Carey CD. He was grinning like a Cheshire cat that had just eaten an entire can of Elmlea in one go.

"Bad luck!" he sympathised (insincerely). "So near and yet …" He let the words trail off.

"Mariah Carey eh? I never thought I'd see the day! Do wait until I have left before you put the thing on won't you? And I want a screenshot of those play counts on your iTunes playlist: no cheating!" I let him carry on a bit. With an unnecessary flourish he began to present me with a CD shaped packaged that he had wrapped in paper and had tied a little bow of ribbon around.

But I had an ace up my sleeve.

"Just before I take the CD from you Chris, let me tell you about a funny thing that happened to me today." I began. I wore a poker face. Chris looked at me. He hesitated. "I took a call from Bob – from

Leigh Records – just a couple of hours ago. He told me that a bloke came in with fifteen copies of Sgt Pepper yesterday. Isn't it amazing what people come in with...?"

Chris looked wary all of a sudden. He waited for me to finish. He suspected something was up. "He also had something else. Would you believe it?! He had a copy of *Past Masters Vol 1&2* ..." I let the words hang in the air for a while. "... which Bob let me have for thirty-five quid." My triumph was palpable. I allowed myself a smirk. I may have raised a mirthful eyebrow.

"And guess what else he had? A very rare double vinyl LP...of something called *The Emancipation of Mimi* by Ms Mariah Carey. Which he let me have for nothing!" This was true. Bob had been sufficiently tickled by the idea of the bet – and forfeit – to gift me this LP, which had been in stock for "quite a few years" without having been sold. He doubted it ever would be of interest to anyone.

Chris looked stunned. But he's made of stern stuff. He wasn't finished yet. "Did he have the book?" he asked quietly. The book! I had forgotten about the book! I thought quickly.

"Er, I have the book. Wait here."

I ran upstairs and pulled out my copy of *The Beatles: An Illustrated Record* by Roy Carr and Tony Tyler. It's a great glossy history of the Beatles that covers each of their records in turn – and is LP sized. Surely a reasonable replacement?

To cut a long story short, after a steward's enquiry, (and an assessment of the book's value on eBay/Amazon) the book was allowed. I had won the bet! Mariah Carey could wait another day. And another. And another.

So what did I learn from this adventure? Not only did I manage to buy an entire set of the Beatles' albums on vinyl for just (just?) £235, but a good proportion were early (i.e. sixties) or first pressings, that should hold their value. Will the new box set records be as good an investment? I don't know[2]. The seventies re-pressings clearly haven't held their value like the sixties originals – but they are pressed on noticeably thinner vinyl: this will be the first time the complete set will be available on heavy 180g vinyl – so maybe that might help. I am sure audiophiles will enjoy the chance to play these records crackle-free on heavy vinyl, although I rather take the view that many songs were most often first heard on mono AM radios – and the magic of a record like *Please, Please*

---

[2] 2019 footnote: Mono reissues of Beatles albums subsequently went out of print and are now fetching high prices (over £50 for mono copies of Sgt, Pepper et al).

*Me* may be enhanced little by playing it on an expensive turntable in stereo. Not that I have one. I can't afford it having shelled out all that money on the records.

Walking around the record fairs and bric-a-brac shops also got me lovely copies of *Imagine*, *Aladdin Sane*, *Sound Affects*, Bowie's *Stage* and *Low*, the *Red* and *Blue* 'Best-of' albums, plus classic books such as *Diary Of A Rock'n'Roll Star, Shaky* and *Our Band Could Be Your Life* – all for just over twenty quid. The Bowie record alone is apparently worth far more.

Of the new pressings in the box set, *The White Album* looks like it will be the biggest bargain – I struggled to find a first pressing for less than £60 with the poster and photos, so the re-release (as an individual record) ought to be a good way to buy this LP for less money. I think *Abbey Road* and *Sgt. Pepper's Lonely Hearts Club Band* might also benefit from a 180g version.

And Chris? We shared a good bottle of wine to drown his sorrows. He's probably listening to Mariah right now. I think he secretly likes it ...

# 2

## Some stories, beginning with...

## B.B. King, Hells Angels and the Naked Hippie Girl

## The story behind Indianola Mississippi Seeds by B.B. King....

In a used record shop in Nottingham I found a 1970 B.B. King LP with a picture of a guitar made from a watermelon on the cover. It cost £8 and was called *Indianola Mississippi Seeds.* Inside the beautiful gatefold cover is a photo of the birth certificate of Riley King, and amongst the musicians playing on the album are Carole King, Joe Walsh of The Eagles and Leon Russell. As I handed over the cash it had me wondering: how did Riley become B.B.? And how did Carole King get to play on a B.B. King album before she released *Tapestry*?

There are two things that stand out in the story of B.B. King. One is that the man never changed his style, despite living through unprecedented change. The second is that although B.B. eventually achieved huge mainstream success (both in the early '70s with 'The Thrill Is Gone' and stints in Las Vegas and with U2 in the late eighties), it isn't the acceptance from the mainstream community that makes him special; it's the music he made throughout his career, which remains constant, and individual to the point that you could hear B.B. King play a single note on a guitar and know it's him.

Actually, there's a third thing I learned about the life of B.B. King: People really had no idea about Health and Safety back in the day. It's a wonder that any of us are still here...

It's 1970. Fresh from the chart success of "Indianola Mississippi Seeds" BB King is about to play what he calls "the most amazing gig of all" his career, at an outdoor rock festival in Macon, Georgia. After many years of successful but gruelling touring in front of mainly black crowds BB King is gaining a new following. A mainly white, hippie, rock loving one, who "discover" BB King thanks to the Beatles and the Rolling Stones acknowledging his influence.

B.B. King flies in from California, and has a limo drive him to the outdoor festival. The limo is stuck in traffic so a couple of Hells Angels offer him a lift on the back of their bikes. This is the year after

Altamont. A Hells Angel is carrying a black man on the back of his hog in one of the Southern states of America at a rock festival. (I bet he didn't give him a helmet).

When King arrives, his band members are giggling mysteriously, but don't say why, and then leave. There's a knock on the door. King answers.

Outside is a young white girl in her twenties without a stitch of clothing. She explains she's King's escort for the festival. Not a groupie as it turns out- but an innocent flower-child way to welcome the musicians to the festival.

Bloody hippies.

King is nervous even though he can hear his band still laughing. "I'm nervous because this is Georgia," he later reflects, "What does a gentleman do in a situation like this?"

Perhaps he was thinking about 1944, when King enlisted into the US army. His bus, filled with newly enlisted black soldiers, passes some white women and one of the men calls out to them. At the next stop an enraged white man threatens them all with a shotgun.

It seems extraordinary now to read of the injustices of the time, but King found that after "growing up in a segregated world of uptight attitudes and prejudice" he welcomed being in a world where both he and his music were embraced.

Riley King of Blue Lake, near Indianola, Mississippi was a shy boy and had a stutter. His dad Albert named him partly after his brother and partly after Jim O'Reilly, the white plantation owner whose tractor he drove, and who found the midwife as Riley was being born. When little Riley asked why he dropped the O' his dad replied, "Because you didn't look Irish".

His dad was quite the wit.

Riley looks forward to church because he can sit next to a pretty girl, and because of the music. Imagine looking forward to church because you like the girls and the music... He buys his first guitar aged twelve. It costs him $15: two months wages. As a teenager Riley travels to the nearest city, Indianola. For ten cents he sees a three-minute clip of Charlie Christian play guitar. "A miracle man doing things to a guitar I never imagined possible."

At Indianola's club, The Jones Night Spot he is too young to gain admittance, but he peers through the cracks in the wall to see the ladies dancing amongst the four hundred people crammed in, and hears touring bands including Charlie "Bird" Parker and Sonny Boy Williamson.

Riley starts singing and playing guitar on Saturday afternoons to earn a little extra money. He begins to sing gospel songs and draws appreciation, but no-one leaves even a nickel. Bloody church-goers... He soon learns an important lesson: he switches the words from "My Lord" to "My baby" and personalises the songs he heard Sonny Boy play the week before. He gets the same praise, but also a few dimes. "Real life songs," he realises, "have cash value".

The Second World War comes. King is used to segregation, but it still hurts when the German prisoners of war are rested and treated better than the black plantation workers. He's twenty years old and "starting to feel the weight of the system".

King might have stayed in Indianola, but something happens that makes him move. It isn't being threatened with guns, or being treated badly; he crashes his tractor. The thought that he has let down his boss, Mr Johnson, makes King panic and he worries Mr Johnson will want to shoot him. And despite the fact he has a wife at home, he grabs his guitar and $2.50, and runs. All the way to Memphis.

And there he stays with his mum's cousin Bukka White for seven months, near the main musical hub of Beale Street. He tries to play like Bukka does with a slide, but he can't get the hang of it. Instead he develops a vibrato sound with his left hand, which later becomes his trademark.

He returns back to his wife for a while, but Memphis calls again, and this time he has paid off the damage to the tractor and he starts afresh.

But where to start? Get a press agent? Release some demos and build up a following on social media? Not in 1948 it would seem...

King calls on Sonny Boy Williamson, now presenting a radio show in West Memphis. He turns up at the radio station, guitar in hand, and asks Sonny if he can play a song, live, on the show. He auditions, and a few hours later he plays on the show. Just like that.

What's more, an impressed Williamson is double-booked for a gig and sends King to one of the venues to cover for him for the then king's ransom of $12.

Boosted by this, King goes to another radio station, WDIA and asks to play. This time, the owner asks him to write a jingle for a tonic called Pepticon. He hums, and sings "Pepticon sure is good, and you can get it anywhere in your neighbourhood."

On the back of this B.B. King now has his own ten-minute radio show, playing songs and promoting a so-called health tonic that actually had the same alcohol content as wine. Soon he has a second slot at 12.30.

For the next five years, BB King is a DJ. He gets up, picks cotton, plugs Pepticon, then heads back to the fields for another couple of hours. People like the show, and King gains a nickname, the Beale Street Blues Boy. This becomes Blues Boy, Bee Bee and then B.B.

Before Memphis he didn't even own a record player. Now he is surrounded by thousands of records. Salesmen give him his own personal copies. "I hoarded those records like a squirrel hoarding nuts" he said. By the time he moved to Las Vegas in the mid '70s he had a record collection of over twenty thousand shellac 78s.

In the winter of 1949, B.B. King plays a gig in Twist, Arkansas. It's not a club, just a big room in a house, with a bucket of kerosene in the middle of the floor to heat the place up. Here's what I mean about health and safety: there's a club being heated by a garbage pail containing lighted aeroplane fuel that stands in the middle of the dance floor. Just imagine the conversations...

**Health and Safety Inspector**: *"Couldn't you move that away from where people are dancing?"*

**Club owner**: *"Don't worry, it's fine..."*

**H&SI**: *"I don't know, it might get knocked. It's jet fuel. It doesn't seem awfully safe..."*

**Club owner**: *"Well I can't move it to the side – it might set alight to the wall. Here, have a drink, what's the worst that can happen...?"*

A fight breaks out and the garbage pail of kerosene is kicked over, setting the house ablaze with "an incredible river of fire". Panic. Everyone stampedes out in a crush, elbowing each other out of the way. Then B.B. realises he has left his guitar in the burning building. He doesn't have the money to buy another, and heads back into the fire. A beam crashes in front of him just as he finds the guitar. He jumps over the beam and a wall collapses as he rushes to the exit. Two people are trapped in the building and are not so lucky.

"Damn" says one of the crowd, "you wouldn't think two guys would near kill each other over a gal like Lucille".

B.B.'s guitar is christened "Lucille" from that moment on to remind King not to go and do anything quite so foolish again. Lucky the girl was called Lucille. It wouldn't be as good a story if they had been fighting over a bloke called Gavin. As it happens, the guitar is stolen not long afterwards.

Soon afterwards, King shows up late to a show, and there's Ike Turner waiting for him. Ike offers to help out and sits in with the band, playing piano. Ike is also a talent scout for the Bihari brothers, who own Modern Records, and they sign up King, who records for Modern for the next decade. B.B.'s seventh single, a cover of Lowell Fulson's 'Three O'clock Blues' hits number one on the R'n'B charts. For eighteen weeks.

A big hit means King can play bigger cities, for more money and so for the next eighteen years that's what he does. 330 shows a year on the circuit for many years, often because the taxman is after him. By 1955 he has his own branded bus, presumably called the B.B.mobile. In 1956 King plays 342 one-nighters, which is a ridiculous number of dates and we can strongly suspect King was liable to attract disapproving looks from his wife.

Over the next decade or so he's sometimes popular, sometimes out of favour. He's the outsider bluesman during the rock 'n' roll years and the outsider bluesman during the soul years at the height of the civil rights movement. He is booed by a young crowd impatiently waiting for Sam Cooke, and who see King's blues as old fashioned.

Bloody kids ...

Yet King keeps doing his thing. Despite all the external change, the fashions and the social change all around, B.B. King keeps playing the blues. In 1964 he plays the Regal Theatre in Chicago. "I've probably played hundreds of better concerts" he says. Only this time they record the show. The subsequent album *Live At The Regal* wins critical favour and keeps B.B. King's name in the R'n'B charts. This album is still the best way to introduce yourself to BB King's music.

With new manager Sid Seidenberg on board to sort out King's money problems, King receives more appreciation from mainstream musicians only now hearing his work. John Lennon name-checks him, then Mike Bloomfield, Johnny Winter and the Rolling Stones.

King looks to expand his audience and his manager books him in to play the Fillmore. He feels out of place amongst the weed-smoking hippy contingent. He takes a drink to steady his nerves.

He's introduced onstage by Bill Graham. Walks out onstage. And for the first time ever receives a standing ovation before he's even played a note. Overcome, and with tears in his eyes, BB King plays for three hours. The times they are a-changing...

King records the *Live And Well* album. Half the album is with B.B. King's band but, at the request of his manager, the other half King agrees can feature white session musicians. It's an attempt to broaden B.B.'s appeal.

For the next album *Completely Well* BB King agrees to have the whole album feature session musicians. King's producer adds strings on a track called 'The Thrill Is Gone'. It's a smash hit. Number 15 in the pop charts. He supports the Rolling Stones on tour. B.B. King has now officially "crossed over" attracting mainstream attention.

For the follow up *Indianola Mississippi Seeds,* session musicians return. But what session musicians ...

"Getting people to play with B.B. was never a problem" said his producer. That was an understatement.

On piano, Carole King is just working up her *Tapestry* album. She takes time out to play on a few tracks and there's a fantastic moment on the fourth song on the album where you hear a piano chord so recognisable that you can tell it's Carole playing. Also on piano comes Leon Russell, who brings his song Hummingbird, which also features a pre-Eagles Joe Walsh.

The songs are strong and slightly skewed to a potential mainstream audience with fresh interest in the 'Thrill Is Gone' star. Perhaps Leon Russell's 'Hummingbird' is the biggest expansion of B.B.'s sound, featuring a choir at its climax, just like Russell's original. But in contrast to these slick touches, the album begins with King accompanied only by a piano with the deathless couplet "Nobody loves me but my mother / and she could be jivin' too".

Was it B.B.'s idea to bring people like Carole King and Leon Russell in on the sessions? 'No, that was my previous producer Bill Szymczyk's idea; but he did ask me if I would like to have them. I already knew of Carole King and I knew Leon Russell when he played with Joe Cocker. At that time we were looking for a follow-up to 'The Thrill Is Gone'.... I'd heard 'Hummingbird', but didn't see how I could do it. So Leon came out and played it for me on the session. I learned so much from him; that guy is really out of sight'.

*Indianola Mississippi Seeds* reached number 26 on the Billboard Charts and the single 'Hummingbird' reached number 48 in August 1970. 'Chains And Things' followed and reached number 45 in December of that year. The album was B.B. King's crossover album – capturing the time immediately after his biggest breakthrough and pitched to a wide audience of rock, pop and blues fans. But despite all the changes of personnel going on around him, all the expensive production and studio flourishes, the rock and pop influence, it's still a B.B. King album. It's still B.B.'s voice, B.B.'s unmistakable playing and many of B.B.'s best songs too. It's still a great blues album. You could take the man out of Mississippi, but you couldn't take Mississippi out of the man, or his music.

## The Star Club, Hamburg, and Black Sabbath: The Other Fab Four...

### The story behind Black Sabbath by Black Sabbath

They were four lads from a tough industrial British city. They formed a band, and went to Hamburg in Germany to play at The Star Club on the Reeperbahn for a residency. Up to seven sets a day. They lived together in a room above the stage. Starting at noon and finishing at 2am. Gruelling stuff. But it was the making of the Fab Four. John, Terry, Bill and Tony.

Hang on a minute. No Paul or George? Doesn't one of them criticise George Martin's tie at some point?

John "Ozzy" Osbourne, Terry "Geezer" Butler (so called because he always called people "geezer"), Bill Ward, and Tony Iommi. That industrial city is Birmingham, not Liverpool, and these are the Fab Four members of Black Sabbath. And yes, they played a long residency in Hamburg – more shows than The Beatles in fact.

But we are getting ahead of ourselves. Let's start with Ozzy. Ozzy had some terrible jobs when he left school, aged 15, all set for a life as a factory worker. For a time he worked as a car horn tuner. His co-worker had been there thirty years and was as deaf as a post. Imagine deafness being the thing you have to look forward to after thirty years. Ozzy's jobs were so awful, his best job was working in an abattoir. Imagine that being your favourite job. How awful was Birmingham's job market that dispatching cows to the great pasture in the sky was the most enjoyable job on offer? He was there eighteen months. He only left after attacking a co-worker with a pole after his colleague cut his apron strings for a prank. Well, we've all done it... Inflicting hearing damage and killing animals: Ozzy's first jobs were not as entirely unrelated to his musical career as you might at first think.

A 20-year-old Ozzy put an ad in Ringway Music shop window in Birmingham's Bull Ring. "Ozzy Zig Needs Gig" it said, for no real reason. Soon afterwards there was a knock on Ozzy's door. Geezer Butler was a trainee accountant but sported fashionable bell-bottomed velvet trousers and a luxurious moustache, all which would have given away to Sherlock Holmes that in his spare time he was a part time musician, if the callouses on his left hand and whiff of "herbal" cigarettes didn't already point that way. His band were named Rare Breed, and they had just lost their singer. After a brief discussion Ozzy was in the band. Unfortunately, Rare Breed were terrible, and Ozzy left three songs into his first gig, when the manager of the working men's club in Walsall they were playing asked them to stop. Geezer quit the following day.

Geezer did know everyone in the Birmingham music scene however, including Robert Plant, whom he bumped into one day when walking around town with Ozzy. Plant had a difficult decision to make: whether to join the Yardbirds with Jimmy Page, or a local band called Hobbstweedle.

Tricky decision. I think it worked out okay for him.

Although Rare Breed petered out, Ozzy soon had another moustachioed knock on his door in answer to his advert in Ringway Music. It was Tony Iommi and Bill Ward, whose band Mythology had just broken up after a police bust for marijuana possession had left them with a bad reputation and no gigs. Iommi recognised Ozzy from school, where he had regularly hit the younger boy to keep him in his place.

He greeted Ozzy with warmth.

Actually, he didn't. What he said was "Aw, f–ing hell! It's you!" upon recognising Ozzy.

But Ozzy worked his charm, noticing something had happened to Iommi's hand and asking about it in a concerned fashion. Tony Iommi had been a sheet metal worker but the machine had come down on his right hand and severed the tips of the middle and ring fingers. There's never a good hand to lose a finger or two from, but as a left-handed guitar player, the right hand is definitely the worst option.

What's more, the accident occurred on the day he was due to quit the job to take up music as a full-time profession. His guitar playing days were effectively over before they had begun.

A friend bought a profoundly depressed Iommi an album by Django Reinhardt. Django played gypsy jazz and used just two fingers to fret chords after burning his hand in a fire, and played the most intricate melodies. He was an extraordinary player.

This inspired Iommi. He still couldn't play with two fingers, but like when the A-Team were trapped by gangsters in a garage with just their van, a couple of conveniently discarded sheets of metal and a welder's torch, he got busy on his escape. Iommi made a couple of thimbles from melted fairy liquid bottles, glued on leather to the sanded down tips and finally – and crucially – loosened the strings so he didn't need to press so hard. Slowly and surely Iommi gained his confidence and technique with these *Blue Peter*-esque improvised finger tips. A deeper tone and slower sound began to emerge as a result.

Back on Ozzy's doorstep, against his better judgement, and perhaps only because Ozzy now had a PA system and microphone, Iommi welcomed Ozzy into the fold. Geezer soon joined after agreeing to switch from rhythm guitar to bass. After briefly flirting with Polka Tulk Blues Band – named after a brand of talcum powder used by Ozzy's mum – they settled on Earth as the band name.

They tried to get gigs using the novel, and frankly ridiculous strategy of turning up with all their stuff in a van outside venues wherever a big band was coming into town just in case they didn't show. And once, in 1968, this insane, lunatic strategy for stardom actually worked. With Jethro Tull.

The Tull were a no-show and were uncontactable when due to go on, so Ozzy and co got shoved onstage in their place, to keep the crowd happy. Eventually Ian Anderson did show up – his van had broken down on the M6 – and while Earth were whipping up a storm onstage, Ozzy saw Anderson nodding his head in approval; praise indeed. On the back of that gig, they found a manager who at the end of 1968 booked them a tour with Ten Years After. But just as they were all set, Iommi quit the band. To join Jethro Tull.

That's the soon-to-be heaviest most demonic guitarist in the world playing with what we might uncharitably describe as Rock's greatest flute playing flamingo impressionist. You can see Iommi on the Rolling Stones' *Rock And Roll Circus*, wearing a white cowboy hat, alongside Jagger and Lennon and the rest of them. He lasted just four days. But what a great four days to be in Jethro Tull. After the incredible high of playing with rock royalty Iommi decided he didn't like being a side man to a flamboyant, slightly potty show-off of a front man.

So he rejoined Ozzy. Hmm ... Not sure he thought that through. Iommi became more determined to make a success of the band, having had a taste of life with Jethro Tull, and a Hamburg Star Club residency was the result. Having to fill four or more sets per night stretched Earth's material, but this shaped the songs. One jam became a forty minute version of something they called 'War Pigs'.

Back in Aston, Iommi noticed queues going around the corner of the nearby Orient cinema for a horror film near where they were rehearsing.

"Isn't it strange how people will pay money to frighten themselves?" said Iommi. "Maybe we should stop doing the blues and write scary music instead".

Off went Bill and Ozzy to write 'Black Sabbath', based upon a vision Geezer reckons he saw one night at the end of his bed of a "figure in black which points at me". It was probably Ozzy getting up to go to the toilet. Geezer nicked the title from a Boris Karloff film, *Three Faces Of Fear*.

It turned out there was another local cover band called Earth, so a name change was proposed to go with the new song. Their manager, Jim Simpson, was not convinced calling the band Black Sabbath would be a great idea.

"I don't think you'll get anywhere with that, lads" he said.

Ozzy remembers the first time they played the song because all the girls in the venue ran out screaming, much to his chagrin.

"Isn't the whole point of being in a band to get a shag?" complained Ozzy.

"They'll get used to it" reckoned Geezer, who remembered the audience stopping dead in a trance until the end of the song, and then erupting and going nuts as it finished.

With the new name, Black Sabbath went back to the Star Club for another residency. When Ozzy once went through the numbers, he reckoned Black Sabbath ended up playing more shows in Hamburg than the Beatles. Not that I'd trust Ozzy to be able to work that out ... The recording of the debut album was at Regent Sound Studios in Denmark Street. The same studio in which the Rolling Stones recorded their debut album. Black Sabbath had a budget of £500.

Simpson took the album to fourteen labels and got fourteen "no"s in reply. Until ... Vertigo, a new swirly-labelled part of the Philips group, said "yes." Their advance was princely: £105 to each band member. Ozzy knew exactly how to celebrate: he bought himself a bottle of Brut aftershave. To smell nice, not to drink, in case you were wondering. That all came later.

Black Sabbath was released on Friday 13th February 1970. The critics hated it, but it reached number eight in the UK charts and number twenty-three in the USA. But as unexpectedly successful as it was, the album isn't a success because of how many it sold. It's a success because of what followed and the influence it eventually had. Judas Priest, Metallica, Iron Maiden, Nirvana, Slayer, Mastodon and countless others all owe their careers to this album. An entire genre of music invented by a guitarist without a full set of fingers, a jazz drummer, a former abattoir worker and, best of all, a trainee accountant.

And the most amazing part of this story? They recorded the whole album in just eight hours in a tiny studio at the back of what is now a guitar shop in Soho. Eight hours. It took them eight hours to invent heavy metal. (Well, eight hours, plus the two years before it, hustling for gigs, working in rubbish jobs in a tough industrial city.) After a run through of their live set and a couple of hours double tracking vocals and guitar lines it was done.

"We were in the pub in time for last orders" said Ozzy....

**Collectors' Note:** If you are a vinyl enthusiast, the first four LPs, including *Paranoid,* were released on the Vertigo label – recognisable by the distinctive psychedelic swirl. The first pressings have a large swirl on the label. Later ones have a smaller swirl and the word "Vertigo" directly underneath. The *Master of Reality* album comes in a card 'box' sleeve with the lyrics on the back and early copies came with a poster of the band also. The box is a bit fragile and weedy, like the quiet one in the Wanted. Rather like the rock stars of 1972, it's becoming increasingly tricky to find one in good condition and with few creases or blemishes but they do still exist. *Sabbath Bloody Sabbath* came in a gatefold cover originally with a lyric-clad inner sleeve so look out for one of those, as there are plenty of later non-gatefold versions.

## Sliding Doors

## The story of *Roxy Music* by Roxy Music

Brian Eno was waiting for the tube at Maida Vale. A train stopped, leaving Brian equidistant between two carriages. He didn't know it, but his destiny awaited: enter one carriage, and he would become a pop star, an innovator of ambient recording, and eventually collaborate on some of David Bowie's most remarkable albums, using a deck of cards with cleverly worded "oblique strategies" that would encourage the Thin White Duke to move out of his comfort zone. Go into the other carriage, and he would remain an art student with big ideas, a high forehead and a pack of cards with weird instructions that would encourage people to believe he was slightly touched.

This was his Gwyneth-Paltrow-in-sliding-doors moment, although his destiny would be to reach the giddy heights of producing Coldplay, rather than producing Coldplay's children. Thankfully –

not least for the sake of this story – he didn't fluff his lines. I like to imagine Eno consulted his strategy cards before boarding the train:

"*Flap your hands like a bird*" says the first one.

"Massively unhelpful" thinks Brian. "These cards are going to need a bit of work…".

It's amusing to think of Eno strolling around London for years reading cards that tell him to do all sorts of odd things, ("wear a coat with feathers on the back"), but sadly there is absolutely no evidence to support this whimsical theory. The cards were reportedly developed in 1975.

He stepped onto the train. In the carriage he chose stood Andy Mackay. They knew each other just a little, enough to recognise each other. Mackay told Eno he had just started a band with a guy called Bryan Ferry, and they wanted to record their music. The trouble was, they didn't know anyone with a tape recorder. As luck would have it, Eno was playing around with such machines as only someone like Eno would have been back then.

From that moment, Eno was part of Roxy Music.

Roxy Music appeared in 1972, apparently from nowhere and seemingly fully formed. At a time when authenticity was a key measurement of the quality of rock music, Roxy Music showed up with daft clothes, odd yet romantic songs about growing potatoes, a singer who warbled strangely and a geezer who 'played' what looked like a console ripped out of Heathrow's air traffic control room. It wasn't an obvious template with which to form a band. Just picture the scene:

**Bryan Ferry**: "*Thank you everyone for coming. I have this idea for a rock band, and I'm looking for volunteers. We've got guitar, drums and bass, so there are just two missing ingredients. First, I need a bloke who can dress up strangely in a feather boa and be a knob-twiddler*".

*(Brian Eno consults card. It says "Honour thy error as a hidden intention"). Confused, Eno raises his hand.*

**Bryan Ferry**: "*Cheers Brian. You're in. Now, who can play the oboe?*"

It wasn't just the instruments that were unique. The lyrics weren't the regular type either.

*Bryan Ferry:* "Okay everyone. I have written this romantic song called 'In Every Dream Home a Heartache'. Any questions?"

*Graham Simpson:* "What's it about Bryan?"

*Bryan:* "Er, it's a romantic song about a blow up doll ... "

*Simpson:* " ... are you alright Bryan ... do you need a rest?"

*Bryan:* "Um, it can wait for the second album. I've got one about growing potatoes instead. By the score. It's really romantic."

*Andy Mackay* "Well, that's not right for a start. By the score? Who goes to the greengrocers and asks for a "score" of potatoes? They're sold by the pound, Bryan."

The potato song, or 'If There Is Something' as it is better known, made the first album.

The other thing you should know about Roxy Music is their story really begins with the Beatles' *The White Album*. Because the artist who designed that cover was Richard Hamilton, and Richard Hamilton happened to be not only one of Bryan Ferry's teachers at Newcastle University, but a hugely influential driver of the pop art movement. In his last year at Newcastle, Hamilton would work on a piece titled 'Large Glass', a statement of romanticism which featured a mechanised bride figure. This, and other such ideas – especially that of art being about many things; sculpture, fashion, music, rather than simply painting – took root in the young Bryan Ferry's mind. Ferry left Newcastle for London looking to form a new kind of band.

He had a vision – one of romanticism and glamour – which was far removed from the singer-songwriters and progressive rock virtuosos of the time, for whom such artifice was inauthentic. This singular vision didn't prevent Ferry auditioning for King Crimson at one stage, mind you. Roxy Music met through friends of friends, band members came and went. Their first drummer, Dexter Lloyd, left to join the Oxford Playhouse's pit orchestra for a production of *Aladdin*. Great decision.

*Dexter Lloyd's wife:* "Honey, don't those fellas on Top Of the Pops look like your old band mates?"

*Dexter Lloyd* (humming 'A Whole New World'): "Don't worry love, they won't get far. They had songs about potatoes and blow up dolls. Bunch of weirdos."

Eno was another friend of a friend, having stepped on the right train carriage, and bought into Ferry's vision. If art school had taught Eno anything, it was that you didn't need to be an expert painter to be a great artist. He was pretty sure the same applied to pop music. At Winchester School of Art he joined a "scratch orchestra" which allowed people of little talent to play along with those of greater ability. His art teachers were divided as to his qualities, some seeing him as a "bad influence", others as "an interesting student" "hampered by intellectual considerations".

This is why Roxy Music emerged seemingly fully formed. All these life experiences brewing around the various band members came together. Ferry was nearer thirty than twenty. Their art-school friends shot the cover art. They even credited their hairdressers in the sleeve notes. Roxy Music wasn't just a band, it was a concept. A lifestyle.

They also weren't afraid of a little hard work. They spent eighteen months rehearsing the same dozen songs. The line-up changed, with Phil Manzanera joining just three weeks before the debut album was recorded, but the songs were the same – just honed to perfection. They played the somewhat strange songs so much they sounded normal to the players. When they finally appeared on TV they were a well-oiled machine, looking alien, yet exotic, playing songs with prog-level complexity, beautifully executed. For everybody else, who hadn't heard them before, it all sounded fresh, strange and exciting.

**Collectors' Note:** First pressings of the first four Roxy Music LPs are on Island records, with later pressings on red Polydor labels. The Island labels have a pink rim around the edge. The debut, Stranded and For Your Pleasure all have gatefold, laminated, covers. The fourth album retains the pink rim label but doesn't stick to the gatefold formula.

# 3

## Peak Vinyl? Is It Time to Start Buying CDs Again?

*But why records? What about CDs? Compared with streaming, new vinyl is an expensive option. If you want real value, surely CDs are the way to go? Or at least that's what I want to explore in this chapter.*

## PART 1

As with many bad ideas, this one started in a pub. History is littered with Bad Ideas That Started In Pubs. The Pet Rock was an idea that began in a pub, naturally. You'd have to be pretty pie-eyed to think that was a sensible business idea, even if it did turn out pretty well.

Quidditch was reportedly invented in the pub when JK Rowling was drowning her sorrows after arguing with a boyfriend. She pictured him being knocked off a broomstick with a bludger, and the world's most mystifying sport was born. The Iron Man Triathlon was concocted in Hawaii in 1977, after John Collins and Judy Collins presumably had one too many Tom Collins and calculated if they did the 2.4-mile Waikiki Rough Water Swim followed by the 115-mile Round the Island bike race, they would be near the start line of the Honolulu Marathon. And wouldn't that be fun? Honestly... Some people shouldn't be allowed near alcohol.

I was beginning to realise that one of those people might be me, when I found myself in the unlikely position of darting constantly in and out of charity shops looking for R.E.M. CDs. It turns out it's quite an annoying habit when you are in company. There are few more grating habits than charity shop visiting, it seems.

The irritation stems, I understand, from when your loved one thinks they are strolling down the high street with you, only to find they have been walking on their own for the last quarter of an hour. After ten vexed minutes of looking around, considering filing a missing person's report, and wondering which picture they should use of you on those "Have You Seen This Person?" adverts on the side of bottles of milk that you see in Hollywood films, they see you popping blithely out of The British Heart Foundation shop muttering something about how many copies of Dido's *Life For Rent* are cluttering up the place.

Apparently, it's also "insensitive" when they are trying on a particularly lovely dress in the changing room of a nice boutique-y shop and they swish back the curtain wearing said dress to ask your thoughts on how lovely the material is, only to find you are next door talking to some old dear on the Cats Protection League counter, scrabbling around for change.

I don't even like CDs. Never have done, with their irritating clickety-clacking of jewel cases that shatter upon impact with human skin, a feature which contradicts the myth of their indestructibility. I have never known anything so fragile as a CD jewel case. Have you ever spread jam on a CD? No. me neither. And yet this was the big selling point when the introduction of the CD was announced on TV in the Seventies, as if everyone was going around spilling marmalade over records whilst tucking into the breakfast egg and toast. You could spread jam on CDs and they would still play, we were told.

Or were we? If you ask people of a certain age in the U.K. plenty will swear blind that they remember just a few things from their childhood vividly, including perhaps where they were when Kennedy was shot, the dry summer of '76, Live Aid, and the moment when Judith Hanna spread strawberry jam on a Bee Gees CD, in an attempt, presumably, to make it less sugary.

I remember it well. At least I thought I did. Imagine my surprise when I learned it is an urban myth. It's as real as that story about Marc Almond. Or, as this is 2020 and we're all very angry with each other, it's FAKE NEWS.

I digress. Where was I? CDs..bad ideas in pubs...ah, yes, I remember now. Back to the story.

I was chatting with a couple of pals. Andy is a casual music fan who has embraced Spotify and the wireless system Sonos. Chris, on the other hand, still likes buying CDs. We were discussing the general flaws around CDs and the fact that CDs have now never been cheaper. For items that used to fetch £15.99 or more in the shops in 1990, cash converting websites will now offer you the princely sum of thirty English pence – just 2% of its original value.

The only items to have fallen more dramatically in value than CDs since the nineties are books detailing how to fix the millennium bug, Beanie Babies and shares in Nokia phones. I mentioned I wanted to start building a collection of R.E.M. albums on vinyl.

"What's the point of buying all those albums on vinyl when they're all on Spotify?" asked Spotify Andy, as always genuinely bewildered at the fuss I make about vinyl. "I know you like playing the records but let's be honest, they're a real pain ..." he added.

"I like to have a physical copy of it." countered CD-buying Chris.

"It's just so ... Pointless ..." retorted Andy, rolling his eyes.

"Until your wifi goes down." replied Chris smugly. Turning to me, Chris asked in all seriousness "Why don't you just buy R.E.M. albums on CD?"

"Why would I, when I can buy records?" I asked.

"Because CDs are so cheap" he answered. "Vinyl is really expensive. It's become so popular, prices are going up – £20 or more for albums. If you like the music and want a physical copy with the liner notes and all that, you should be going around charity shops buying the CDs for a pound. I bet you could buy the whole of R.E.M.'s back catalogue for less than twenty quid now. The same albums on vinyl will probably set you back two hundred quid"

Well. He had a point. And beneath it all there's a challenge. Is it true?

Are we wasting our time on records when the real value is in the CDs? We've been here before haven't we, with vinyl? Everyone sold their record collections in the nineties. We couldn't give them away... Are we falling into the same trap?

To find out, I spent a fair bit of time trying to buy the back catalogue of R.E.M. on vinyl and CD, in order to answer the following questions:

- Are CDs a tiny fraction of the cost of vinyl?
- What's the point of CDs?
- Would all the jewel cases shatter at the slightest touch? And
- Would I be better off just listening on Spotify?

Here's what happened...

## Part 2: Buying R.E.M. on CD

If you are looking for CDs, there's one place you are guaranteed to find some. I went to the first place any self-respecting CD hunter would go.

No, not a record shop.

The loft.

People's attics are where approximately 76% of all the world's CDs can now be found according to a survey I just fabricated. There the doomed discs all are, packed like sardines, taped up in boxes upon which the legend "CDs: loft" has been scribbled. Right next to the box of DVDs, I dare say. All destined never to see daylight again.

Sure enough, a brief search in my loft revealed vast quantities of CDs. A time capsule of my (and my wife's) '90s musical tastes. And equally sure enough, amidst the Shine compilations (1 and 5), the Forrest Gump soundtrack and a collection by Dodgy nestled two R.E.M. CDs. Both of which belonged to my wife. *Monster* and (because she was always cooler than I was) the 'Early Years' IRS best of compilation.

That was £2 saved then. They had probably cost more than £30 back in the day...

Having exhausted the attic, I tramped around the sunny streets of Leigh-on-Sea and nipped into its various charity shops. It wasn't quite as simple as I thought it might be. After six charity shops without a single R.E.M. CD, I was beginning to wonder whether my theory had been the right one. Perhaps R.E.M. fans don't sell their CDs quite so readily as Kylie fans or Steps fans? I certainly wouldn't have had any trouble had I been collecting Dido CDs.

I have never seen so many Dido CDs in the same place as in a charity shop. Every shop had dozens of them. They were everywhere: in the CDs racks (obviously), propping up tables, being used as coasters; one shop had even made a lampshade out of them. I could tell they were Dido CDs as the light it cast made everything seem blander. The only time I ever saw such a concentration of unwanted CDs was in the Notting Hill Video and Music Exchange two months after the release of Oasis' *Be Here Now*.

There was also a decent amount of Busted, JLS and Enya.

I had barely looked at a CD for over thirteen years. It had been so long that I had forgotten why I hadn't paid them much attention. I know I'm into vinyl so may not be representative of the population as a whole, but I do remember the last time I played a CD in a CD player at home. It was September 2003, just before I bought a 3rd Generation 40gb iPod. After that epochal moment, there didn't seem much point in CDs.

After thirteen years of not really looking at CDs aside from ripping them onto an iPod, putting them back into their jewel case, sweeping up the shards of shattered jewel case that came off as I closed the case and then leaving them in a pile to go into the loft, I wondered whether my current lack of interest in CDs was fair. If I could ignite a love for CDs perhaps I could buy up swathes of interesting music from charity shops for a pound a time just as everyone else was exiting the market. I saw myself perhaps as a Wall Street trader, buying calmly whilst everyone else panicked, safe in the knowledge that these stocks had intrinsic value.

Then, in the next charity shop, I found a couple of R.E.M. CDs. Looking closely at the CD for *New Adventures In Hifi* I realised why such things currently fetch a pound a time. It was shiny. I'll give it that much. You couldn't fault it for shininess. It was as shiny as Bob Monkhouse's forehead on reruns of *Bob's Full House*.

The CD artwork was tiny, a photo of a vast expanse captured uselessly in as small a format as possible. The effect felt similar to trying to appreciate the Sistine Chapel by viewing it on a Nokia flip phone from 2004. The CD itself was a circular, featureless, afterthought, a yawn of bytes and binary code, a digital shrug, an unlovable consumable. It really was the most boring thing I had set eyes on in years. And I've watched *Take Me Out*.

Sure, CDs store their bits and bytes and replay them perfectly satisfactorily. This is not an argument about sound quality. But being able to replay what is stored on something is really a minimum requirement for any medium. In a world of hard drives and lossy formats we ask a little more of our physical media.

I saw that, in order for me to love the CD format, I would have to be attracted to bright, shiny, featureless, bland things. And I'm just not. My eyesight's going. I can't see a four-inch paper sleeve. I like those big black slabs of plastic and their massive twelve-inch cardboard sleeves, with all the storage problems and dust they come with.

I gave up the Great R.E.M. CD Hunt there and then. There just didn't seem much point. I couldn't see why listening on Spotify wouldn't just serve the same purpose. Good luck to you if you like CDs for their quality of music or their um, compact size and disc-like shape. It's fine. It's me, not you. In fact, the world is your oyster because it's never been cheaper to buy the things. Fill your boots.

But what kind of people would truly, madly, deeply love these little shiny discs? There are probably others, but I could think of two groups. Magpies; they love shiny things. That was one group. The other? Fans of Dido.

Postscript: *In the months after writing this, I stumbled across plenty of R.E.M. CDs, all for a pound or so each... there's no question you can currently pick them all up very cheaply indeed.*

# Part 3: Should You Buy Nineties Vinyl?

## (Also: Buying R.E.M. on Vinyl)

With no R.E.M. albums to my name, I began my search for R.E.M. in March 2016, at Spitalfields Record Fair, where a copy of *Document* popped up for just £5. It felt like such a bargain. Surely R.E.M. albums weren't all that cheap?

They weren't, but a month later I did find a copy of *Out Of Time* for £10 in a shop called Bulldog Records in Bletchley, near Milton Keynes. In May I found *Green* for £7 in Carmel Records, Southend, and in the same month, *Reckoning* for £10 at the Southend Record Fair. That was four albums for £32 – an average of just £8 each.

In July I found a lovely copy of *Automatic For The People* for £25 (I haggled) at Southend Record Fair. It was £25, so I used 'Record Collector's Logic' to justify the purchase. You may or may not be familiar with Record Collector's Logic. It is an excellent formula used to justify expensive purchases. Research has shown that almost all record collectors use it. It goes like this:

Q. How much does the record cost?

A. £25

Q. If I buy another record costing £5, what is the average price of the two records?

A. £30

Q. So how much does the first record really cost?

A. (Using Record Collector's Logic) £15: an instant saving of £10!

I thought about that £5 copy of *Document* and figured the two came to £15 each. It made the £25 cost seem so much more palatable. *Document* still cost £5, of course...

Formulae are useful in life. Here's another you may find useful:

**R = D-1**

This flexible and adaptable formula is used to calculate the maximum number of things (record players, records or indeed bicycles, cats etc) that one may safely keep in one's collection. In the formula, R equals the maximum number of records (or turntables, cats etc) that one may have in a collection, and D is the number of records or turntables (or cats) in your collection that, were you to own that many, would result in your loved one divorcing you. So long as you always have one less (D-1) than that fateful step, that's the maximum you are allowed to have in your collection.

I digress.

For *six months* I then failed to spot a single R.E.M. album that I didn't own, or that was in decent condition. A drier spell than that of a man whose wife has found his name on the Ashley Madison website.

And then just when I was losing hope, I popped into my local second hand record shop (Leigh Records) just as someone had apparently sold their entire collection of R.E.M. albums and there were half a dozen of the things in immaculate condition including *Fables of The Reconstruction* for £10, something called *Eponymous* for £15 and *Life's Rich Pageant* for £20, which felt a bit eye watering, but it was very clean and the record collector instinct in me knew you don't flinch when there's three together like that. It was like the old adage of waiting around for ages for a bus only for three to come along all at once, only the wait was six months, so more like if Southern Rail were running a bus service.

After this stroke of good fortune all I had left to find of the classic IRS run was the debut album *Murmur*, which I felt might be tricky and expensive, and then the '90s run of albums from *Monster* onwards which would be merely nose-bleedingly expensive. As luck would have it, and much to the detriment of any tension in this story, just two weeks later Leigh Records had *Murmur*, and for just £5. I rejoiced, like any self-respecting record collector nowadays would: by bragging about it on Instagram. I have no idea why that was £5 and *Life's Rich Pageant* was £20, or why *Murmur* wasn't there the first time. It was as though Leigh on Sea had introduced an R.E.M. Vinyl Amnesty and people had started handing in their record collections. Sometimes it's best not to think too deeply about Life's Big Questions.

And then came *Monster*.

The follow up to *Automatic For The People*, *Monster* was released in 1994, just as vinyl sales were beginning a decade-long trough (sales of vinyl albums fell from a peak of 1.1 billion worldwide in 1981 to 109 million in 1993 and just 33 million in 1995. By 1997, they were down to 17 million, and plunged as low as 3 million in 2006). Despite it selling in decent quantities, in line with many albums released in the nineties, most sales of *Monster* were of CDs. The vinyl run was not large and due to R.E.M.'s enduring popularity there is high demand for the album on vinyl. On the record collector catalogue and trading site Discogs, recent sales of the album averaged £45.77, with a highest price of £61. So, when I saw it at Southend Record Fair for £35 it felt like a fair price – notwithstanding the £1 price for a CD in a charity shop and the fact that £35 for a single album is a huge sum of money in itself – it's funny how value is relative – and I snapped it up.

Nineties vinyl is an odd thing. It's expensive now – often upwards of £40 for anything remotely popular – but the recordings were often not analogue, so there is far less of an audiophile argument for collecting the first pressings of nineties vinyl as there might be for analogue-only early pressings of, say, Nick Drake or Led Zeppelin. In the case of Nick Drake the original tapes have degraded so there really can be a discernible difference in an old pressing of Drake's debut album and a newer copy. Digital recordings don't degrade the same way analogue recordings can, so there ought not be any discernible difference in quality between one digital recording and another. The desirability of an album is therefore purely an issue of owning an original and / or of scarcity.

And interestingly, when nineties albums are reissued, there is evidence the price of the originals does comes down. The best time to buy an original copy of an old album is just after a reissue. For example, when The Black Crowes' *Southern Harmony and Musical Companion* was reissued, original copies stopped selling for £40 and fell to around £25 – not that much more than the reissue. In 2017 HMV released a pink vinyl 500-copy-only run of Teenage Fanclub's *Bandwagonesque*, and now you can buy original copies of the album for £25-£30 instead of £50. In contrast, Teenage Fanclub's subsequent album, *Grand Prix*, was not reissued at that time and would still have set you back £120. If you had taken leave of your senses, obviously[3].

On the other hand, despite a recent reissue, a copy of the 1994 original *Definitely Maybe* LP by Oasis on Creation will set you back upwards of £75. In this case, the comparative scarcity of the debut album relative to the popularity of Oasis means there is a sufficient market of people who want "the original" to push the price up. Other Britpop albums now fetch £40-£50, including the debuts by Supergrass and Elastica (the latter with poster and flexi-single). Pulp's *Different Class* meanwhile regularly reaches over £100 mainly because re-issues don't have the same "cut out window" that features in the original album. Nothing to do with how the record sounds. Indeed, original copies of previous album *His 'N' Hers* are still more than double the price (£53 average) of a double vinyl re-issue (£24) despite the latter featuring an extra track: hit single 'Babies' on the

---

[3] Since the reissue in 2018 of *Grand Prix*, there has been a clear reduction in the average sale price of original copies so that two years after I wrote this, the last copy sold was down to £60, which will surprise no-one with an elementary knowledge of supply and demand economic theory, or who has attempted to buy an umbrella on an unexpectedly rainy day from an unscrupulous street vendor in Tottenham Court Road and then looked at the prices when it's sunny.

album proper and having an extra LP of b-sides and rarities. The re-issue is a demonstrably better LP to own – and is cheaper!

Record collecting logic, eh?

So, is it worth picking up R.E.M. Albums on vinyl? My conclusion is this: the eighties albums are relatively inexpensive – I paid £92 for everything up to *Automatic For The People* – an eight album stretch – which is a bargain. The packaging isn't always breathtaking – *Murmur* doesn't even have a printed inner sleeve – R.E.M. weren't really a lavish gatefold sleeve kind of band. There don't appear to be any quirky "collector's items" out there. No variant sleeves, fan club inserts or "loud" pressings such as you might find with Beatles or Bowie vinyl. The nineties albums? These are now not great value. *Up* may be a brilliant and under-rated record, but it is too expensive (GBP100-plus) for anyone other than their biggest fans, so it's worth waiting for a reissue, either to buy new or to see if the price of original copies falls.

So why buy the albums on vinyl? I came to the realisation it is this: that I have liked R.E.M.'s music for years, but I have never taken time out to really listen to the back catalogue. For nearly thirty years I have not listened to R.E.M. very much. It seems that buying a few albums has given me a reason to play R.E.M.'s music. I spent money on it. And that made me want to get my money's worth. Mainly because I'm tight like that.

Streaming services are great, but can make us lazy. Stumbling across a record spurs me on to actually play the thing properly. To get into it. To play it multiple times rather than moving on to the next thing. And as a result, I have a collection of R.E.M. records that I bought inexpensively enough that they will always be worth at least what I paid for them and which even if they don't appreciate in value, I will appreciate all the more – which is what it's all about, right?

And to top it all, I also have the upside of a CD of *New Adventures In Hi-Fi* that can't be worth any less, and which might just be worth squirreling away just in case CDs become retrospectively and unfathomably popular again ...

# 4

## Three more stories, then, starting with The Story of Clube da Esquina by Milton Nascimento and Lô Borges

*Clube da Esquina by Milton Nascimento and Lô Borges was one of only five Brazilian albums to be featured in the book "1001 Albums You Must Hear Before You Die".*

*If you have yet to hear this fusion of Brazilian music and Beatles-inflected pop, this may whet your appetite...*

1971. Rural northern Rio de Janeiro, just across the border from the mining state of Minas Gerais. Seven year old José Antônio Rimes, known to his friends as Tonho, is playing with his friend Antônio Carlos Rosa de Oliveira, known as Cacau. Two guys pull up in a VW Beetle, someone calls out to him, and he smiles. The driver takes a picture, and beetles off. Tonho carries on with the rest of his life, unaware he and his friend will be the cover stars of one of Brazil's most celebrated records.

When he was young, like José Antonio Rimes, Milton Nascimento had a nickname. His was "Bituca", which translates as "Cigarette Butt" – hardly the most flattering nickname. Born to poor, working class black parents in Rio he was adopted by white middle class parents on the death of his birth mother when he was just three years old. Growing up, Bituca would attempt to learn to play songs he heard on the radio. The only problem was the songs were often incomplete because the signal would cut out mid-song. He would snatch fragments of songs, transcribe them and wait for them to be repeated. If they weren't he would imagine the rest, making up his own harmonies. Only years later, when he heard other musicians play the songs did he realise he was playing them differently to everyone else. Being different turned out not to be a bad move.

Aside from the radio, the other place he and his friends could hear music was the cinema, in stereophonic sound. The cinema became a ritual. These temples of magic with their large screens didn't just impress with their visuals, but also with their music. Bituca's father was a director at a local radio station, Ràdio ZYV36, and at just fourteen years old Bituca became a DJ, playing music from around the world. He played in bands, covering pop songs from Brazil and America.

Moving to the city of Belo Horizonte for work, he rented a room close to an expanse of pavement on a corner downtown called Ponto dos Músicos. It was the Denmark Street of Belo Horizonte – a place where musicians would congregate, be hired to perform bailes (balls/dances), and to meet, and be seen. Here he met a number of musicians who, in 1971/72 would join him to record an album called *Clube da Esqiuna* – the "Corner Club".

Nascimento got a break at the 1967 Festival Internacional da Canção, a national song contest – think Eurovision for Brazilians, but with fewer Finnish heavy metal bands dressed in masks. His song 'Travessia' was voted second best song. The following year, he was a finalist again, this time at TV Record's IV Festival De MPB, but his song was ignored by the judges in the middle of a storm between more traditional, conservative singers and a new wave of Brazilian music makers, the Tropicalistas – a movement of musicians that included Os Mutantes and Tom Zè – whose music was upsetting both the ruling dictatorship and Marxist-influenced students on Brazil's left, whose aesthetic agenda was strongly nationalistic. This was mainly because a) it didn't say how great everything was being Brazilian and living under a military regime and b) contained electric fuzzy guitars associated with American music. It seemed that "going electric" wasn't just controversial in the Northern hemisphere...

Tropicalia vanguards Caetano Veloso and Os Mutantes' performances that year were the Brazilian equivalent of Bob Dylan's infamous "Judas" concert, albeit because this is Brazil, they were even more tumultuous, as both were festooned in outlandish green costumes. Such behaviour resulted in their being pelted with fruit, vegetables, eggs and a rain of paper balls, while the audience expressed their disapproval by standing up and turning their backs to the performers, prompting Os Mutantes to respond in kind by turning their backs on the audience. It's the Brazilian equivalent of Bob Dylan at the Albert Hall, only the punters don't dress as leprechauns or do the Poznań at the R.A.H, even at the London Symphony Orchestra's more raucous gigs.

Despite being overlooked at the 1968 contest, Nascimento had done enough to sign a record deal and he released a modestly successful album every year for four years, growing his fan base. But, that year saw the military government pass strict censorship laws. Many Brazilian musicians went into exile. The period is sometimes referred to as one of "cultural emptiness." Nascimento and his fellow musicians were watched with suspicion by the authorities – and with good reason – they would shelter activists and dissidents in their apartments. He was prohibited from seeing his son in São Paulo – the government threatened to kidnap his son "forever" were he to do so.

The atmosphere in the streets became paranoid. Gathering in groups on a street corner was now seen as suspicious. If someone reported your owning the wrong sort of book, something subversive, you might be arrested, or disappear. People became mistrustful and cautious, resigned to a future without hope. It was established by the Truth Commission Report in 2014 that the military government subjected as many as 20,000 people to torture between 1965 and 1985. That's quite an atmosphere in which to be a musician.

In response, Nascimento wanted to do something different. A collaborative effort with people he knew from the Minas Gerais region of Brazil, and to blend this regional music with Brazil's national musical forms such as samba and bossa nova, and with jazz, music from cinema and Beatles-influenced pop. He also wanted to reflect the times in his lyrics, while walking a thin tightrope with censors. He pulled together a team of people who had the sort of football-friendly names that would have Graeme Souness sign them on four year £100k per week contracts, sight unseen, with or without an endorsement from George Weah.

These included two drummers, one called Rubinho and the other Robertinho Silva, a bassist called Luis Alves, lyricist Marcio Borges, guitarists Beto Guedes, Lô Borges and Nelson Àngelo, keyboards/piano from Wagner Tiso and to cap it all, a lyricist called Ronaldo. Well, Ronaldo Bastos. Either way, you would fancy them to beat West Ham nine times out of ten. Even now, at their age.

They had mostly met each other from the corner club, and were a close-knit team. Having convinced the record label, Odeon, to fund a double album – a first for Brazilian popular music – the musicians took to a studio, rehearsing and composing as they went. Instruments would be swapped and songs would be put together as the friends gathered over lunch in bars and restaurants that would spill out into the street corners. Àngelo described such gatherings in 2012: "We had many meetings...we met and said 'So this song will be like this, it will open and so on..' Then Nascimento would say 'No, let's see if we can get a choir singing something there.' Then someone else, 'Let's splice this song with that other one'."

Lyrics in songs such as 'Nada Será Como Antes' ('Nothing Will Be As It Was') reflected the group's experiences and were seen as subtle protests. Thus the Clube da Esquina of the title represented the literal corners of the city of Belo Horizonte where Nascimento and his co-musicians met. And while it wasn't possible in such an oppressive regime to be openly critical, the album projected a more subtle meaning.

From its cover of two friends, its cinematic expansiveness, its use of a whole team of individual talents, its bringing together regional, national and international influences to create something that transcends them all, indeed its very name – the club on the corner, where the collective all met and came together to create something extraordinary – is one of achieving something greater than the sum of its parts through openness and cooperation.

The resulting album is a true collaboration, with multiple lyric writers, half a dozen guitarists, an equal number of percussionists, vocals from Lo Borges, Alaide Costa and Nascimento... all swapping roles from time to time. The subtle message is that by working together, through friendship, life's obstacles can be overcome. Including, no doubt, military dictatorships. The album became one of Brazil's most celebrated, and remains an extraordinary listen.

Which brings us back to the beginning of the story.

2012 marked the fortieth anniversary of the release of Clube da Esquina. The hunt was on for *os meninos da capa*: the boys from the [album] cover. They were tracked down by a journalist. Tonho worked in a supermarket. Cacau as a gardener. Tonho had been unaware of the album, and was delighted to discover the photo, meaningful to so many Brazilians as a symbol of friendship across racial divides, but for a different reason: "We never had photos from when I was a boy". More meaningfully he reflected that his own friendship with Antônio Carlos had lasted as long as the image: "We each took a different path, but when we see each other it's always a riot. A friend is a friend, right? For life."

**Collectors' Note:** Until very recently it has been prohibitively expensive to find a copy of Clube da Esquina on vinyl. Original copies are scarce. But a 2017 official Brazilian reissue by Polysom has changed this. Released on 180 gram vinyl in a gatefold sleeve and remastered from the original analogue tapes, this is a double album that would grace any collection and, although postage from Brazil is nothing to be sniffed at, is now more affordable than ever before.

## The Story of Bohemian Rhapsody by Queen

It's worth considering the near-disastrous position Queen were in on 24th August 1975, as they checked in to a former farm called Rockfield Studios in the Wye Valley, near Monmouth to record their fourth album, the one that included the extraordinary 'Bohemian Rhapsody. Queen were more broke, as the saying goes, than the Ten Commandments. They were massively in debt. They had lost their manager; a future US tour had been cancelled and it looked like it might be the end of the road for this quirky band.

Sparks, a band Queen had shared a bill with at The Marquee a few years previously, had just scored a hit with 'This Town Ain't Big Enough For The Both Of Us' and sensed there might be an opportunity to enter the transfer window. They offered Brian May a way out.

"They came round and said, 'Look, it's pretty obvious that Queen are washed up, we'd like to offer you a position in our band if you want,'" said Brian May "and I said, 'Well I don't think we're quite dead yet.'"

Despite May's optimism, it's fair to say that success and Queen were yet to be wearing matching jumpers and skipping along together hand in hand. Whilst Queen's last U.S. tour had seen the *Sheer Heart Attack* album reach No 12 in the charts, it looked like it might be tougher for Queen to crack the States than it would be for Victoria Beckham to crack a smile. It hadn't helped that throughout the tour lead singer Freddie Mercury had suffered throat problems.

Better was the Japanese tour, where they had become pop stars for the first time, had been wildly successful and had played the Budokan twice in front of 14,000 screaming fans. However that success brought their situation elsewhere more starkly into focus. Mercury, May, Taylor and Deacon returned to the UK facing huge debts and, more immediately, mould growing in their pitiful basement flats in London, which were grimmer than England's 2015 Rugby World Cup campaign. Three albums into their career they were earning £60 a week each.

The money problems were genuine. The band owed their management company, recording studio and publisher Trident the huge sum of £200,000 and were frustrated with Trident's ability to promote them internationally. £200k might not get you even the mouldiest basement apartment in London nowadays, but in 1975 it was a sum so vast it could buy a small island, six classic and now priceless Ferraris, or even cover Black Sabbath's alleged cocaine bill for six months.

To move forward, Queen decided to exit the deal with Trident. EMI took over the contract, but at a cost. The band would pay royalties to Trident to repay the debt over their next six albums. To prepare for the studio, Queen rehearsed for three weeks in a house in Hertfordshire owned by a lady who rented out the property to rock stars to pay her bills.

The lady's daughter, a six year old little girl called Tiffany recalled Freddie playing her a piece of music on the piano.

"Do you like it?" he asked.

"It's fantastic" replied Tiffany.

"It's a bit long..." he replied.

You can probably guess the song he was playing. Yet, Tiffany was not the first person to hear the song. In fact, 'Bohemian Rhapsody' pre-dates *Sgt. Pepper's Lonely Hearts Club Band* in its origins. That's right. Freddie Mercury had begun writing 'Bohemian Rhapsody' before Lennon and McCartney had written their own multi-part Magnum Opus 'A Day In The Life'. The Beatles get credits for finishing theirs a bit quicker, mind you. Take nothing away from them, those Beatles.

In 1967, Freddie Bulsara would take his friend, Chris Smith from college to a music shop on Ealing Broadway. If Freddie had written a song, he'd grab a guitar off the wall and play it to his friend. The shop got pretty unhappy about this rather *laissez faire* attitude to the use of their equipment, but not before Freddie had played his friend a song called 'The Cowboy Song'. Its opening line was "Mama, just killed a man."

When 'Bohemian Rhapsody' was finally released Chris Smith's first thought was: "Oh. Freddie's finished the song..." To put how long it took to write and release 'Bohemian Rhapsody' into perspective, it's a longer period of time than there was between the release of the Beatles' first album and their last. A week after it was released, the Sex Pistols played their first gig.

Back to 1975 and now in the studio, Freddie played the song to producer Roy Thomas Baker. After the piano led introduction, Mercury paused, saying "And this is where the opera section comes in". Baker and Mercury both laughed at the absurdity of it all, but Baker reflected "I had worked with the D'Oyly Carte Opera at Decca... so I was probably one of the few people in the pop world who knew what he was talking about."

If there's one story that stands out about the making of 'Bohemian Rhapsody' and the lengths that Queen would go to in their search of perfection, it's this: there were parts of the song that required one hundred and eighty overdubs. Nowadays, you could sing a line a couple of times onto a digital mixer and multi-track it to create a chorus in minutes. Probably. In 1975, the members of Queen had to sing the same line a hundred and eighty times. This sounds an insane labour of love until you consider that Brian May built his own guitar from a mahogany fireplace with fret markers made from sanded down mother of pearl buttons, a tremolo arm made from a piece of steel used to hold up the saddle on a bike and capped by a knitting needle, and two valve springs from a 1928 Panther motorbike to balance the string tension. You suspect May might have a pretty good attention span.

One hundred and eighty overdubs and the recording tape was becoming threadbare and transparent. "People think it's this legendary story but you could hold the tape up to the light and see through it" said May. "Every time Freddie came up with another Galileo I would add another piece of tape to the reel which was beginning to look like a zebra crossing whizzing by".

Added Mercury, "between the three (Brian, Roger, Freddie) we created a 160-200 piece choir effect ... There was a section of "No, no, no" to do. Those were the days of 16 track studios. We did so many overdubs on the 16 tracks for that song, we just kept piling it on and on, that the tape went transparent because it just couldn't take any more. I think it snapped in two places as well."

Once the overdubs had been done, the mixing was still to be done. Studio engineer Robert Lee was there for the mixing. "So many faders had to be precisely cued, it was really tricky. They spent hours and hours trying to get it right, never quite succeeding. And then, miracle, this was the one. Everything was going perfectly ... nearly at the end. Everyone was tense with adrenaline but very happy. And then, suddenly the lights went out and in walks Jill (the sister of the owner of the studio) proudly carrying a huge cake aglow with candles and she was singing "Happy Birthday dear Freddie, Happy Birthday to you!"

"And they had to start over again..."

The single was famously picked up by DJ Kenny Everett who played it multiple times on his radio show, leading to Queen's first number one chart position. Yet at the time the single was not an obvious choice. It seems incredible now, but 'Bohemian Rhapsody' might not even have been released as a single. Said Brian May, "There were contenders (for first single). We were thinking of 'The Prophet's Song' at one point..."

That would have been the equivalent of having Lionel Messi on the subs bench in your football team's cup final in which you're a goal down, and then choosing to bring on Dame Maggie Smith for the last twenty minutes.

"I'd say something like 'Rhapsody' was a big risk, and it worked," said Freddie Mercury, looking back. "It had a very big risk factor. The radio people didn't like it initially because it was too long, and the record companies said they couldn't market it that way.... We had numerous rows. EMI were shocked... "a six minute single? You must be joking!" they said. But it worked.... That single sold over a million and a quarter copies in Britain alone, which is just outrageous. Imagine all those grandmothers grooving to it ..."

On a final note, perhaps what is most revealing about the internal tensions of the band at the time is the story of the b-side. Roger Taylor had a less than mature reaction to Mercury's composition being the first single. According to Roy Thomas Baker he locked himself in a cupboard until his own composition 'I'm In Love With My Car' was allowed to be the b-side (and would therefore get the same royalties as the a-side). It took Queen a dozen years to get that out of their system. By the time of *The Miracle* album Queen decided to split all songwriting credits – and therefore royalties – equally between them.

## The Story of *Different Class* by Pulp: a play in seven parts

Pulp's defining album, *Different Class* reached the top of the charts in November 1995, more than two decades ago, in a move designed solely to now make us all feel rather old. In a year when the rest of Britain was deciding whether Blur's 'Country House' or Oasis' 'Roll With It' should be number one, Pulp slipped out of the wardrobe and quietly wrote the defining song of the times, the mix of righteous anger and danceability that was 'Common People'. Most of the album that followed – *Different Class* – was written after 'Common People' soared to number 2 in the charts and the boost to Cocker's confidence gave us that ode to the late '80s rave scene ('Sorted for E's and Whizz') and the combination of real-life story and Laura Brannigan's 'Gloria' that was 'Disco 2000', not to mention one of the finest love songs anyone ever wrote, in 'Something Changed'.

It took Pulp sixteen years to become an overnight success. But the journey was what, in the end, made them great.

## 1.   The low point

Picking out the toughest time in the life of Jarvis Cocker is like trying to pick your least favourite candidate in *The Apprentice*. There's just so many to choose from. Aged five, Cocker narrowly survived a bout of meningitis, permanently damaging his eyesight. Only slightly less traumatically, when Jarvis turned seven years old his mother made him wear lederhosen to school. His uncle had married a German woman and they sent him the leather shorts as a gift. "I was mortified" said Cocker, understandably.

Cocker's childhood in Sheffield was not an unhappy one, although the spectacles and his lanky frame made him stand out from the crowd. Like many towns and cities in Britain at the time, Sheffield was a city where in Cocker's words "You'd get these packs of blokes, all dressed the same in the white short-sleeved shirt, black trousers and loafers, and they'd call you a queer or want to smack you 'cos they didn't like your jacket."

He and his friends would pretend to be in a band long before they had instruments "It just made it seem more interesting when you were walking down the corridor, imagining that we were a group and all the kids were clapping us," explained Cocker, but it didn't impress the girls, especially Deborah Bone, whom Cocker took a liking to. Deborah was, as Jarvis later explained "a girl who was born about two days after me in the same hospital. My mother and her mother knew each other, and I really fancied her when I got to about 13. Unfortunately, everybody else in the school fancied her as well, and we never got it together."[4]

After leaving school things didn't get any easier. Perhaps a low point was in November 1985 when he fell out of a window while trying to impress another girl called Adrienne with his Spiderman impression. Jarvis fell 20 feet to the ground, breaking his wrist and ankle and fracturing his pelvis. Like a lanky Dave Grohl, Cocker fronted his next shows from a wheelchair, albeit a National Health one rather than a custom-designed Guitar Throne. Jarvis was told the injuries sustained would

---

[4] *Deborah Bone went on to be a pioneering mental health worker, and was awarded an MBE in the New Year honours list shortly before her death aged 51. She had been diagnosed with multiple myeloma, a type of bone marrow cancer, and died hours after receiving the honour for her services to children and young people. Bone developed ways to help young people cope with high stress and anxiety. She was also, as you have probably guessed, the Deborah in "Disco 2000". In a nice touch, Cocker sang the song to her at her fiftieth birthday party. They never did meet at the fountain down the road. It was demolished in 1998.*

eventually be debilitating. "When they took the plaster off me legs, the doctor said, 'We've tried to put (your bones) back in place, but it's impossible to do properly, so you'll always have pain there. And in the end you'll be in so much pain that we'll have to fuse your foot to your ankle. Then you'll never be able to move your foot again.'

On the other hand Jarvis Cocker's lowest ebb might have been 1989. Nine years in, Pulp had failed to release a record in the previous two years, the band was shedding members every six months and their audience was dwindling. By now, some gigs were more deserted than the Friends Reunited page for Pompeii High School: Class of AD78.

A disillusioned Cocker decided to leave Sheffield, having had his application for a degree course at St. Martin's College accepted, but this meant putting the band on hold and living in a squalid flat in a hostile and unfriendly Mile End. Cocker described the flat in the song 'Mile End', a b-side to 'Something Changed' which also featured on the *Trainspotting* soundtrack. "It smelled as if someone had died / the living room was full of flies".

Pulp guitarist Steve Mackey reflected: "It was the end of the Eighties, a really bad time for us as nothing good had happened." Cocker and Mackey meanwhile took refuge in the rave scene including one event that took place in a tunnel under the M25 originally built for wild animals to cross safely. "You'd go to these raves and it was like a spaceship had landed! Lights were flashing, there were sexy girls, the music was like Kraftwerk ... it was like the future and you were part of it".

Cocker described living in Mile End as "without any question, the worst nine months of my entire life". But perhaps the nadir was in 1991, when Pulp were now twelve years into their music career and were still going nowhere fast. They'd just sacked their manager, Jarvis had borrowed £5k off his grandma to make some demos, they wanted to exit a five album record contract just one album in. Having finally attracted major record company interest Pulp couldn't cash the advance cheque as it would represent a breach of their existing contract. They were in a mess.

## 2. The Rise of Pulp

In 1991 Rough Trade offered to manage Pulp, and a major label contract was the target. From then on, the story of Pulp was one of a momentous rise in fortunes:

Single 'Babies' was released on October 5th 1992, 'Razzmatazz' followed in Feb 1993 and in July of that year Pulp finally signed to Island Records. 'Lipgloss' reached number fifty in the charts – a first for the band– in November 1993 and then Pulp had their first top 40 entry in March 1994 when 'Do You Remember The First Time which reached  number thirty-three.

*His 'n' Hers* would be the big breakthrough. Twelve years, eight months and four days after Jarvis first stepped into a studio, Pulp had finally made their "real" debut album. *His 'n' Hers* entered the album charts at number nine. The momentum was building. In July 1994 Jarvis presented an edition of *Top Of The Pops* and cheekily pinned a note to the inside of his jacket that read "I Hate Wet Wet Wet", a band whose cover of 'Love Is All Around' had spent an interminable time at the top of the U.K. Charts. This prompted Marti Pellow, the lead singer of the Scottish pop band, to describe Pulp as "indie nobodies". Ah, poor Marti. Fame is a fickle mistress. In 2013 Wet Wet Wet's final album (a greatest hits compilation) charted at number 53 - and sank without trace.

### 3. Common People

The origins of 'Common People' seemingly date back to when Jarvis was at the Notting Hill Music and Video exchange swapping some records for a Casio keyboard. He played a riff to Steve Mackey who said "Oh yeah, that sounds like 'Fanfare For The Common Man'". A seed was planted.

As we now know, the song's lyrics were inspired by a rich girl, believed to be Danae Stratou, the wife of a former Greek Finance Minister Yanis Varoufakis, and who Cocker met at St Martin's college. "She thought of the lower classes as something quite exotic, and something she could go and see as a tourist... and use it in her own work. I told her she wasn't trapped like they are ... She never wanted to sleep with me, unfortunately." Pulp finally recorded the song in January 1995. It was an obvious hit, so Island wanted to delay releasing it until just before the next LP would be ready, in September of that year. Had that happened, it's doubtful Pulp would have been in the frame for their famous headline appearance at Glastonbury.

In the end, Common People was released on May 22nd 1995. It sold 70,000 copies in the first week and reached number 2 in the charts.

### 4. Stand Out Stand Ins part 1: Oasis

In April 1994 Pulp were asked by Oasis to step in for The Verve at Sheffield Arena after Nick McCabe broke a finger.

Pulp played the still unreleased 'Common People'.

Noel Gallagher said "The whole audience went beserk and even me Mam...went "God I like that one, what's that one called?" and I went "I don't even know who they are – I don't know what the song's called."

Never short of confidence, Noel added "And we all sort of looked at one another and went "F— hell. It's a good job we're good".

## 5. Stand out Stand ins part 2: Glastonbury

Towards the end of June 1995 Pulp got a phone call. John Squire of the Stone Roses had broken a collar bone and the band's Glastonbury headline appearance would have to be cancelled. Rod Stewart wasn't available, so could Pulp step up to replace them?

It was so last minute, all the hotels were booked up, so the band bought a couple of large frame tents and some sleeping bags. The set was triumphant, a mixture of *His 'n' Hers* tunes and a few songs never heard before being played for the first time. Jarvis Cocker introduced new song 'Mis-Shapes' as a song about people who "laugh at you because they think you're the weird one. And this is how we are going to have our revenge on them". And then 'Common People', the last song of the night; said Cocker, introducing the song, "If you want something to happen enough then it actually will happen. And I believe that. In fact that's why we're stood on this stage after fifteen years. So if a lanky get like me can do it, and us lot, then you can do it too."

Drummer Nick Banks said "the crowd roared and it was amazing. As Jarvis started singing, basically you could hear the crowd louder than you could hear him and that was ... the hairs at the back of your neck just went. "

## 6. *Different Class*

"In late 1994 me and Jarvis had this concept to make an LP that was 12 pop songs and every one could be a single" said Steve Mackey. "We even talked about getting Benny from Abba to produce it".

Jarvis Cocker had overcome childhood illness, his awkwardness, being picked on for looking different, having no money, being told he might not be able to walk, an East End flat suited to a serial killer, endless nights of no audiences, no record deals, and being sent to a school in Sheffield wearing leather shorts. He'd then turned things around, headlined Glastonbury and written the best song of the nineties. All he had to do now was write an album to go with it. And what's amazing about this, what is extraordinary about the *Different Class* album, is how those years of frustration, bullying, humour and endurance came pouring out. Because Jarvis Cocker wrote the rest of the album – eight songs in total – to make a timeless, classic album that reflected upon all these events in Cocker's life, and he did it in just two nights.

"I did five one night and three the next night. I just sat in me sister's kitchen with this brandy me mother had brought back from Spain and I just kind of necked that..."

## 7. Something Changed

Pulp's low points turned out to be the things that made the band special. Like Cocker's musings on the happenstance of love in 'Something Changed', where would Pulp have been if these things hadn't occurred? Looking back, the key to what made Pulp special was the change that occurred in Jarvis during his spell in a wheelchair in 1985.

"In the hospital, I had a lot of time to think. And there was a miner in the bed next to me who'd been in an accident. He was a right nice bloke. The only contact I had with miners before was during the strike. I wanted to support it, but I always remember I was sat outside this pub and these striking miners came by and took the p*ss out of me because they thought I looked an idiot. Well, I did look an idiot at the time actually. So it was like, I support you in theory but you probably want to cave my head in. Of course, it was just four blokes, not the entire mining community. And I was guilty of generalisation and almost despising my own background.

"But meeting that bloke in the hospital encouraged me to think I'd been looking in the wrong direction for inspiration. I'd been in Pulp since I'd left school. I'd had this attitude of ignoring day-to-day things, I was hiding from life really, thinking I didn't have to deal with it because I'd become famous soon. I turned round the other way after that. I tried to get into the tiniest details of life, trying to scrutinise everything – I started to write lyrics that way too."

In other words, had Cocker not fallen out of a window trying to impress a girl, he might never have written such beautifully crafted vignettes of people's lives like 'Disco 2000'. Had he not stood out from the crowd, he might not have felt such a 'Mis-Shape'. Had he not moved to London in despair at his lack of success in 1989, he would never have caught the eye of a girl at St Martin's College studying sculpture, or experienced the rave scene described in 'Sorted For E's And Whizz'. Or lived in that flat in Mile End.

And Cocker's lowest point? Actually that came later, after all the success. In 1996 Jarvis was enjoying himself perhaps a little too much. He was living the dream in a club off Oxford Street, "doing some drugs in a toilet" when Cocker heard a voice from the other side of the cubicle. It was the drummer from Dodgy, and he said simply "Have you been larging it a lot recently?" At that moment it hit home. "No disrespect to Dodgy's drummer" Cocker later mused, "but that kind of made me think, 'No, you've taken a wrong turning here....'"

*Pulp's Different Class reached Number One in the UK album charts in November 1995. It won the Mercury Music Prize in 1996 and has sold over a million copies in the UK alone.*

# 5

## Is It Cheaper to Buy Vinyl Online or In Record Fairs and Shops?

*As you begin to acquire records second hand, or pre-loved, or used, depending upon your preference, you will be wanting to make your money stretch, in order to buy more records or perhaps food, shelter and clothing, depending upon which is more important to you. In 2016, our friend Chris and I therefore conducted a field experiment to see which method was best. Online or in record shops? We did this with the unknowing help of the late Aretha Franklin.*

### Part 1

I *thought* the answer to this question was self-evident.

"It has to be cheaper buying from used record shops and record fairs." I somewhat patronisingly advised Chris. "Buying records online is more expensive, because eBay is a global marketplace. It is designed to bring together the biggest number of buyers: the more buyers, the more demand. The greater the demand, the higher the price. It's basic economic theory. It's the perfect market." I can be a right bore sometimes...

Chris scratched his head. We were having this chat over a coffee, and he didn't look convinced by my argument. "But doesn't that mean It's cheaper then?" he asked slyly. Deliberately trolling me, I suspected. "After all, there might be greater demand, but – to take your slightly dull economic theory point one step further," and here he rolled his eyes rather too witheringly I thought, "there's also more supply. That brings prices down. Loads of competition. Whereas in a shop, there's usually only one copy and you pay the price the shopkeeper wants for it, which is often higher than you'd expect, because he has overheads."

I admit I winced slightly at the emphasis on the word "dull", but could he have a point? We have these "stimulating" conversations sometimes. Usually however, economic theory stays where it belongs. In a textbook. More precisely in a textbook that belongs to, and is read by other people. And anyway, since when did an economist know anything? We are, after all, living in a world where we are apparently all fed up with experts, and people who, God forbid, know what they are talking about. Far better, so they say, to listen to some ill-informed nonsense from random strangers. (And you couldn't have come to a better place for that, dear reader).

Nevertheless, the question as to whether it is better to buy online or in-store is a good one. If you are building up a collection, and assuming like the rest of us you're not absolutely swimming in money, how can you acquire these black discs of wonder in the least expensive manner? These are crucial life skills. After all, there's nothing that dampens the ardour of even the most spirited loved one than when they learn you can't go on a romantic night out because you just spent the evening's dinner money on a rare first pressing of Throbbing Gristle's debut LP.

There's also something strangely satisfying about finding an album for not very much money. I am certain the pleasure I take listening to my original copies of the Beach Boys' *Surf's Up* and Motörhead's *No Sleep 'til Hammersmith* is greatly enhanced by knowing I found both for a pound each. Record collecting for the super-rich must be so much less satisfying. If you can afford everything, where's the fun in that? I pity the oligarchs who will never know the pure adrenaline rush and utter joy of uncovering an original laminated-and-orange-labelled copy of Bowie's *Heroes* for a fiver at a record fair.

And it must be hellish trying to stop the needle skipping on your yacht in a heavy storm.

Poor souls.

Anyway, back to the matter in hand. To discover whether it is cheaper to build a record collection online or in person, what we need is a scientific experiment. Perhaps, as the late great Paul Daniels might have put it, "Under Laboratory Conditions". Or more precisely, two people who could go out and buy an identical record collection over the same time period. One would buy online, from all the sellers on eBay, and Discogs and so on. The other would trawl record fairs, record shops and anywhere else that might carry such items. We could then compare what they paid online and in person and reach a conclusion. But where in the wide, wide world of record collecting could we find such individuals?

I'm glad you asked.

## Part 2: Aretha Franklin's Emotional First Performance … and Why It Took Nine Albums to Score Aretha's First Hit

Aretha Franklin sat at a piano in her father's church, just days after her mother's death. She was just ten years old and about to make her first ever public performance. There were two thousand people in the congregation waiting to hear this recently bereaved child play the piano and sing. She had been crying her eyes out all week. After pausing for a minute, she sang 'Jesus Be A Fence Around Me', a song that Sam Cooke had sang as lead singer of the Soul Stirrers. It all came pouring out. All her pain. All her grief. And not for the last time, when she was suffering the most trauma in her life, Aretha would produce one of her finest moments.

The maturity and pain you hear in Aretha Franklin's voice comes from bitter experience. Two teenage pregnancies, a religious background, parents who both had children by other partners and a mother who moved out when Aretha was six years old and who died of a heart attack just four years later.

Simon Cowell eat your heart out: Aretha had the greatest ever back story, way before X-Factor. "What's that? Your nan's got angina and can't come to see your audition? Do you not realise what Aretha Franklin had to go through? That's what you're up against! Now go away and come back when something *really* bad happens ... "

Aretha Franklin grew up the daughter of a preacher man, at a time when R'n'B music was evolving from its gospel roots, leaving the church behind. Her father was not just any preacher man. The Rev C. L. Franklin was a big cheese. A liberal minister who preached about black pride before James Brown. A peer of Dr. King, he was a charismatic genius and a man B.B. King called the "bluesman's preacher" – a holy man who didn't treat the blues players as enemies of the gospel.

There was a lot of suspicion about R'n'B in the church. Take Jesse Belvin. He wrote 'Earth Angel', that song you'll know from *Back To The Future.* He and his wife were killed in a car crash and people said it was because he'd left the church to write R'n'B. That his driver had a history of being drunk and falling asleep at the wheel was irrelevant...

"See?" said Marvin Gaye's dad (also a minister) to his son when Sam Cooke was shot. "See what happens when you displease God".

That's right. Marvin Gaye's *dad* said that.

Aretha was a child prodigy. From age seven she would learn complex church chords on her father's grand piano in the living room. Guests including Oscar Peterson, Ella Fitzgerald and Duke Ellington would visit and play at parties. They almost didn't need to play records at Rev. Franklin's house, they just called up the people who played on them. The young Aretha would look on, soaking it all in, and, when the parties had finished, immerse herself in her record collection. Before long, Aretha could hear a song once and play it back on the piano straight away, note perfect.

Aged 12, Aretha would join her father on his preaching tours, singing and playing piano before and during her father's incendiary sermons. Here she was exposed to a promiscuous culture (at one point on tour her father found her in Sam Cooke's motel room – she insisted it was all innocent, a story not corroborated by Etta James or Sam Cooke) and she would fight over the same men with her sister Erma.

It's hard to imagine how she must have felt when she fell pregnant aged just 13. A religious background, a strict parent, no mother. Thankfully her father was understanding. Her son, Clarence, was looked after by the family, and Aretha went straight back to school. That first experience might have made her second pregnancy, aged 15, easier to bear, but perhaps not. This time she did drop out of school, not just to look after her second child but also to join her father's out of town services.

An important moment in Aretha's life came when Sam Cooke performed on the Ed Sullivan show in 1957 – when Aretha was fifteen. Cooke helped the Franklin sisters see the attractions of the world outside of the church. Aretha adored Sam. He had transitioned from gospel singing to more worldly concerns and was being noticed by mainstream America. Aretha's sister Erma even bought a dress especially for the TV show, just in case Cooke might see her through the screen.

As she turned 18, there was talk of Berry Gordy at Motown being interested in signing Aretha, but in 1960 she signed to Columbia Records at her father's recommendation. Yet it is remarkable to note that Aretha was at Columbia for six years and eight albums without a single hit song.

Her voice may have been amazing, but Columbia perhaps saw her as a rival, and then successor, to Dina Washington, especially after the latter's untimely death in 1963. Indeed, Aretha recorded a tribute to Washington in 1964.

Aretha was singing beautifully, but her material was all a bit polite, looking to attract a sophisticated jazz loving crowd, and a long way from the passionate singing Aretha would perform in church. As Etta James said "Aretha's Columbia s--- wasn't black enough for blacks and too black for whites ... Columbia didn't know nothing about crossing over." While Etta James was reaching the upper echelons of the charts with 'At Last', Aretha's version of 'Lucky Old Sun' made no impact. It didn't hurt Etta James that her record label, Chess, knew how to reach a black audience. Columbia had no such idea. Eight albums in five years; some great performances, but no hits. It was 1966. Since Aretha had signed with Columbia, Kennedy had been shot, the Beatles had conquered America and Dylan had gone electric. The times they were a-changing. There was a war in Vietnam, and both civil rights and women's rights were being fought for. This was no time for gentle jazz-tinged torch songs. It was time for flaming-torch-and-pitchfork songs. It was time, in short, for Aretha to make her mark, and capture the mood of the times.

Meanwhile, back to the question of whether to buy records online or in shops. I had travelled to a number of shops across the UK, but the UK didn't seem overstocked with Aretha Franklin LPs. I asked a couple of dealers why her records were a bit tricky to track down. "R'n'B collectors tend to buy singles" suggested one, "so there's less call for the albums – if you do see them they won't be silly money." "Her albums do come in, but they get snapped up quite quickly," offered another, not entirely consistently with the first guy. I carried on digging.

The albums on Columbia were easier to find, as is always the way with records you don't actually want. Also freely available and veritably clogging up record stores across the land, it seemed, were Aretha's mid '70s to mid '80s work, the latter in the bargain bins. I did find one late sixties release early on though. A single, on Atlantic, of '(You Make Me Feel Like) A Natural Woman'. It was £1.

In a charity shop a week or so later, I found a lovely Atlantic sleeve housing a Carole King single (coincidentally, King co-wrote the Aretha track I'd just bought) so I picked that up for 50p and swapped the sleeves around so the Aretha one matched. Try doing that online! I re-doubled my efforts and crossed my fingers Chris hadn't already snapped everything up on eBay.

## Part 3: The Story of 'I Never Loved A Man (The Way I Love You)' by Aretha Franklin

Wilson Pickett moved towards Percy Sledge, ready to punch him, hard.

Sledge had popped in during one of Pickett's recording sessions at the Muscle Shoals Fame Studios, and as his name would suggest, began to sledge Pickett, telling him first he sounded like Otis Redding, and then like James Brown. That's the best way to annoy a singer, apparently. Tell them they are derivative of someone else. Unless you the singer is Bjork, of course, when you just need to say "Welcome to Bangkok"... Not that Sledge used the word "derivative".

*"I say Wilson old chap – you're a little derivative, don't you know?"*

We can safely assume he was a little more forthright, and Pickett was having none of it. Jerry Wexler, the head of Atlantic Records was also present and was looking at two of his prize assets about to murder each other. This might not go down well with the shareholders, he decided, and he stepped in. The wicked Pickett flung him out of the way. An impressive show of force from Pickett, but Sledge was a former boxer. Who would win, in this heavyweight boxing contest between two of the most celebrated R'n'B singers of all time?

We will never know, because right at that moment the phone rang. Wexler politely told them both to *"calm the f— down"*, and answered.

The story of Aretha Franklin's first Atlantic Records album hinges on two phone calls. This was the first. On the other end of the line was the message Wexler had been waiting six years to hear: Aretha Franklin was ready to join Atlantic Records. Franklin had spent a frustrating, hit-less six years at Columbia and was desperate to cross over to the mainstream. She had a couple of ideas that might help her do that already. In particular, a revamped version of an Otis Redding song she had been working on.

It was called 'Respect'. Aretha had this little piece that wasn't in Otis' version where she would spell out the word. R-E-S-P-E-C-T. It was catchy.

Looking back at Aretha's later success, it all appears inevitable. It was anything but. The first Atlantic album very nearly didn't get made at all. Wexler's idea was to take Aretha to Fame studios in Muscle Shoals, Alabama, the scene of Sledge's recording of 'When A Man Loves A Woman'. Rich Hall, the owner, was a big personality, and had recorded some wildly successful hit songs. What could possibly go wrong?

Everything. That's what. It was fine at first. Dan Penn and Chips Moman – two of the musicians at Muscle Shoals – wrote a song on the spot: 'Do Right Woman – Do Right Man'. The first day's work went so well, some celebratory drinking took place. Then it all went wrong. An argument began with one of the trumpet players, Rich Hall got involved, Aretha's husband Ted White – a difficult personality whose relationship with Aretha was later described as abusive – only made things worse and in no time at all Aretha and her husband bolted, and would not be persuaded to return to Muscle Shoals.

It looked like a disaster for Wexler. His new signing had run off, and he was responsible. All Jerry had in the can was half a version of 'Do Right Woman – Do Right Man' and a completed 'I Never Loved A Man (The Way I Love You)'. Aretha's first recording session for the new label with a team that had produced a succession of hits for other artists – who had produced magic and a feeling that hadn't been replicated anywhere else – and there had been a massive fight. Ted White was seething that Wexler had insisted they record there.

Wexler had no album. All he had were one and a half recordings and an artist refusing to come back to record any more songs. Wexler acted decisively. He printed twenty or thirty acetates of the finished song, 'I Never Loved A Man (The Way I Love You)' and sent them to key DJs, who immediately played the song on the airwaves. Radio listeners loved the new Aretha sound. Distributors cried out for copies of the song to sell. Wexler stalled.

It was 1967. To release the single, he couldn't load it up on iTunes. He needed two songs, an A-side and a B-side. And the problem was, he only had one and a half songs. The good news was that on their first attempt Wexler and Aretha Franklin at last had a hit. The bad news was that it was only a hit on the radio. He spent ten nervous days avoiding calls from irate distributors unable to get copies of what looked like a certain sales hit.

And then came the second phone call of this story. Aretha had been impressed by how much her song was gaining significant radio play, and finally called Wexler. She told him she would agree to record more songs, and to play with the Muscle Shoals musicians. But in New York. Jerry Wexler's gamble had paid off. Wexler no doubt breathed a huge sigh of relief and prepared for the recording session in the big apple. This time, in New York, there was no more nonsense. Aretha meant business. She walked in, sat at the piano, played over the half-finished 'Do Right Woman – Do Right Man' track, sang harmonies with her sisters and then sang the lead. Once. She may only have been 24 years old, but she was on her eleventh studio album and in complete command.

The finished song became the b-side to 'I Never Loved A Man (The Way I Love You)' and Aretha – in just two songs and two days in the studio (not counting the two weeks in between) – had the top ten hit for which she had waited six fruitless years at Columbia, mixing with the Beatles' 'Penny Lane'/'Strawberry Fields Forever' and the Rolling Stones' 'Ruby Tuesday'. 'I Never Loved A Man (The Way I Love You)' sold a million copies.

The rest was plain sailing. The next single, 'Respect' hit the top spot in the pop charts and won two Grammys, catching the mood of the times. The album *I Never Loved A Man (The Way I Love You)* was impressive. What's more, some of the best songs on the album were written or co-written by Aretha: 'Save Me', 'Dr Feelgood', 'Baby, Baby, Baby' and 'Don't Let Me Lose This Dream'. It's a classic.

So ... Could I find copies to buy now? And for how much? As a reminder, all this talk about Aretha Franklin has another purpose. Could I track down her albums, and would they be cheaper on eBay or in used record shops?

I was feeling good about this one. I had snagged a nice UK mono original copy of the LP for £10 at Spitalfields Record Fair in London, which I thought was a bargain. There hadn't been many copies in the used record shops I had travelled to over the past six months and those I had seen tended to fetch £20 or more. I had also sneaked a look at Discogs, which (for the uninitiated) is probably the largest online seller of vinyl. Indeed, many used record shops sell their stock on Discogs also. It helps those shops to reach a wider market place, and is extremely useful for those less able or willing to trawl around the country trying to find old records.

Discogs has a useful statistics section showing the average of the last ten copies of any individual record sold. Aretha's Atlantic debut averaged £16.94 for the last ten copies, which, when you add postage, took the average price to around the £20 mark. They had a couple of copies still on sale as cheap as £10, but not in acceptable condition, and with postage on top, there was, I reasoned, little chance of Chris finding a cheaper copy than mine. On eBay, a mint UK first pressing had fetched £122.

"I spent a tenner" I gloated in front of Chris. "How much did you spend?"

"£8.50" he replied.

"Rubbish!" I said. Actually, that wasn't my exact retort but this is a family-friendly publication. I examined his album. It wasn't a UK mono pressing. It was a brand-new pressing. He'd cheated!

"We never said anything about not buying new ones," protested Chris. "If you wanted to go about buying original copies you should have said so! eBay is perfect for picking up stuff like this – a fiver plus postage. It's a total bargain!"

"How are we supposed to compare prices scientifically if you go around buying different versions?" I argued, not unreasonably. But there it was.

- eBay: £8.50 (for a new pressing in NM condition)

- Record fair: £10 (for a UK original)

# Part 4

The day came for us to finally resolve the question: is it cheaper to buy vinyl online or in record shops and fairs? We had a couple of minor rules – we would try to buy a) Aretha Franklin's Atlantic albums up to 1972, b) copies should be in VG+ condition or better, and c) we should try to pay less than £10 per LP.

To set you the picture, we met in a cafe, sat facing each other at a table, with a pile of LPs in front of us. It was like the scene in *Heat* with De Niro and Al Pacino, only really rubbish, and with a stack of LPs cluttering up the table. I bet De Niro didn't have to be careful there wasn't any ketchup or coffee stains on his table. We asked the waitress to affect a Brooklyn accent but, correctly, she just looked at us blankly.

We had begun this quest more than six months ago, to see who had picked up the most albums, and for the least cost. The atmosphere was electric. Mainly due to one of those ultraviolet fly catcher things in the corner of the cafe. A mortally wounded fly landed on the table, legs kicking, adding to the tension.

We had already established Chris had paid £8.50 for *I Never Loved A Man (The Way I Love You)*, although of course his was a modern copy whereas I had paid £10 for a UK 1967 original. Chris claimed victory, but because my copy was a near-fifty year old original we called it a draw... I reckon I scored the moral victory however.

We moved on to Aretha's next release: *Aretha Arrives*. I picked my copy up for £10, again from Spitalfields record fair. Nice Atlantic label in plum. It was in great condition. I thought this good, until I saw the Discogs average was £4.50. I asked Chris how much he paid, expecting the worst. I was right.

"£4.70 plus 1.80 postage on eBay. £6.50 in total".

He laughed a little too loudly when he heard I had paid a tenner. I felt better when I saw his copy wasn't quite as pristine as mine. Nevertheless, one point to buying online. *Aretha Now* was next. I had paid £10 at the same time and from the same Spitalfields stall at which I found *Aretha Arrives*. (I had also found a copy of Jimmy Reed's *Live at Carnegie Hall* for £10. It had been a good day's shopping, that one. )

"I couldn't find this one online for less than £10, if you include postage" confessed Chris. "I got very close a couple of times, and missed a couple that did go for around £10. There are a lot of copies in not very good condition too, if Discogs is anything is go by. I didn't end up buying a copy." This was a fail on Chris' part, and a win for buying in record shops, but I wasn't getting too excited just yet. Scores: one for Chris, one for me and a half point for the tie. One and a half points each.

On *Lady Soul* I had paid £10 again. It was the same stall, but a different day, and again it was a lovely original Atlantic plum coloured label UK pressing. I asked Chris how he had fared. I was feeling better about this. The Discogs average was £13.50 (plus postage).

"Ah, this was a good one. I found a US copy for just £6 and ... at the same time I found a copy of *Aretha In Paris* from the same seller for £7-ish. He lived in Denmark, but with the two albums together, postage was only £7. The exact amount was £19.89 for the two albums, so unless you picked up *Aretha In Paris* for less than a tenner, I think I win both. By a whisker."

I smiled. I had indeed picked up Aretha In Paris for less than a tenner. In fact, I found a copy for £6 at Southend Record Fair. Chris looked suitably gutted. I worked out he had paid less than I had for

*Lady Soul* – but only by 11p – and for a US copy at that – and had paid more for the live album. I charitably agreed *Lady Soul* was a draw, so the score was now 3-2 to record shops and fairs versus online.

I saw a copy of *Soul '69* next on the pile. "How much was that one?" I asked.

"This seemed to be the most expensive – I couldn't find it under £10" confessed Chris, "so I had a look at Discogs and got creative." He showed me the reverse. It was written in Spanish. My inner Miss Marple deduced this was a copy from Spain. It's difficult to get these little details past me. "It was €19.50, including postage from a seller in Holland. You can save money going for foreign copies. At least you could until the pound crashed... I bought a Kinks LP at the same time, which brought the cost down and at the time the euro rate was okay, so it was just over £14."

I brought out my copy of *Soul '69*. UK Atlantic plum label, of course.

However, I too had a confession: "I paid £14 for this one, so slightly cheaper than yours – and for a UK copy."

"Oh, okay. Where did you get it?"

I shifted uneasily in my seat.

"I bought it in person in Rayleigh".

Chris looked at me suspiciously. He knows me too well. He raised a sceptical eyebrow. "In person?" he repeated. "I didn't know there was a record shop in Rayleigh?"

"Er, well, there isn't, technically," I squirmed, "I sort of found it online. I say online... It was on, um, well, eBay." Chris gave me a look I had previously only observed in a taxi driver after I tried to pay for a £7 cab journey with a Scottish £50 note. "I wouldn't have bothered but the guy selling it was just down the road, so when I won the auction I drove to his house and picked it up in person, saving on the £4 postage. It kind of counts as I picked it up in person, right?"

In truth, I hadn't seen this album for sale at all in shops or record fairs. I thought £14, whilst above our general limit, was a decent price. For this album, eBay and Discogs had been the only way to get the LP. One back to online. The score was now 3-3.

"What about *Don't Play That Song*?" I asked. "I paid £13 for mine".

"I actually found one for £10 plus postage, and managed to get a "Best Offer" accepted on eBay to get a copy for £10 including postage" Chris said, but he didn't sound quite as happy as I thought he should.

"Why aren't you crowing about it?" I asked suspiciously.

"It came through – but when I played it I saw it was scratched. It was clicking – I couldn't fix it – and I had to send it back. I haven't found a better priced copy since, so I'm empty handed on that one. And it cost me £3 for the return postage."

I found my copy again at Spitalfields record fair – a different stall this time. It was a UK original priced at £18, but managed to haggle it down to £13. I think the stall owner left with grudging respect for my persistence / tight-fistedness. On this occasion, buying from a record fair paid off: 4-3.

*This Girl's In Love With You* was next. Chris laid his cards on the table. "I paid £6.99 plus postage – so £10.99 in total."

"Well", I countered. "I paid £7.90 for mine. So I win."

Chris looked sceptical. "That's an odd amount. Why £7.90?" I was rumbled.

"Oh, okay. I may have found it on eBay..."

"What?! Again?! You're supposed to be buying in record shops!" It was true. But I couldn't find this one anywhere. And £7.90 (including postage) was too good to pass up for a genuine original UK pressing. It was in great condition too. I looked shamefully towards the floor ... 4-all.

There were three albums left: *Live At Fillmore West, Young, Gifted And Black* and a Greatest Hits collection.

"Next?"

"Okay, I'm pleased with this one, announced Chris. "*Live at Fillmore West* cost me £9.04, and it comes with a story." I pretended to look interested. "Imagine you're a US serviceman in Taiwan in the late sixties. You're stationed over there, but all you have to listen to is the bloke out of *Good Morning Vietnam* who has now been posted in Taiwan and plays Polkas on the radio all day. You need some music. And in Taiwan, there's a record factory that makes bootleg pressings of all the latest albums. Well, this is one of those albums. And it sounds surprisingly good."

"You have a Taiwanese bootleg?" I was half appalled and half interested. It was wrapped in a paper bag-type sleeve.

"Try finding that in a record shop! Proof that online shopping can come up with a more diverse collection." Chris had started to wax lyrical. "You might have UK stuff, but my collection has copies from Spain, Taiwan, America. New and old. It's a bit more interesting."

"All highly fascinating Chris. But you overpaid. I picked my copy up for £7 at Carmel Records in Southend." 5-4 to the record shops.

*Young, Gifted and Black* was next – a cracking LP, but one I just hadn't been able to find. Chris simply needed to produce his copy and it would be 5-all ... "This was a funny one" confessed Chris. "I just couldn't get one at the right price, and when it did sell for a good price, I was never in, or was busy, or beaten by a sniper. So I never pinned it down."

I breathed a sigh of relief.

"But now I know you haven't got a copy ..." My chest tightened.

Chris pulled out his phone with exaggerated deliberation. He opened his eBay app. And as (bad) luck would have it, there was a copy of *Young, Gifted And Black* in what looked like immaculate condition on a "Buy It Now" offer of £9.99 plus £3.50 postage. He clicked the button with inner glee. "Five-all" he said with a smile.

It had all come down to the "Best of" collections.

I had found the *Greatest Hits* for just a fiver or so, but didn't buy it. In the end I plumped for a more interesting collection, an LP called *I Say A Little Prayer* on Atlantic's budget 99 Series. I paid £8 at Carmel Records. Despite the "budget" label, it is a lovely heavyweight piece of vinyl and a plum label. Chris had gone for the traditional *Greatest Hits*. He paid £5, plus £3.50 postage. For the sake of 50p we called it a draw. Five and a half to each side. Eight studio albums, two live and a Hits package.

I had all the UK originals. Chris had the exotic variants. Overall, it was much of a muchness price-wise.

What Chris didn't have was about a dozen other albums that I had found whilst searching in record shops and fairs for those Aretha Franklin albums. I had an Otis Redding collection called *Remembering* on the 99 budget label found at the same time as the Aretha collection. I had a *Muddy Waters Folk Singer* album on Chess that I bought for £10 at Spitalfields the same day as the *Live At Fillmore West* album. I had a Kinks album, and a B.B. King *Completely Well* LP from the early seventies which is great. I had also found a collection in Carmel Records called *Soul From The City vol. 1*, a lovely black label *This Is Chess* compilation with tracks by Maurice and Mack, Sugar Pie Desanto and Koko Taylor which I heard playing through the oversized speakers in that tiny shop one day, and a *This Is Loma Volume 6* compilation of soul artists, none of whom I knew, on Warner Brothers' soul label Loma.

In conclusion, I'm afraid the whole thing hasn't been much help: sometimes it is cheaper on eBay. Sometimes it is cheaper in record shops and fairs. Buying online might be better for finding records you know you want...but if this exercise showed me anything it is that buying at record shops and fairs is much better for discovering music you never knew existed.

# 6

## Three more stories, this time starting with The Flaming Lips ... and the secret behind their success

It's difficult to know where to start with the story of The Flaming Lips; we could start with a van. But then again, there's so much else to consider. For example, we could mention the time Wayne Coyne's enthusiasm for music found him queueing outside a venue for *three days* to see Led Zeppelin. Three days? I get impatient waiting for YouTube clips to load. Or the epiphany he had listening to punk and realising he could make his own music. Before then, music was only made by *real* musicians. Or the *eleven years* he spent working in a fast food seafood restaurant whilst the band was getting off the ground. He can fry a mean fish, can Wayne Coyne. And when he came back from work smelling of fish and oil, he still kept a romantic world view. He even told his girlfriend he wrote his first EP so she would fall in love with him.

I should mention the fact that Wayne Coyne isn't quite the drug taking hippy he makes out. He might sound like he is consistently between acid trips, but he is said to rarely indulge in anything much stronger than coffee.

And what about Michael Ivins? Here's a source of inspiration, because he actually did a Brian May and tried to build his own guitar. What is appealing about Ivins' attempt is that he failed, because like most of us he isn't a rocket scientist. Crucially, that failure didn't put Ivins off being a guitarist though as, let's face it, anyone, including many rocket scientists, would likely fail in such an attempt. In fact, probably only Brian May and his dad could possibly have ever built their own guitar from scratch. The show-offs.

And what about Steven Drozd? Perhaps I should talk about the way Steven Drozd got so good at playing the piano. Not through playing in the band, but by playing songs by the Rolling Stones or Journey every night for hours to his older brother Tony, who had been paralysed in a car accident. (I'm hoping his brother liked Journey, or that heart-warming story of familial devotion takes quite the sinister twist.)

The Flaming Lips took a while to make an impression. It wasn't easy. There was the time in 1988 when The Flaming Lips played in front of six people in Portland, Maine. That was *five years* into being a band. Imagine doing something for five years and only six people being interested. Also that yearThe Flaming Lips visited the U.K. The UK border agency discovered they didn't have work visas, which the band's management had deemed superfluous to requirements, and as a result the U.K. wouldn't allow them in, marking their passports with an "X", which then meant Belgium wouldn't allow them in either. To recap, the band had been around five years, and not only was their audience only twice the size of the band itself, the band were *persona non grata* in two European countries.

Then there's Jonathan Donahue. He joined the band in 1987 as their roadie but fell out with Coyne after a year or so over the latter's lack of interest in Neil Young – and ability to argue incessantly about it. But Donahue came back, and at a crucial point. In the aftermath of an album called *Telepathic Surgery* which failed to set the world alight, The Flaming Lips consisted of just two people, Coyne and Ivins. No drummer. He'd left. You can hardly blame him. They were going nowhere. At least his leaving meant the audience was now three times the size of the band.

After five years and three actual albums, Coyne and Ivins were beginning to wonder whether, in fact, they could be a band. They weren't the greatest singing group. They weren't the greatest players. Coyne was twenty eight years old. Let's face it, when Paul McCartney was that age, The Beatles had already split up having changed the world. Coyne had barely changed his underpants. He went back to his job frying fish in Oklahoma, and bumped into Donahue. They got working on some new songs. Donahue – their roadie let's not forget – saw something in the new songs.

Coyne, Ivins and Donahue were joined by a new drummer called Nathan Roberts. Roberts, an unusual combination of barber and a classically trained percussionist, had just been kicked out of college for general unchristian-like behaviour. By the end of the first song of his first rehearsal he had broken every cymbal, skin and stick. He was in.

Donahue asked a friend, Dave Fridmann, to mix some new songs and the result was their fourth album called *In A Priest Driven Ambulance (With Silver Sunshine Stares)*. It was September 1989 and The Flaming Lips had finally recorded their masterpiece. Everything was set for take off. Stardom awaited.

And then the record company, Enigma Records, got divested from Capitol/EMI, the album was shelved for a year, and the whole thing lost momentum. Masterpiece? They didn't know it yet, but The Flaming Lips were still a decade away from recording their *actual* masterpiece.

Things got so bad, the band took to selling their plasma to feed themselves. This worked, until the nurses suspected the marks on their arms were evidence of drug taking. In fact, it was evidence of the previous week's donation. As we now know, life got better.

Shortly afterwards they signed to Warner Bros. and it would be nice to say that, with the odd exception, the Flaming Lips never looked back. Even that isn't true of course. Before their first Warner Bros. album was released both Donahue and Roberts had quit, the former to find success with Mercury Rev. But drummer Steven Drozd joined and The Flaming Lips as we now know them were born. They got there in the end, thanks to the 1993 fluke success of a song, 'She Don't Use Jelly', becoming a hit after being featured on Beavis and Butt-head (which gave them time), and the subsequent all-conquering genius of 1999 album *The Soft Bulletin*.

And what about that van mentioned earlier? Maybe the tour van the band bought in the early eighties tells us most about The Flaming Lips. It was a blue Ford Econoline. They paid $8,900 and paid for it in instalments. When they bought it the van had 27,000 miles on the clock. When it was sold eight years later, it had travelled 485,000 miles. That's the equivalent of over eighteen times around the world.

And that, more than anything, more than all the confetti, hamster balls, spider bites and songs about life and death, tells you all you need to know about why the Flaming Lips have succeeded. As you can see, the story of the Flaming Lips is not one of incredible genius that floated effortlessly through life tossing off three deathless songs every morning before breakfast. What most of the things mentioned above have in common is how much hard work and relentless toil has played its part. That, and a stubborn refusal to give up.

## The Story of The White Stripes (with a little help from 'Don't Stop Believin'' by Journey)

Those who believe Jack White is a Rock 'n' Roll Messiah may be interested to know he has his own John The Revelator. And luckily for us, Jack White's own prophet captured Jack's own story in a song, written nearly two decades earlier. The prophet's name is Steve Perry. And that song is 'Don't Stop Believin'' by Journey.

I'm serious. Well, fairly serious. Here's how: *"Just a small-town girl, livin' in a lonely world."* Meg White, born in Grosse Point Farms, a town with a population of 9,479 – making her very much a small-town girl. She had progressed from college to culinary school, paying her way by working in bars and restaurants such as the Memphis Smoke blues bar in Royal Oak, north of downtown Detroit. I like to think she went there by the Detroit rail system, *"taking the midnight train goin' anywhere"* where she met Future Electric Six-er Cory, then playing in a band called The Wildbunch.

*"Just a city boy, born and raised in South Detroit."* Jack Gillis was born and raised in South Detroit. Okay, South West Detroit – apparently there's no such place as South Detroit, you just end up in the Detroit River. I was rather sceptical of this, but Google Maps has confirmed it, amusingly citing

South Detroit as "permanently closed". We can forgive Steve Perry's suspect geographical knowledge. He was born and raised in California.

Jack was the youngest of ten children, and, ideally for a bluesman, the seventh son. He apprenticed as an upholsterer in 1991, and opened his own upholstery shop in 1996, painting the shop in three colours: black, yellow and white. Jack began to learn the guitar whilst a teenager, and played in various bands. He slipped poems (and recordings) into the furniture he revived, his yellow and black business cards containing the slogan "Your furniture's not dead".

Meg met Jack, they hit it off, and the pair married in 1996. The story of how they first played music together is simple. Meg was waiting tables, Jack was in various bands or performing solo. One day Jack was playing music in his attic and Meg was at his house. She sat down on the drums. They jammed on a Bowie song, 'Moonage Daydream'. It all just clicked. They doubtless smiled, and played all night. *"For a smile they can share the night / It goes on and on, and on, and on."*

The rest is history. And myth, of which there is plenty:

The matching outfits idea may have originated from the Doll Rods, a local band who wore matching outfits, played a simple drum kit, and had onlookers speculating whether the guitarist and lead singer were brother and sister.

They weren't always the White Stripes. In contention for the Band Name Sweep Stake were Soda Power and Bazooka.

They played their first gig – three songs – on Bastille Day, July 14 1997. An open mic spot at a venue called The Gold Dollar. It was recorded by the proprietor, Neil Yee, and Jack paid him for the recording by upholstering and refurbishing a rocking chair.

At the time, the venue was known for its experimental acts. My favourite story about the Gold Dollar is when they booked two punk bands and put on a magician in between. I'm not sure who would have been more discombobulated, the punk band whose name appeared below the magician on the bill, or David Blaine. Okay, it wasn't Blaine.

The Gold Dollar was a bit rough, as most good venues are, and you were likely to end the evening dealing with your car having been broken into, but at least you might have got to see the earliest shows of the White Stripes. Because these were the days before smoking was banned in venues, and because it wasn't a male-only venue, there is little doubt that an observer at that first show would have seen *"A singer in a smoky room / A smell of wine and cheap perfume."* And, presumably, various touring magicians, which isn't in the Journey song, but perhaps should have been, if Steve Perry could find a word to rhyme with magicians: nuclear fissions perhaps? Missions? Cushions? Might have needed some work.

To add further interest to the venue, police would, when they weren't stopping people breaking into vehicles, use the car park to entrap people looking to secure the services of working girls. *"Strangers waiting / Up and down the boulevard / Their shadows* (okay, police torches) *searching in the night / Streetlights, people / Living just to find emotion / Hiding somewhere in the night"* (presumably from the police).

The White Stripes' first full show was a month later at the same venue, 15th August 1997 in a support slot. Of all the Detroit bands that were around at that time, many disappeared, and some went on the have a measure of success, including the Von Bondies and the Electric Six. But only the White Stripes lasted the course. Or as Steve Perry put it, *"Some will win, some will lose / Some were born to sing the blues."*

However much the story of the White Stripes may chime with that Journey song, perhaps their real story of is the one story that Jack White has spent his career NOT telling. The story of The White Stripes is not 'Don't Stop Believin''. It's that they released their first ground-breaking album slap bang in the middle of their divorce.

What kind of band would stay together despite such personal turmoil and then make such great art? I can't think of any. It's extraordinary. Yeah, all right, I'll grant you Fleetwood Mac is one band that would stay together after a divorce. Well, yeah, obviously Abba. I mean Abba goes without saying doesn't it? But apart from Fleetwood Mac and Abba ...

Johnny Hentch, of the Hentchmen, a Detroit Band who Jack would play with from time to time, described this time: "She's very quiet. I spent a lot of time with her over the years ... They're different kinds of people ... it didn't surprise me.

"So they divorced and they had a gig and they cancelled it. And then Meg said she wanted to do the last gig anyway. That's when it started taking off...

"The show was sold out, at a venue called Paycheck's. They played 'Sugar Never Tasted So Good' and the crowd started singing along. This was way before the first album. Jack was completely taken by surprise. He stopped singing and started laughing."

Perhaps it was at that moment, or perhaps when they played 'Not The Marrying Kind' that both Jack and Meg realised the noise they were making onstage was something that would outlast their marriage.

The first record was recorded for $2,000 in early 1999 on two inch tape and a mixing board that had been found in a barn, left discarded by the music school that had owned it for nearly twenty years. White used guitar microphones because vocal mics sounded too polished. It took just six days. A month after recording the album Jack and Meg began divorce proceedings, with the divorce going through the courts in March 2000. The wedding rings were said to have been airbrushed from the record cover artwork.

So why did they carry on, despite the turmoil that their broken marriage must have caused? And why did they then create a myth? Jack White hinted at the reason in a Rolling Stone interview in 2005. For him, it was to keep the focus away from his private life and towards the music: "When you see a band that is two pieces, husband and wife, boyfriend and girlfriend, you think, 'Oh, I see ...' When they're brother and sister, you go, 'Oh, that's interesting.' You care more about the music, not the relationship—whether they're trying to save their relationship by being in a band."

## The story of Josh Homme and Kyuss

Chris Goss was driving through the Palm Desert in 1988, a couple of hours drive from LA, on his way to launching the career of one of rock's most important figures of the next thirty years. He just didn't know it yet. Goss was the producer and band leader of Masters of Reality. He was on his way to a generator party in the middle of the desert, to see a band he had thus far only heard on a demo cassette.

Generator parties were a way for Palm Desert kids to meet, drink, and hear bands play, all out of sight of parents, police and general interference. Bands played miles out of town around a raging bonfire in the open air, the hot desert wind blowing sand everywhere, with just beer, a barbecue, some possibly illicit substances and an audience for company, all thirsty for music and fun – with a diesel-powered generator providing the electricity.

Despite being the middle of the night, it was over a hundred degrees outside and Goss drove through the desert, feeling totally lost, until he saw a car parked by the side of the road, like it had been abandoned. That was his first clue. Then he saw someone stumble out of the darkness. He was getting closer. Then a glow – a single light on a tall pole. This was it ...

He got out of the car and walked towards the bonfires and the band. As he approached, Goss was surrounded by a couple of hundred kids jumping around, dancing, creating a whirlwind of sand around them. He later mused "the sound of it, like you're listening to them in a tornado, and you could only see this cacophony of bodies... slamming into each other. It was like stumbling on the Plains Indians doing a war dance."

The band he went to see called themselves Sons of Kyuss (rhymes with "pious") and featured a teenage Josh Homme. Josh Homme grew up in Palm Springs and was given his first guitar when he was 10 years old. He learned how to play polkas on the acoustic instrument for two weeks. Polkas are what Robin Williams' nemesis in *Good Morning Vietnam* used to play to the troops in what appeared to be a precursor to later military forms of torture such as water boarding.

After two weeks Homme had had his fill of polkas. It's a bit surprising it took him a fortnight to be honest, but there you go. However, rather than follow Robin Williams' lead in the film and start playing Thunderclap Newman songs he switched his attention to hardcore punk. *Good Morning Vietnam* would have been a very different film if Homme had played the Williams role.

In 1984, the twelve year old Josh Homme met the thirteen year old Nick Oliveri. They met at school, after Nick's family moved from LA to Palm Springs. Nick liked Ozzy Osborne and Judas Priest, Homme preferred Black Flag and Minor Threat. Homme formed a band with friends John Garcia, Chris Cockrell and Brant Bjork – who sadly is no relation to the Icelandic singer. They called themselves Katzenjammer, rehearsing in garages which served a dual purpose at night – as meth labs.

The band evolved – Oliveri was recruited on guitar before moving to bass when Cockrell departed – and the group moved their sound away from hard core punk because of their demanding audiences. Anything that was too derivative would be picked up on and criticised by kids at the generator parties, and the band switched from punk to extended heavy jams, taking Black Sabbath riffs and mixing them up with trance-like Hawkwind rhythms. Instead of John Garcia shouting the words punk-style, Brant Bjork suggested that he just sing the melody.

And, somewhat by accident, the guitars got tuned down, accenting a lower, heavy growl which Homme emphasised by playing his guitar through both guitar and bass amplifiers. I say "accident". It was more circumstance. Without the money to buy guitar tuners, the guitars kept being tuned downwards, and they would all tune to each other and then start. "That was the main thing in the desert. You had to sound like yourself, or else people would talk s— about you".

The result was a Darwinian evolution of their own sound, a heavy sound, but isolated from either the LA metal scene or the nascent Seattle grunge scene. Sons of Kyuss recorded a few songs. The production was poor, but the cassette found its way to Chris Goss – which brings us back to the start of this tale.

Goss' interest was piqued. Sons of Kyuss began to make the two hour journey to LA to play gigs. Their first LA show, in 1988, was not well attended. Five people showed up, including Chris Goss. But, like the Sex Pistols at the Manchester Free Trade Hall, sometimes it isn't about how many people show up, but who. Goss walked up to Homme after the show, marvelling at the Black Sabbath-style heavy swing coming from the band.

"Are you a Sabbath fan?" he asked Homme.

"No. I've never really listened to Sabbath" replied Homme.

"It was then that I knew we were on to something" remarked Goss later, "This was coming from them."

After a self-released LP made precious few waves, it took nearly three years for the band to win a record deal. Dropping the "Sons of" moniker, Kyuss recorded *Wretch*, an LP cobbled together from songs on that initial self-released LP with a few newer songs. But Goss knew the record wasn't capturing the band's sound. Kyuss had a rumble, a giant sound-wave that Goss likened to "sitting in the middle of a bowling alley when the balls are rolling down the wood". Now a friend and supporter of Kyuss, he pleaded to and won agreement from the Chameleon record label boss to be allowed to produce the next LP. *Blues For The Red Sun* was the result. Released in June 1992, Goss' production captured the band perfectly. And the band hit their peak at the same time. It's hard to describe just how strange the album sounded back then. It was so unlike anything that came before it or that was released contemporaneously. It's also interesting how well the album has aged. It still sounds immediate, unique, and had it been released this year, it would still have been described as contemporary. There's still little out there quite like it: a modern classic that has only improved as the years have flown by.

Here's Kerrang! Magazine's end of year list for 1992 – the year the album was released in the US:

1.    Alice In Chains – *Dirt*

2.    The Black Crowes – *The Southern Harmony And Musical Companion*

3.    Kyuss – *Blues For The Red Sun*

4.    Pearl Jam – *Ten*

Third best album of the year from a bunch of unknown desert kids. The LP didn't even get a release in the UK until the following year.

*Blues For The Red Sun* appeared ahead of such now classic heavy albums such as Pearl Jam's debut, Pantera's *Vulgar Display of Power,* Faith No More's *Angel Dust,* Soul Asylum's *Grave Dancer's Union,* Screaming Trees, Body Count and er, a Marillion singles compilation. Josh Homme was still just 18 years old. A punk kid from a desert town. It was quite a statement.

Kyuss broke up when Homme was only 21. Not because they fell out. Not through musical differences. But because they had got bored. In the meantime, they got as far as supporting Metallica in stadiums. Homme went on to join Mark Lanegan's Screaming Trees as a touring musician before finally conquering the world with Queens Of The Stone Age

"We made four records and we just wanted to have a good solid ending with a finishing point" said Homme years later, still amazed at what happened. "Someone handed me a picture of John Garcia and I from 1993..." he remarked. "I just sat and looked at it for 20 minutes without saying a word, you know. And I never thought all this would come of it. We never even planned on leaving the desert, to tell you the truth."

# 7

## The Bowie Bet: Some Thoughts On Record Collecting

Record collecting can sometimes be somewhat infuriating if you are looking for something specific. A record can nestle untouched in the racks of a shop for years, it seems, when I am looking for something else. Copies will get in the way of what I am actually looking for. I can be searching through a rack in an entirely different genre and a copy of this same album will be there, misfiled. Three copies, all discounted by fifty percent will be in the next rack. "Good grief," I think to myself; "Will no-one buy this album?"

The next time I am there, there are seven copies, with the albums having apparently bred, like rabbits, in the rack. As I'm looking around the shop, three people will come in, all carrying copies of the same album, looking to sell to the owner, who will look regretfully at their copies, and wave them away, saying "Sorry mate, it's not even worth me giving you a quid for it – I've already got seven copies of that one."

The owner begins to use several copies of the album as a door-stop, or to level a wonky table. They begin to outnumber copies of Paul Young's *No Parlez* at boot sales.

And then comes the day I hear a song, and realise it's on that album I have previously overlooked. Given the plethora of copies scattered about in the "£2 and under" rack I go to buy it at the record shop only to discover that very weekend there appears to have been an unfathomable run on the album of the kind previously only seen outside Icelandic banks and small provincial building societies in the early days of the financial crisis. I travel to a couple of other shops, but there's not a copy in any of them, each and every one having been apparently stockpiled by "a bloke from London", doubtless a hedge fund manager or Bond villain. What copies you can unearth are battered and incomplete, tripled in price, with the album having become rare overnight. eBay copies suddenly fetch ridiculous sums. Every playable copy has vanished like the occupants of the Marie Celeste, or the career of Steve Guttenburg.

I wait a week or so and decide I will redouble my efforts. As I am about to do so, there's a story in the press saying the album was one of the last things Kurt Cobain played – on vinyl of course – before his death. Demand skyrockets. People are knocking each other out of the way at record fairs to find copies. It's like Black Friday at the Edmonton branch of ASDA. Then Rod Stewart and Robbie Williams announce they will cover the whole album as duets. I panic and buy a copy of the original at a sky-high price. The covers album reaches number one. Bublé then gets in the act and his cover of one of the songs makes the Christmas Number One. And just as it does, the record company releases the original album on vinyl for £16.99, and all the original vinyl copies go back to being £2 again, and my investment is worthless.

And I'm not exaggerating when I say this exact scenario happens *every single time.* Well ... You know what I mean ... For example, I found a copy of a '60s Kinks compilation called *Sunny Afternoon* a couple of years ago at a record fair in London. It was just £5, but I dithered. I put it back for two minutes thinking "I don't need a Kinks compilation," and when, five minutes later I decided my life would probably be incomplete and somewhat bereft without it, I went back to the stall only to find someone else had waltzed off with it, no doubt tap dancing and singing a comic song as they did so. Less than a week later, I was in a market in Cambridge and found the album on sale for £8. I was hardly going to pay more than I could have paid a few days earlier, so I passed again, thinking these things were clearly as common as the cast of *EastEnders* and I would stumble across another in no time at all. I didn't see another copy for two years.

In the end, after the most extensive search since John Speke woke up one morning and thought "I wonder where the Nile begins?", I bought a copy online. For £8. Literally the very next day after I bought the album online and two years since I had seen an actual, physical copy of the record, I was in a record shop and another punter plonked a pristine, almost mint condition copy of *Sunny Afternoon* on the counter to sell to the owner. It was in such good condition I bought that one too.

Moving on, here's a story about David Bowie records. Demand for Bowie has sky-rocketed over the last few years, but this is a reminder that there was a time when you could attempt to build up a collection of Bowie LPs for less than a hundred pounds ...

# THE BOWIE BET

# PART 1

Just how cheaply can you buy a full set of Bowie's '70's vinyl records?

"The trouble with buying old records" said my friend Chris after several pints of Adnams, (if I can paint you a brief picture), "is that everyone suspects they're worth something, so it is difficult to get a real collector's item unless you spend a lot of money. And if you do buy something old and in mint condition, why would you then play it? You'd reduce its value."

I considered the statement carefully, like a drunk considering a pint of beer. "It's a fair point," I said, "but not every old record is a collector's item. Those Beatles singles sold in the millions – so you can still buy a sixties original for a pound or two and play them all the time. Elton John's albums are regularly in charity shops."

"That's because they're awful..."

"No they're not! *Honky Chateau, Tumbleweed Connection, Goodbye Yellow Brick Road* – all classics."

"He lost my respect when he put that wig on."

"Do you remember that? It was shockingly hilarious at the time, but I told my son the other day that Elton used to be bald and he didn't believe me."

"We've all fallen into Elton's trap. He's got away with it."

We stared into our beers whilst we reflected on the inner truth of these words.

"Well – what about David Bowie's records?" I piped up, "I reckon most of them are probably all still pretty inexpensive. It's just the sixties bands that fetch the really big prices."

So Chris began to thresh out a challenge: just how cheaply could you buy a full set of Bowie's '70's records? In top condition. All the extras – lyric sheets and the like. First pressings.

I neglected to mention it on the night, but I knew that my local used record store, Leigh Records, had a decent stack of Bowie records for about a fiver each. I also had a bit of a head start this time. I had picked up copies of *Aladdin Sane*, *Low* and *Stage* six months ago (the latter two in a brick-a-brak shop) when I was buying the Beatles records. *Stage* cost me just £1; *Aladdin Sane* was £3. However, I thought the version of *Low* – also £1 – was a later reissue, so might not count – although I didn't know if there was any difference in buying the original.

The question was: how to make it interesting. Chris was still a keen sportsman and was out for revenge after our last bet. He began by suggesting I pay just £1 for each record. "I'm not that daft" I replied. "Even charity shops want more than that for most things nowadays."

I pretended to think hard – and doubtfully – like a cowboy builder poised to deliver an inflated quote for a new bathroom to a vulnerable old lady. "What about £10 per record? I think it might be possible to get copies of most Bowie records for that much – but getting the originals with correct inner sleeves in mint condition might be more of a challenge?"

Neither of us were sure whether this was too hard or too easy. I had a doubt in my mind that the early ones might be a bit pricier.

"I'll tell you what. That sounds too easy – so let's make it a fiver each – and just give you 24 hours to do it in." Chris kindly suggested. "That might stop some doubtful last-minute intervention from 'helpful' local record store owners too," he muttered darkly…

"I don't think so. No-one's going to have them all – it'll need a bit of digging around … Especially if I am going to get all the original bits and pieces."

We counted the albums. After about thirty minutes of coming up with different numbers, one of us had the remarkable (some might say genius) idea of looking up the answer on Wikipedia. Bowie's remarkable run in the seventies comprised of fourteen albums from *The Man Who Sold The World* (1970) to *Scary Monsters (And Super Creeps)* in 1980. Including two double live albums. And *Pin Ups* – the covers album with Twiggy on the cover.

"What's the prize?"

"You mean 'forfeit' don't you?"

"I don't know. Do you have a Bowie-in-'King-of-the-Goblins' *Labyrinth* costume? You – er, I mean the loser could wear that for a day…"

"No I don't have one! And I don't intend to get one either!"

Chris made a proposal: "What about this. Fourteen albums from *The Man Who Sold The World* to *Scary Monsters*. You have to buy them in fourteen days. A day per album. You have to spend less than a hundred quid. If you underspend, I pay you the difference between what you spend and £100 – in wine or beer. If you overspend, you buy me a bottle that costs the difference between £100 and what you overspend by."

I thought about this for a minute. It appeared heavily weighted against me. Chris' downside was capped, whereas my downside was unlimited – depending upon the cost of the records. On the other hand, I'd had a few beers myself by now, and I thought about the £5 records I had seen in Bob's shop. It might be possible. Perhaps the worst outcome might be that we get within three quid either way and have to drink some dreadful Bulgarian paint-stripper? Either way, I'd have some nice Bowie records.

And then before I could stop myself I uttered some ill-advised and potentially fateful words: "And the loser has to wear a Westlife T-Shirt at the occasion of the winner's choice."

Why did I say that? What possible reason would I have to say that?

So I took on the bet. What's the worst that could happen?

## Part 2

The day after making the bet I took stock of what was already in the bag.

1. A copy of *Aladdin Sane*, bought six months ago for £3.

2. A copy of *Stage* bought six months ago for £1.

3. A re-issue of *Low* (that probably didn't count for the bet as I didn't think it was an original release) that cost £1.

So twelve albums to go, and £96 to play with. Accepting that a couple of records might be harder to find, I still thought it might be possible. The spectre of having to wear a Westlife T-Shirt weighed heavily, but, like an Arsenal fan at the start of each season I was full of cautious optimism. As a start, I had snaffled a first pressing of *The Rise And Fall Of Ziggy Stardust And The Spiders From Mars* on eBay for £8.70 (plus P&P). "*Ziggy*" was a huge commercial success and is thus reasonably priced because it isn't all that rare. We all know Bowie retired the character soon afterwards, but for a while, Ziggy was a huge phenomenon. The cover, photographed in Heddon Street (off Regent Street, in London) in black and white (it was later tinted, giving it that unusual, futuristic look) is now a classic. Seeing it on a 12" record certainly does it more justice than on CD. A plaque was erected in Heddon St. in 2012 to celebrate the 40th anniversary of the album, although the street now looks very different.

The concept of Ziggy Stardust only came together at the last minute, after many of the songs had been written, according to Bowie biographer Paul Trynka. Two of the key 'concept' songs – about Ziggy's rise and fall – 'Rock n Roll Suicide' and 'Suffragette City' were among the last songs to be recorded, with Chuck Berry's 'Around And Around' still on the track listing.

Perhaps Bowie's biggest challenge was to persuade his three musicians from working class Hull to wear the costumes. Trynka explains that Bowie took the sceptical Spiders to see *A Clockwork Orange* and explained Freddie Buretti's costumes "were "futuristic" rather than something "poofs" would wear. When the three were presented with their catsuits – blue for Trevor, gold for Woody and pink for Ronson ... Bolder frankly admits he was not impressed – "To be honest it took a lot to wear that stuff" – and remembers Mick, destined for the pink jacket, as the most vociferous objector. "Mick was not up for it. Not at all."

The band played Friars Aylesbury to launch the new image on 29th January 1972 and after a stunning show the local paper declared "A Star Is Born". First pressings of *The Rise And Fall Of Ziggy Stardust And The Spiders From Mars* are identifiable by the lack of a "MainMan" credit on the reverse of the cover (in the top right). If your copy has the word "MainMan" on it, it's a later copy. MainMan was the management company Bowie's then manager, Tony Defries had set up, so all later pressings contained this credit. Many early copies have a nice inner sleeve also – with photos and lyrics.

It's worth the extra hunting around (and couple of quid if you are lucky) to get the inner sleeve. It's great to get a copy that sounds good – but as part of the attraction is holding the record and reading the credits it seems a shame not to enjoy the whole experience – which with the *Ziggy Stardust* LP doesn't cost much more. An orange RCA label is also preferred over the later black coloured labels – again because orange labels were earlier UK pressings. So: I finally had Ziggy in the bag. Eleven albums to go. Going well. Or so I thought.

# Part 3

I called Chris to discuss Bowie's first album of the seventies, *The Man Who Sold The World*.

Chris sounded amused, so I knew something was up. "Did you know that the first UK pressing of *The Man Who Sold The World* is er, not overly cheap?" he asked with all the innocence of an escaped convict found climbing half-way through a window at midnight.

"I don't know about that – I think I have seen them for about a fiver."

"Hmmm. You might want to check that... whilst I go shopping for a larger wine decanter and a Westlife T-Shirt. What size are you again?" He can be quite insufferable at times.

We had agreed that first pressings would be part of the bet. Chris had rather irritatingly discovered that the first UK pressing of *The Man Who Sold The World* was a) very expensive and b) had a controversial cover: of Bowie draped louchely (if that's a word; if not it should be) on a sofa wearing a dress. Not a tight-fitting little black cocktail number, either. One that might have made a rather fetching pair of silk curtains. It would have struggled to flatter Twiggy. On Bowie it struggled even more. Perhaps a better title for the album would have been *The Man Who Sold His Trousers*.

The story behind the dress is that it was one of six "men's dresses", made by a Mr. Fish of London, leader of the "peacock revolution", that Bowie purchased in 1970. Journalist Nick Kent described Bowie walking through New York airport immigration in one of the dresses in February 1971 as "looking for all the world like a young Lauren Bacall." Given the aggressiveness of New York immigration officials even now, you have to admire Bowie's *cajones*. If that wasn't enough, Bowie then travelled (wearing the dresses) across America – including a visit to that well-known forward-thinking liberal US state, Texas, in what might have ended up as a crazy suicide mission. Bowie later recalled "In Texas, one guy pulled a gun and called me a fag. But I thought the dress looked beautiful."

Despite the controversial look of Bowie in a man-dress, and because of the scarcity of the record, which wasn't a huge commercial success until it was re-released following the success of *The Rise And Fall Of Ziggy Stardust And The Spiders From Mars*, a new copy of *The Man Who Sold The World* in mint condition will cost a collector up to £500. I checked there and then – sure enough there was one on eBay for £400.

This was Extremely Bad News. The thought of exceeding the budget by £400 on just one album filled me with horror. The Heath Robinson-esque financial part of the bet meant that if I went £400 over budget I would also have to buy Chris a £400 bottle of wine. Financial ruin stared me in the face. And then kneed me in the testicles. However, a second version of *The Man Who Saved The World* was released in 1972 with a proto-Ziggy picture of Bowie in black and white. I had seen this 'kicking cover' in used-record shops for around a fiver and it was this that I had in mind for the bet. To learn it was not the original 1970 album, but a 1972 re-release was an unwelcome knock to an already stretched budget. I also discovered that even this album came with a lyric sheet and a poster – and a copy with the complete set might cost me £20 rather than £5. I had no intention of buying the £500 version.

I resolved I would have to buy the 'kicking cover' at a sensible price and smooth-talk Chris into seeing sense. I wasn't sure it was going to work ...

# Part 4

With brow furrowed, I called in to see Bob at Leigh Records. Bob saved my bacon last time, and I knew from popping in to Bob's shop from time to time that he had a good selection of Bowie records for around a fiver. I had a quick flick through the "B" section, but something was up. The stocks of eighties and nineties Bowie vinyl were still plentiful, but there were no *Heroes, Low, Diamond Dogs, Hunky Dory, Aladdin Sane, The Rise And Fall Of Ziggy Stardust And The Spiders From Mars* etc – in fact most of the Bowie vinyl had gone. This was a bitter blow: Bob was my 'banker'. I was certain I would be able to pick most things up in there for around £5. I asked Bob what was up.

"Since Bowie released his comeback single [*Bowie had just released his comeback* The Next Day *LP*], I've had a load of people buying Bowie, and no-one's brought any in." Bob told me. "I'm hoping for a laminated *Hunky Dory* to come in one of these days," he continued. "I had one a few years ago..." he mused wistfully. Truly – only vinyl could get men of a certain age looking romantically skywards. Or was it money?

"I suppose that's a few quid is it?" I asked. Bob chuckled and looked at me pityingly.

"With no 'MainMan logo and with the lyric sheet? About three hundred ..."

I gulped. "So what about those versions that you used to have for a fiver? What were they?"

"Oh, they're still pressings from the same year – just a bit later. After the first batch they stopped laminating the covers – and *The Rise And Fall Of Ziggy Stardust And The Spiders From Mars* was released only six months after *Hunky Dory*, at which point *Hunky Dory* got a new lease of life and was released in a matt cover – so you ought to be able to pick up one of those copies with a lyric insert for not much more than a tenner."

I breathed again – it might still count. I asked Bob about *The Man Who Sold The World*. He confirmed the Dress Covers were expensive – and that he didn't have one. "You know there's a third cover don't you?" he said. I gave Bob my usual blank stare, which some have likened to that of a goldfish.

"The record was released in America on Mercury records – naturally the Americans weren't going to have a man in a dress on an album cover, so someone at Mercury came up with 'The Cartoon Cover'. Bob started to resemble a magician who has just produced a dove from mid-air ... "As luck would have it, I have a copy in stock. It's in great condition too." Bob pulled out the record from the garish sleeve. "Look at the sheen on that", he continued, showing me the lustrous finish on the forty year old record, which suggested it hadn't been played much.

"How much?" I asked, suspecting the answer would be closer to a hundred pounds than five.

"Thirty-five quid".

Then Bob dropped a minor detail into the mix. "Technically the "Cartoon Cover" is the very first pressing as the record was released first in the USA. This was good. It might stretch the budget, but not half as much as the 'Dress Cover'. I decided to splash the cash – £35 – and left the shop with four albums under my arm – the other three each costing £5 and all first pressings:

First was *Scary Monsters (And Super Creeps)* in a gatefold sleeve ... then *Lodger* – in a nice laminated gatefold sleeve and with an all-important lyric sheet. *Lodger* is an underrated '70's Bowie album. The last of what is now known as the Berlin Trilogy too, even though it was actually made in Montreux and New York. It contained the amazing single 'Boys Keep Swinging' which had a startling (and potentially career ending) video. If you have never seen it, then do check it out on YouTube: Bowie's live performance is enhanced by his being his own backing singers – a trick Phil Collins perhaps had in mind when he made the video to 'You Can't Hurry Love'. The two videos have little else in common however: Bowie is dressed as three different female backing singers who hilariously rip off their wigs and smear lipstick over their face ... except the last one who just hobbles on with a walking stick. All very bizarre. When it was aired on *Top Of The Pops* at 7pm on a Thursday night, it put the nation off their collective teas sufficiently for the song to actually go down the charts – an almost unprecedented event. On the same episode that night was Gary Numan with 'Are Friends Electric'. Numan's single made number one...

'Lodger' contains typical Eno experimentalism: song 'Move On' is actually 'All The Young Dudes' backwards, which sounds unlikely, but search the internet for the *"Move On Bowie Backwards"* video for proof.

*Young Americans* completed the haul. I had spent more than half my budget now, but was still only halfway through – and with a week of the challenge left. The Westlife T-Shirt forfeit was looking a very real possibility.

## Part 5

For people who believe happiness is contained within thin vinyl discs, London is a good place to be. Despite HMV's troubles, vinyl lovers can still find a number of independent record shops to spend their hours of leisure merrily flicking through reams of old Barry Manilow and Cliff Richard albums in the (usually) vain hope that something decent will be hidden in between.

In order to track down inexpensive copies of Bowie's back catalogue I decided I would need to go to London, and Reckless Records in particular.

Reckless Records delivered – sort of. *Low* (with insert and stickered sleeve) was £15, (take that, eBay!) *Hunky Dory* was £25, *The Man Who Stole The World* wanted to set me back £20 whilst *Stage* sought to take a further £15 out of my wallet. All too expensive for my self-imposed budget, but they were all in fantastic condition. A *Heroes* picture disc was £12 and *David Live!* was £20 for a first pressing with inner sleeves. It was the sort of shop where you could spend inordinate amounts of money and still exit with a smile on your face.

However, quite aside from the bet, I was pretty reluctant to buy *David Live!* for the twenty quid that people seemed to want for it. The main reason for this was that, shorn of the visuals of the *Diamond Dogs* show, it is more an interesting document rather than a great rock 'n' roll live album (although it does contain great versions of 'All The Young Dudes', 'Here Today Gone Tomorrow' and 'Rock 'n' Roll With Me').

To enjoy the album properly – and to put it into context – you really need to watch *Cracked Actor,* a superb hour long documentary produced by Alan Yentob which covered the *Diamond Dogs* tour and which was broadcast on 26 January 1975. Yentob persuaded Tony DeFries, Bowie's manager, to allow filming because "it would be an exploration of a significant, serious artist in his new, American setting". It features some mesmerising performances from Bowie, including his singing Major Tom from a chair which is elevated above the heads of the crowd by a cherry picker and which looks magical. Bowie has shed his Ziggy and Aladdin Sane personas and appears to be somewhere in between Ziggy and his Thin White Duke character, which wouldn't properly formulate itself until *Station To Station*. During an interview Bowie drinks from a carton of milk and compares his adventure in the USA to a fly in the carton, soaking up what is around him. It's a fascinating snapshot of Bowie who was famously living on a diet of milk, red peppers and cocaine. The *Diamond Dogs* tour had jettisoned The Spiders From Mars in favour of a more considered and theatrical show.

In that context, *David Live!* is an interesting document – but it needs the visuals. Of Bowie's live albums perhaps the best are the *1976 Nassau Coliseum* recording that was in the *Station To Station* re-issue, or the *Santa Monica '72* album, the latter of which features the Spiders. The mark of a true Bowie fan used to be whether you had a copy of this Santa Monica bootleg. Although recorded from a radio show in 1972, it was finally released officially in 2008, so it wasn't an album I had to track down for the bet.

Whilst searching I also found a bootleg of Bowie's 50th birthday show (*Live At 50* – guest starring Robert Smith, Dave Grohl, Frank Black and Lou Reed) and rehearsals for the *Serious Moonlight* tour which featured Stevie Ray Vaughan on guitar. Vaughan played on *Let's Dance* but did not tour – pulling out after these rehearsals apparently at the behest of his management who wanted him to be a star in his own right. He released his debut album *Texas Flood* in 1983 – the same year as these rehearsals. This is an unusual bootleg, in that it is listenable. It sounds great, with a real variety of songs - 31 across the whole of Bowie's career to that point. Bowie appears to forget the words to 'Life On Mars' which is pretty funny, and changes the opening lyrics of 'Station To Station'. Stevie Ray Vaughan seems somewhat buried within the constraints of being in someone else's band – save for a blistering 'White Light White Heat'. However, the bootleg is still worth looking for online...

Overall however it was clear that Record Shops were not going to solve my problem of buying Bowie's albums inexpensively. Next step? The record fair at London's Spitalfields Market, which was on Friday – the day before my deadline. Time was running out if I was going to win the bet ...

Before setting off to Spitalfields market, I bought *Diamond Dogs* for £3.50 on eBay from the same seller who sold me *The Rise And Fall Of Ziggy Stardust And The Spiders From Mars*, thus saving on postage. The two records had cost me (including P&P) £16.70. I couldn't have bought all the albums off eBay or Discogs: the postage alone might have come to nearly £50 with fourteen albums to buy. As it was, I had eight albums for £70.70. I hoped that 70p wouldn't cost me – I now had six albums to buy for £29.30.

*Diamond Dogs* itself received mixed reviews, but was Bowie's most successful album in the US to date, peaking at Number 5. Blending the Stones-ey 'Rebel Rebel' with a dystopian Orwell-based concept album was never going to be straightforward, although we should be grateful it was *1984* rather than *Down and Out In Paris And London* that Bowie based some of the tracks on. I'm not sure how well a concept album about homeless people in the inter-war years would have gone down with the glam rock generation.

However, I had more pressing matters on my mind than unlikely concept album ideas. If I didn't pick up decent copies of the remaining albums for a fiver each not only would I soon have a large bill outstanding at the local wine merchants but perhaps more troublingly, I would have to wear a Westlife T-Shirt for the first (and hopefully only) time in my life – at an age when wearing Westlife T-Shirts is not dignified Leaving such worrying thoughts to one side, I hit Spitalfields early, and soon found several copies of covers album *Pin Ups* from £3 – although many were in poor condition and didn't have the insert. The insert was key to the bet – everything had to be included.

Released at a time when rock was finally old enough to look back at itself, as cover version albums by John Lennon and Bryan Ferry demonstrated, *Pin Ups* was recorded with Spiders Ronson and Bolder (invited at the last minute when Jack Bruce was unavailable) but not Woodmansey. The back cover includes a handscribed note from Bowie acknowledging the bands covered and the clubs they played: indeed Bowie had played at many of the clubs mentioned in the sixties. In many ways it is now more interesting to hear the originals which are in some cases fairly obscure (The

Mojos?). As Bowie says in his liner notes "These songs are among my favourites from the '64-'67 period of London".

After forty-five minutes of wandering around Spitalfields without finding anything more promising I began to get worried that there was more chance of seeing Bowie do karate with the Fonz as I had of finding all of Bowie's records for a fiver each. (there really is a clip of Bowie doing karate with Henry Winkler, on the *Dinah! Show*). One of the fun things about record fairs (aside from being elbowed and trodden on by middle-aged record dealers in sub-zero temperatures that would make a penguin's eyes water whilst you search in vain for a copy of a record that isn't there) is finding records that you never knew existed. Some of them are terrible of course – I can live without seeing a Portuguese-only release of Celine Dion's debut album. However, there are also some occasional gems: such was the case with *Christiane F* – the soundtrack to a German film which consists entirely of mid to late seventies Bowie songs, (some with slightly different versions to the album tracks) including a German language version of 'Heroes', renamed '*Helden*'. I found this 1981 release and snapped it up: not part of the bet, but how cool was that?

One stall had opened, and people were swarming over it. A dealer was selling all his records for a pound each. It was carnage. I saw one guy buy fifty albums – clearly this was the place where record dealers came to buy stock. Promising. I looked through, but no Bowie. The stall holder explained, "I just bought a guy's collection and I want rid of them (I assume he had cherry picked the good ones) – the vinyl is good, but the covers are a bit tatty". It's all about the condition of the package when it comes to the value of records ...

I then noticed a stall that was still setting itself up, yet also had hoards of people beginning to assemble around it. They all appeared to be record dealers, judging from their chat and banter with each other. As it opened these record dealers swarmed over the stock like a plague of locusts devouring crops, forcing me to stand back. In fact, as I waited behind these professional vinyl-ferreters I overheard what I thought was quite a touching conversation that spoke volumes about the lure of vinyl records and people's willingness to go truffling about in all weathers looking for them:

"So if you won a million on the lottery would you still come up here and do this?"

"... Yeah, I think I probably would ..."

"... Yeah – me too..."

They're mad – the lot of them.

When eventually I was able to get near, I knew at once this was the stall I had been looking for. There was *'Heroes'* – in fantastic condition with a tan label: an Italian pressing, but with lyric sheet. That would do. The UK version (with orange label) could wait another day.

Behind it was a copy of *Low*, UK pressing complete with insert and sticker on the back. And for less money than at Reckless Records. *Low* was originally called *New Music Night And Day* – the name change coming so late that some cassettes went out still labelled with the original title. They didn't have any at the record fair – that would have been a find! The cover comes from a teaser poster for *The Man Who Fell To Earth* and it is the first pressing of the album that comes with the track listing stuck on the back.

And finally there were nice clean copies of *Pin Ups*, *Station To Station* and *Hunky Dory*: success!

Just *David Live!* to go – but could I find it? Just as I was giving up hope, lurking in a box underneath the stall I saw it... for just £5. *David Live!* was in the bag!

## Part 6

I met up with Chris to settle the bet two weeks to the day from his challenge. Chris looked pensive. On his mind, I suspect, was my rather fortuitous last minute win the time we had a bet on those Beatles records. He looked like an expectant father.

"Come on then," Chris challenged me somewhat suspiciously. "What last minute surprises do you have for me?"

I played along. "Well – first things first: you know you told me that a first pressing of *The Man Who Sold The World* would cost me £400? It turns out that the first pressing is not the dress cover. That might have been the first UK pressing, but the US version came out a couple of months earlier." I fished into my bag like an enthusiastic conjurer, "And I have a first pressing of this lovely 'Cartoon' cover..."

Chris groaned, and swore. "Prove it."

I was mildly hurt at his lack of faith, but didn't let it show. There was a brief pause whilst he looked up the minutiae of 'Cartoon' covers. Chris also perked up a bit when I told him it had cost me £35.

"OK", he smiled, "so no killer blow – but that's over a third of your budget. I might have to bring down my sights a bit from a first growth claret, but it sounds like you might have struggled a bit?"

"Well", I continued, "I did find these two for just £4. For both." I pointed to *Stage* and *Aladdin Sane*. "And these were all fiver each." I gestured towards my other finds.

"Come on – how much did you pay in total?"

"Wait," I said. "Let me tell you about the *David Live!* album."

I appreciate this is beginning to sound like a Poirot novel, where the detective launches into an extended monologue before revealing the criminal mastermind behind a shooting in the library, but bear with me.

At Spitalfields, you will remember, I found an amazing record stall which had just opened and was crammed with records of every description in terrific condition. I had already picked up copies of *Heroes*, *Hunky Dory* and *Low* in the cases on the table. Underneath these cases were more records – all for £5. I had bagged *Station To Station* and *Pin Ups* and all I needed now was *David Live!*

And then I saw it – peeking furtively out of a crate like a kitten that has just torn your curtains. A man had been flicking through the records in the case next to me and in between the Rod Stewart and Jethro Tull detritus these few Bowie albums suddenly caught my eye. First *Scary Monsters*, then the kicking cover of *The Man Who Sold The World*. My heart leapt. To my utter dismay the man who was flicking through the crate picked it out and added it to a large pile of records he had already selected. A dealer! Then – right behind it – *David Live!* I immediately pulled the guy back, threw him to the floor and grabbed the record.

No I didn't. Before I could do anything, or even say "Aaaaarrrrrgghh!" (although I believe I said it inwardly) he had picked that one up too. You know the moment in Julius Caesar when Brutus betrays Caesar, stabs Caesar and Caesar says "Et tu Brute?" I imagine Caesar probably felt just as miffed as I did at that moment. To give Caesar his due, he was slightly more eloquent than I was however. I think my (unspoken) language might have startled a ship's parrot.

This dealer had beaten me to it! I checked the case after he had left, resembling the forlorn Japanese Dog Hachiko that waited at the train station for its master's return from work every day even after the man had died – but the moment had passed. There was no more Bowie left.

I wasn't beaten yet. We sportsmen / Bowie vinyl lovers are quick on our feet. I went up to the man and attempted to appeal to his better nature. I said "That *David Live!* album you just picked up: that's the one record I was after today." (I stealthily tried to hide the other records I was carrying). "Can I just see if it's the one I'm looking for and perhaps we can come to an arrangement?" He showed me the record. It was the first pressing with the right inners. But not all record dealers (he told me he bought it so he could sell it) have "better natures". This one had ice in his veins. He wouldn't sell. And with that, I was defeated. Having seen *David Live!* for a fiver, I wasn't going to go elsewhere and pay £20.

Oh, and I probably didn't mention this before, but I was already over my budget. I had lost the bet anyway.

I told Chris the story, and dipped into a bag and produced a reluctant bottle of wine. We counted the *David Live!* record at £20 and this made the total £130.70.

"Well done – you have won the bet", I said, with joy in my heart and a smile on my face. Sort of. "Er, you'll probably need someone to help you drink the wine – so I also brought a corkscrew…"

Chris looked very, very pleased with himself. He's still deciding when I have to wear the Westlife T-Shirt. His current favourite idea is the Download Festival. As I said before, he can be quite insufferable at times…

**Collectors' Note:** Original copies of *Low*, *Heroes* and *Hunky Dory* all cost me £10, with the majority of the rest £5 or less. *The Rise And Fall Of Ziggy Stardust And The Spiders From Mars* was £12.20 including postage but it was that £35 copy of *The Man Who Sold The World* that ultimately cost me – and not getting that *David Live!* album. It turned out the gatefold cover of *Scary Monsters* was a Greek import – but I found a UK copy with an inner lyric sheet for the same price at the same time – I just preferred the gatefold sleeve. My copy of *Pin Ups* was Canadian. It doesn't appear to have affected Bowie's pronunciation of the word "about" on the record.

*Epilogue:*

A week after I had lost the bet I went to the Southend Record Fair. I know I shouldn't have looked for Bowie records, but I couldn't help myself. I found a copy of the kicking cover of *The Man Who Sold The World* without the poster – but with the inner – for just £5. It wouldn't have counted but it was nice to find.

Less pleasing to find (if you know what I mean) were *Pin Ups* (a French copy) for £3 and *David Live!* For £6. Would it have made a difference? Not quite: I would still have lost the bet.... I also picked up the Greatest Hits *ChangesOneBowie* for £3.

It is possible to pick up all that fantastic vinyl for less than £100 if you take the kicking cover of *The Man Who Sold The World* instead of the US cartoon cover version.

In these difficult recessionary times what better investment could there be than a complete set of seventies Bowie vinyl? Even if it doesn't appreciate in value, you can still listen to one of the most diverse, constantly changing, always interesting and incredibly consistent bodies of work in rock n roll history.

# 8

## Why Neil Young Headed for the Ditch: Danny Whitten and *Tonight's The Night*

It's March 1968. Eric Clapton is in a police cell, butt-naked, save for a pair of pink cowboy boots, retained only at the insistence of some affronted police. The members of Buffalo Springfield have been busted for playing their music too loud at Stephen Stills' house in Topanga Canyon with drugs found on the premises. Our cast is completed by Neil Young and the band.

Clapton responds magnificently, delivering an archetypal English stiff upper lip parading in the boots whilst the lawyers arrive. Jamming with Clapton, police raids ... For Neil Young, this was a salutary lesson in just where the heady heights of success can lead you.

Buffalo Springfield split up just two months later. Stephen Stills joined up with Graham Nash of The Hollies and David Crosby, formerly of The Byrds, and, eschewing the chance to form a decently named law firm, Crosby Stills and Nash scored a hugely successful hit album. Young was not so lucky. In December 1968 Young released a solo studio album backed by session musicians that flopped by comparison.

It took until March 1972 – another three years of hard slog – for Young to claw his way to the top. But three solo albums and a team up with Crosby Stills and Nash later, Neil Young achieved his dream. He reached Number One in the singles charts in America with solo hit 'Heart of Gold', and his fourth album, *Harvest* topped the album charts. Life couldn't get any better.

How do you celebrate a number one single? Nowadays it's a call with a Radio One DJ followed by appearances on Breakfast TV. But back in 1972 Neil Young does things with more style.

Young invited Graham Nash over to the ranch to hear the forthcoming album *Harvest*, taking him across a lake to an island on his ranch. Young had fame, money, a 140 acre, $340,000 ranch and, as befits a rock star with a small fortune, the world's biggest stereo system that he was keen to show off to Nash.

How big was Neil Young's stereo? Neil Young converted his entire house and a barn into the world's biggest boom box.

Each building contained huge speakers to blast the album across the water to the two men. The house was the left speaker and the barn the right speaker. Concerned about the balance in the "speakers" Young shouted out the immortal line that only a pop star at number one in the charts can pull off:

"More barn!"

How Young reached this position is one story, but what happened next is perhaps more extraordinary, as Young seemingly sabotaged his career. Or as he put it, 'Heart of Gold' "put me in the middle of the road. Traveling there soon became a bore so I headed for the ditch."

Why did Young veer off the middle of the road?

The answer lies in his band, Crazy Horse, and in particular, guitarist Danny Whitten. As Young himself put it, "Every musician has one guy in the planet that he can play with better than anyone else. You only get one guy. My guy was Danny Whitten". That's quite a statement.

Danny Whitten, Ralph Molina and Billy Talbot had all met in California in August 1963. Danny was a dancer, and they formed a vocal a capella group called Danny and the Memories, singing amongst other things, Jerome Kern show tunes. They even cut a disc, although it failed to set the charts alight. While stardom eluded them, to make ends meet they would earn money by entering Danny into dance contests. In true *A Hard Day's Night* fashion they all moved in next door to each other.

Then they saw The Byrds in concert at a club called 'Mothers' in North Beach. It was a seminal moment. Stunned by what they had seen, there and then they dropped the vocal group idea and all decided to learn instruments. Their approach was a little unorthodox. Molina didn't have a drum kit, so found some spaghetti strainers to tap out rudimentary rhythms on cardboard boxes and phone books. Whitten locked himself in a basement for six months and came out a guitar player. Talbot meanwhile bought a bass; learning how to play it was yet to become a priority.

The three joined a few other, more accomplished musicians and formed a band with three guitars, bass, drums and electric violin. They called themselves The Rockets. They would jam in Billy Talbot's house on a sharp bend on Laurel Canyon Boulevard. If you happened to be stuck in traffic around that time you might have been treated to some of their ear-splitting jams.

They sound like awful people to have living next door for most people. Even the most ardent rock fan would surely tire of it all after a while. If it had been 2016 rather than 1965, there would have been reality TV shows made about them: *Keeping Up With The Rockets, Extreme Makeover: Hippy Neighbours From Hell Edition* or perhaps simply *What Not To Snort.*

The Rockets met Neil Young whilst the latter was still in Buffalo Springfield but it wasn't until March 1968 when The Rockets had released an album that they played in Topanga Canyon and Young picked up on them. In August of that year Young sat in on a show at The Whisky which went so well that by the end of the year Young had persuaded Talbot, Whitten and Molino to join him for an album and tour as Crazy Horse, and in January and March of 1969 *Everybody Knows This Is Nowhere* was recorded and in the can.

What was it about Crazy Horse? They weren't the greatest musicians. But compare Young's debut with the follow up. The first is polite and restrained. *Everybody Knows This Is Nowhere* is slow, heavy and ragged. There was nothing else like it. Neil Young had found his band. The trouble was, he didn't quite realise it, and neither did the public. Young needed a commercial boost, and he soon received one.

Stephen Stills came knocking. CS&N needed to go on tour, and he invited Young to join them. With a broken-up band and two solo albums not selling so well behind him, Young joined up, on condition he could be a "Y" in CSN&Y.

The rest is history. By August 1969 they were playing shows together. A Crosby, Stills, Nash and Young album *Deja Vu*, was released in March 1970 and sold millions. The money rolled in and Young's solo albums began to sell also. But despite the success with CSN&Y, Young had unfinished business with his special one: Danny Whitten. He returned to play shows with Crazy Horse. But whilst Young had been away, Whitten had found heroin.

After nodding off onstage at The Fillmore Whitten's drug problem began to attract attention. Falling asleep onstage during a gig is liable to do that. Once the tour had finished, Young fired the band. A song 'The Needle And The Damage Done' would record his thoughts on a future album.

Young made another solo album, *After The Gold Rush*. Whitten was replaced by teenager Nils Lofgren whilst he tried to sort himself out. Flush with the higher profile given to Young by his role in CSN&Y, the album was a hit. Another CSN&Y tour and an appearance at Woodstock cemented Young's place as Rock Royalty, and paved the way for the blockbuster album *Harvest*. Which takes us back to the start of this piece and Young's showing off in front of Nash with the world's biggest stereo.

Young was subsequently booked on a ninety city tour in support of Harvest. Audiences clamoured to hear the latest singer-songwriter play his hits. But that wasn't where Neil Young was at...

Rather than play a set of songs from the hit albums *After The Gold Rush* and *Harvest*, Young decided to write new songs to play on tour. We all know that feeling in the pit of the stomach when an artist says "Here's a new song we'd like to play". Their attempt to do so at Live 8 is one of the reasons we don't talk about the Scissor Sisters any more.

Young called up Crazy Horse guitarist Danny Whitten to join his *Harvest* band in the autumn of 1972. Young heard Whitten had shrugged off his drug problems and Whitten stayed in a trailer at Young's home, Broken Arrow ranch, to rehearse some new songs for an album to be called *Time Fades Away*. But Whitten hadn't quit drugs. To be fair, he had tried, but only by substituting tequila – not something that doctors typically recommend. Attempting to deal with his addiction by taking a trip to Mexico, when asked if he had anything to declare, Whitten threw up over the customs official.

It didn't take long for things to unravel. During rehearsals Whitten was once again nodding off during songs and by all accounts was in a terrible way. Eventually, Whitten was fired and given money to fly back to LA. The very night he was fired Whitten died, having overdosed on alcohol and Valium. It was a bitter blow. Understandably, Whitten's death hit Young hard. The day after Whitten's death he wrote 'Don't Be Denied', a biographical song encapsulating his disillusionment with success and how dreams can turn sour.

The rehearsals continued gloomily, and Young's *Harvest* band – all crack session musicians – began to argue about money, each demanding $100,000 to tour. They promptly fell out with each other and Young as the tour progressed across America. Egos were bruised. In-fighting and squabbles were the norm. As an example, drummer Kenny Buttrey was told he didn't play loudly enough. He tried bigger and bigger sticks until a music store vendor told him "Son, anything bigger than this is gonna have bark on it!" Young stayed on a separate floor in the hotel to the rest of the band. The trappings of rock 'n' roll took Young further away from real life.

It wasn't all bad, mind you. You can always rely on rock musicians to come up with novel and interesting ways to pass the time. Young and his band hired their own jet and built their own hookah pipe with an aquarium pump. This they christened 'Big Red' and it filled the plane with reefer smoke. (There is a downside to filling an aeroplane with marijuana. It reached the point where one of the band, Ben Keith, forgot what key 'Don't Be Denied' was in, despite the fact he had played it every night for three months. There was also a mild concern the pilots might get stoned from the atmosphere, something the Civil Aviation Authority usually – on balance – tends to discourage.)

On the tour Young realised everything he had wanted, all the success, fame and fortune, had brought him unhappiness. His backing group were bickering over money and he was playing huge, soulless venues such as the Oakland Coliseum. It was at this venue that on 31st March 1973 a fan had been beaten up by cops whilst Young played 'Southern Man'. Young stopped right there and then, mid song, and walked off stage. Show over. What's more, the one band he really wanted to play with had lost their spiritual leader, and all this was a consequence of Young's stardom.

"I was finding out it wasn't me who made the records" said Young. It turned out that Young needed Crazy Horse, he just didn't know it until the *Time Fades Away* tour.

The tour finished, and the album *Time Fades Away* was released that August. The first in what would become The Ditch Trilogy. It is Young's least favourite album, featuring those squabbling session musicians, plus Crosby and Nash in vocals, and no Danny Whitten. As a snapshot of the tour and of the songs Young wrote and recorded whilst dealing with fame however, it is remarkable.

Aside from the haunting piano ballad 'Journey Through The Past' (omitted from the album of the same name) *Time Fades Away* is rough, and couldn't be further from the polished, orchestrated soft rock of *Harvest*. An attempt to record more songs with Crosby Stills and Nash in Hawaii was fruitful, but unfinished, and whilst they were in Hawaii, there was another death; this time of CSN&Y roadie Bruce Berry, also hooked on heroin and who accidentally overdosed.

All this was brewing in Young's head as the CSN&Y sessions moved back to California and got stuck in treacle. So one day, instead of going to the CSN&Y sessions, Young went to the house of David Briggs, his producer, knocked on the door and uttered the immortal words: *"I'm ready to make a rock n roll record".*

If ever someone makes a Neil Young biopic, I think that moment goes in the trailer.

That rock n roll record would become *Tonight's The Night*. The bickering session musicians were ditched, and Crazy Horse were back, with Nils Lofgren and Ben Keith standing in for Whitten.

*Tonight's The Night* was recorded in the aftermath of those deaths of Whitten and Berry. Young's mood had also been affected by a 1972 drug-deal-related double murder near his home, an incident referred to in the song 'Tired Eyes'. These tragedies framed the mood of the album.

A recording session in Sunset Sound studios had gone nowhere, so Young rented a rehearsal room and – as we all would, I'm sure – used a sledgehammer to batter a hole in the wall to allow cables to go through to a mobile recording truck. The band drank tequila, playing in the dark on the rehearsal stage and created an atmosphere in which to honour Berry and Whitten. They were performing as if onstage in a darkened room to a non-existent audience. Young waited until they were sufficiently drunk or stoned before recording, usually in the middle of the night when the vibe would hit them. On the title track Young sings directly about Berry. "Bruce Berry was a working man … a sparkle was in his eye. Late at night when the people were gone, he used to pick up my guitar, and sing a song in a shaky voice that was real as the night was long." It is painfully raw and hauntingly beautiful.

How down was Young? Listen to 'Borrowed Tune': "I'm singing this borrowed tune / I took from the Rolling Stones" he sings to the melody of The Rolling Stones' 'Lady Jane'; "Too wasted to write my own". It's heartbreaking self-pity.

The recording was mostly one take, no fixes, with drunken raps in between. Five of the songs were recorded all in a row in one night without any break between them. Even the album packaging oozes atmosphere, with a black label I stead of the normal yellow one, and an inner sleeve with a photo of the band on stage with a gap to the right where Whitten would have stood had he been alive, with his name underneath.

Whitten was a gifted guitarist and songwriter. He had written 'I Don't Want To Talk About It', later a huge hit for Rod Stewart. Whitten's voice appears during the track 'Come On Baby Let's Go Downtown', an upbeat song he wrote with Young about scoring drugs. When the album was released he'd been dead more than two years. Hearing his voice midway through an album mourning his passing is like hearing a ghost. It may have lacked the sheen and commercial appeal of Harvest, but for all the reasons described, that wasn't Neil Young's mood in 1975. Not many artists have career highs when they are at their lowest ebb, drinking heavily and mourning lost loved ones. Tonight's the Night is unusual because it is all the better for it.

"What we were doing was playing those guys on the way" said Young.

## The Story of Are You Experienced by Jimi Hendrix

Perhaps the most traumatic moment in Hendrix's life was when he first met his father.

Little Johnny Hendrix was born in Seattle in 1942 to a flighty teenage mum, Lucille, who was unprepared for motherhood. His father Al had been drafted into the army before his son was born. Lucille was something of a drinker and had to work to make a living, so struggled to look after Johnny for more than a few days at a time. Johnny was mostly looked after by aunts and people from his church. At two he was taken from Seattle to California to live with a friend of his grandmother. At last Johnny had some stability.

His father returned from the army in 1945 and travelled to California to see his son for the first time. After just a few days Al took Johnny from the family where he had spent the last year or so being nurtured and cared for and took him eight hundred miles by train back to Seattle. On the way back a confused Hendrix cried to his dad "Leave me alone! I want my family!"

If that wasn't unsettling enough, suspecting Johnny may have been named after a boyfriend his wife had taken whilst he was at war, Al renamed the confused nearly four-year-old boy James Marshall Hendrix.

So young Johnny is still not four years old and he is ripped away from his family to live with a stranger who says he is his father, and who gives him a new name, Jimmy. Thanks Dad. You're a brick. New family, new town, new name, and new brothers ... Leon was born a year later, and soon after Lucille had a third son, Joseph. All might have worked out had Al and Lucille been more capable.

But Jimmy's parents – never happily married it seemed – divorced by the time Jimmy was nine years old and Al got custody of James and Leon, whilst Joseph was "fostered out". Concerned neighbours would leave food for the neglected teenage boys as their father would go out gambling. Later Leon too would go to a foster home.

It was a tough, unstable childhood, the sort of subject matter John Steinbeck might have dismissed as being a bit too grim for one of his novels, capped when Jimmy's mother died of a ruptured spleen when he was fifteen years old. Heck, even Morrissey might have thought twice about writing about such matters.

Music was the one thing that could take Jimmy away from his troubles. When he was fourteen years old Hendrix saw Elvis perform at Sick's Stadium in Seattle. What captivated him more than Elvis was the backing band. "They made playing music seem like the best thing in the world" he said. When he turned sixteen – and after playing an acoustic guitar for a couple of years – Jimmy finally got his first electric guitar earned by helping his father in the garden. Jimmy would take his guitar to school, and sit at the steps, endlessly playing and figuring out chords to the latest pop tunes.

Jimmy got into trouble when eighteen, "borrowing" cars and shoplifting. A counsellor took him to one side and Jimmy got the message. If he went to jail, he knew he wouldn't be able to play guitar. In 1961 he signed up for the 101st Airborne Division of the US Army. But wearing a uniform and conforming to his superiors wasn't a natural fit. Within eighteen months he engineered a discharge.

Jimmy travelled to Nashville to find work as a musician and for a couple of years backed Curtis Mayfield, Wilson Pickett, Jackie Wilson and Sam Cooke. In 1964, tired of the circuit and still only 21 years old, Jimmy travelled to New York. He played with the Isley Brothers and Little Richard, but throughout it all, he was broke, and felt a failure. He had been out of the army some time now and success still felt miles away. As it happened, things were about to change...

The second time a stranger renamed Hendrix was in far happier circumstances than the first time.

By 1966, Jimi had followed in the footsteps of Bob Dylan, playing in Greenwich Village in New York. Now billed as Jimmy James and The Blue Flames, an early show was seen by an English model, Linda Keith, who happened to be Keith Richards' girlfriend. Linda told Chas Chandler of The Animals about Jimi. Chas had been looking for a chance to step into management or record production. Chas liked what he saw. He signed him up, and they agreed to go with the new, more striking spelling of "Jimi". Stage names still seemed to be compulsory in the sixties, as Arnold Dorsey[5] found out to his cost.

From this moment Jimi was a fast worker. He left for the UK the day his first passport arrived in the post at the end of September 1966. The night he arrived in England he met Kathy Etchingham, who would be his girlfriend for the next couple of years. Like I said, a fast worker.

The most striking thing about this story now is the pace of Jimi's rise in fortunes: It's the autumn of 1966, and with a few notable exceptions, the pop charts are still mostly rubbish. Jim Reeves' 'Distant Drums' is number one. Ken Dodd is a credible pop star in the Top Thirty. Ken Dodd! It might not know it yet, but the world is crying out for The Next Big Thing, and it feels a decent bet The Next Big Thing won't be hailing from Knotty Ash.

Music is revving up a little. The Beatles have released *Revolver*. The Rolling Stones have released 'Have You Seen Your Mother Baby Standing In The Shadows', the Who 'I'm A Boy' and the Small Faces 'All Or Nothing'. I mean, sure, The New Vaudeville Band is in the Top Ten with something called 'Winchester Cathedral' which is properly, fundamentally terrible, but hey, two months ago Eric Clapton joined forces with Ginger Baker and Jack Bruce in Windsor to debut a band that would explore the blues as a power trio. They've called it Cream.

On October 1st 1966, a week after arriving in the UK, Chas Chandler arranged for Jimi to "sit in" at a Cream concert at London Polytechnic. Ever the Surrey gent, Clapton politely allowed Hendrix to play a song of his choice, Howlin' Wolf's 'Killin' Floor'. As he saw Jimi play, Clapton's jaw banged loudly as it hit the floor. Hendrix fired off his licks whilst Clapton turned pale and by all accounts was rendered speechless. Hendrix admitted "it seems so pushy that I would have barged into

---

[5] The real name of Engelbert Humperdinck

someone else's show that way. I can hardly believe that I treated Clapton – a hero of mine – with so little respect. I knew I was being rude. But at the time I had to get moving."

Jimi still didn't have a band, but just a few days after the Clapton show the line-up for the Experience was finalised. Brilliantly, the choice of taking either Mitch Mitchell or Aynsley Dunbar on drums was decided by the toss of a coin, an approach which would certainly make the X-Factor a briefer experience for all involved without really affecting the end product. After three weeks 'Hey Joe' was released on Track Records, because Decca turned Jimi down, continuing their catastrophic strategy of not signing the world's greatest pop acts, just as they had the Beatles.

Well done them.

Nevertheless, the single failed to chart at first. So just a month after the release of 'Hey Joe', and with his debut single not in the charts, Jimi would have another one of those traumatic moments in his life, only this time for all the right reasons. On November 25 1966 Chas Chandler arranged a showcase gig for the new band. It was a make or break strategy. Invite the press to a lunchtime showcase to show off the new band. Jimi and band would play, and hopefully blow everyone away. Play a bad show, and the only thing they would blow would be the opportunity. What's more, to attract the press, an audience was assembled featuring one or two well-known musicians. No-one important, just Eric Clapton, Jimmy Page, the Beatles, the Rolling Stones and Pete Townsend. No pressure then.

The still virtually unknown Hendrix – just 23 years old and with a hard life behind him – had to perform the gig of his life, at a lunchtime showcase in front of the world's most famous musicians and the assembled press with his hastily assembled six-week-old band. And if they blew it, they were back to the drawing board, and would be branded a failure. Hendrix and co played for forty incendiary minutes. The set included 'Hey Joe', 'Wild Thing', 'Like A Rolling Stone' and 'Johnny B Goode', and they went down a storm. John Lennon was first in the dressing room afterwards to offer his compliments.

Boosted by the press coverage and publicity 'Hey Joe' entered the charts by the end of the year, eventually reaching number six. Two more singles followed, including 'The Wind Cries Mary', which Jimi wrote after arguing with Etchingham (whose middle name is Mary) about her miserable attempt to make mashed potatoes, causing her to smash plates and walk off down the street. This is, I am sure, exactly what you imagined that beautiful song was about.

The debut album *Are You Experienced?* was released in May 1967 and on 4th June the Experience were topping the bill at The Saville Theatre, opening their set with 'Sgt. Pepper's Lonely Hearts Club Band', the title track of the album released just two days before, impressing the onlooking McCartney.

Less than two weeks later Jimi, Mitch and Noel were to appear in the USA at the Monterey Pop Festival, just as their debut album reached number 2 on the UK album charts. Celebrated documentary maker D. A. Pennebaker was hired to film the festival. He was told to shoot one song per performer and Jimi was one of the last to go onstage.

On went Hendrix in front of an expectant audience. The Who had been on already. They had won a coin toss to make sure they wouldn't have to follow Jimi. That's right: the Who *won* the toss and the world's loudest band with the maddest of madcap drummers, alpha male vocalist, ox-like bassist and a guitar-smashing guitarist elected to bat first to avoid being blown offstage by Jimi. And to Pennebaker it quickly became clear that he was witnessing something very special indeed. After the first song, instead of stopping, he decided to keep shooting a second song, so remarkable was the performance. Then a third. And a fourth ... By the end of the set, Hendrix had set fire to his guitar and Pennebaker had just shot every single mesmerising song. Pop history was made and Hendrix had a platform to global stardom.

It took just nine months for Hendrix to go from being on his own, a complete unknown, with no direction home, to being celebrated on both sides of the Atlantic.

## The Story behind The Kinks' Most Famous Fight...

Forget Mayweather versus Pacquiao or even Mills versus McCartney. Whilst some observers will argue the Fight of the Century was Ali versus Frazier at Madison Square Garden in 1971, or for The Rumble In The Jungle, or even The Thrilla in Manila; none of these take into account the real fight of the century, possibly known as The Tiff in Cardiff.

The Tiff in Cardiff saw, in the blue(s) corner, Kinks drummer Mick Avory, and in the (increasingly) red corner Kinks guitarist Dave Davies. Sometimes it is worth reminding ourselves of what, to this day, is one of the most bloody - and at the same time hilarious - fights in rock 'n' roll. The facts are in slight dispute, but most observers agree they are as follows:

1. The Kinks were playing a show in Cardiff as part of a tour playing seventeen gigs in nineteen days. Davies and Avory had already come to blows after the previous show in Taunton, with Dave Davies, who had started the fight, coming off worst, sporting two black eyes.

2. During the Cardiff show, Dave Davies took his revenge, telling Mick Avory in an insult worthy of ~~Oscar Wilde~~ Joey Barton, "You're a useless c— and your drumming's s—. They'd sound better if you played them with your c*ck", and then proceeded to kick Avory's drum kit apart.

3. Mick Avory appeared to not take this as a compliment.

4. Avory picked up his drum pedal (some accounts say it was a cymbal) and struck Davies over the head with it, knocking him, bleeding, to the ground.

5. Avory, believing he may have killed the guitarist, then fled into the crowd wearing full Regency stage costume and onto a train bound for London.

6. Avory then hid from the police for three days, until news reached him that Davies was still alive and wouldn't be pressing charges.

Oasis split up after Liam threw a plum at Noel. They just don't make 'em like they used to....

Rob Jovanovic's Kinks biography *God Save The Kinks* describes Avory's flight from justice like this: "The big drummer panicked when he saw Dave laying there motionless and ran right out of the theatre, disappearing into the Welsh night with his frilly shirt and hunting jacket flapping about him". Nick Hasted, in his own, excellent Kinks biography *You Really Got Me*, agrees: "Avory believed ... he'd murdered him. Running through the crowd and out of the hall, he took a train towards London, surely a hunted man, shrinking into his seat in pink Regency garb."

Dave Davies told Jovanovic "That was outrageous. That was very funny, though not at the time. Imagine Mick trying to hide in the crowd thinking he'd killed me, with that pink hunting jacket and frilly shirt he used to wear." Avory meanwhile generously conceded to Hasted "It obviously wasn't the way to handle it," but denied he had used the more lethal weapon some accuse him of using: a cymbal. "I only used a high hat pedal. It wasn't as bad as it was made out. If I'd hit him with a cymbal obviously that could decapitate someone."

Davies hid at NME journalist Keith Altham's house for a few days. The Cardiff police wanted Dave Davies to press charges for attempted murder, but he declined to do so.

The real punchline to the story, however, was not delivered physically. The next time Davies and Avory saw each other was at a planning meeting for their next tour of the USA. Their tour manager Larry Page decided to ignore the ill-feeling that remained, a task made more difficult by the fact that Dave Davies was sitting in the room with an enormous bandage wrapped around his head.

After running through various points, Page asked the band if they had any questions.

"Yeah," replied Mick Avory. "I'm gonna need a new drum pedal …"

# 9

## Modern Record Collector Dilemmas

### PART 1: Record of the Month Clubs

If you are old enough, cast your mind back to adverts in 1980's magazines. You may remember the following:

1. Franklin Mint's offer for readers to invest monthly in a set of twelve potentially priceless butter dishes celebrating the fairy tale, and no doubt everlasting, marriage of Charles and Diana for just £23.95 +p&p each,

2. a cartoon advert for Bazooka Joe bubblegum,

3. an incredible offer from the Britannia Music Club.

The latter advert offered three albums by popular artists for just £1.49 each (plus p&p). This was a substantial discount, and acted like a Pied Piper to the pocket money of the nation's youth. Stung into action by the chance of ludicrously discounted records, Britain's youths posted freepost coupons in their droves with little heed to a) small print or indeed b) their parent's knowledge. The offer was seemingly a trap: attached was the promise of a "handbook" to explain the club "rules". That list of rules were described as "simple", but then there were ten of them just in the advert itself, suggesting understanding membership terms might require a little focus. The scheme was designed to be fiendishly complicated in order to make it almost impossible to calculate that in fact the buyer would be worse off after taking into account the cost of posting back a letter every month to say no, they would rather cover themselves in jam and dive head first into a nest of wasps than have the *Phantom Of The Opera* soundtrack or worse, Enya, posted and billed to them as the Album of the Month choice.

This was the big catch: having product sent to you unless you said "no thank you". An album was recommended each month by the club – presumably by someone with a pretty mischievous sense of humour around what sort of music you liked ("What's that? You ticked the 'rock music' preference? Here: have a Five Star album") – which would be sent unless you posted a letter within a month to say otherwise.

You had to order six albums over two years, and each time you did you could order another at a discount, diminished by shipping and handling charges that were so high it suggested the warehouse was based in the Outer Hebrides (or perhaps Neptune) and packages were handled by princesses, and what's more, princesses earning considerably more than the National Minimum Wage For Princesses.

After ordering six albums, if you ordered another two you would get a free album. And if you posted your order on a Tuesday, you'd get an extra 10% off.

Okay, I made that last one up. But you get the idea.

All this assumed that you were happy to wait months to receive the latest releases instead of just popping to Boots, WH Smiths, Woolworths, Our Price, Virgin, HMV, or one of hundreds of independent record shops then scattered liberally throughout the land.

It was truly a business model for people who never left the house, except to post letters to request someone not to send them music through the post. Which appears pretty niche if you think about it. There was a ten day free "home trial" – presumably of the potential buyer's sanity in signing up to the deal – a sanity which, in many cases had been temporary suspended by the promise of cheap CDs or tapes.

In the USA the allure was even greater. A skim of US magazines would reveal Americans could buy eleven albums they hadn't thought important enough to buy upon release for just a penny. Or thirteen for a dollar! Who could resist! Especially the millions of Americans who actually lived nowhere a near a record store.

Both Britannia Music and its US equivalent, Columbia House, generated huge profits because many subscribers would forget to mail back their request to skip the latest Milli Vanilli long-player. The offending album would be delivered, unwelcome and unwanted, like a prehistoric version of U2's *Songs Of Innocence,* only you had to actually pay for it. Imagine the bleatings of the people who complained about U2's album appearing on iTunes if they had received Milli Vanilli through the post along with a bill for $16.99...!

Let's face it, being organised enough to send back a form in the mail every month within a set time frame is a big ask for anyone, never mind a teenager. And this was before junk mail was frowned upon. Every day the nations' letter boxes were polluted by so many Readers Digest promotions it was a Herculean task to sift through a kilo of mail every day to find the real letters.

Speaking of Herculean tasks, the story of Hercules may well have turned out very differently had one of his quests been to diligently send back his album of the month cancellations over a three year time period. In the US you also had to buy a set number of albums (nine over three years at "catalogue prices") before cancellation was possible. Many complained that cancellation of the scheme wasn't easy. It was said in some circles (my own) that the one thing Harry Houdini was never able to get out of was his Album of the Month Club subscription.

The scale of these mail order businesses was phenomenal. According to an AV Club[6] article in 1994, 15 percent of all discs in the U.S. sold because of these clubs, while a 2011 Boston Phoenix article about Columbia House Record Club reported that 3 million of the 13 million copies sold of Hootie And The Blowfish's *Cracked Rear View* were sold via Album of the Month clubs. There had to be a reason for the success of that band. So we're unlikely to go back to those bad old days, right?

Wrong. The resurgence of the popularity of vinyl has led to a plethora of companies wanting to revive the old Album of the Month Club format. Not that anyone is offering ten albums for a dollar. With the advent of streaming services, cheap CDs and YouTube, anyone offering an Album of the Month service competing on price is going to fail. With Spotify and Apple Music et al having algorithm-based or curated recommendations, the idea of having an ordinary album forcibly sent to you every month for twice the price of a Spotify account to see if you might like it is also somewhat anachronistic. There are plenty of ways to discover new music – doing so by having one physical album sent through the post months after release doesn't seem to be a tremendously good use of anyone's time.

## PART 2: The Five Golden Rules

An Album of the Month Club is a wonderful thing. It's like having a friend with great musical taste who is compiling, nay, "curating" music ("curating" sounds so much better than "compiling" because er, it sounds like they have taken a bit of time to carefully choose it whereas of course if you compile something that's just the equivalent of throwing a bunch of tunes in the air and seeing which ones land in the bag.) for you to add to your collection. Yay! Or is it? What friend would 'curate' a selection of music and then insist you buy it from them? And then send you letters threatening to take you to court if you don't pay?

---

[6] www.avclub.com

So are Album of the Month clubs more like having a slightly menacing, litigious, overbearing bully of a friend who insists upon imposing their musical opinions on you? This certainly sounds less good, and consequently is an unlikely by-line in any advertising materials for such clubs. So what's the truth? And what makes a good or bad offer?

Having tried out a few of these clubs in recent weeks and months, I feel qualified (in a completely "I'm not in the slightest way qualified to do this" kind of way, but we're all fed up with experts, right?) to advise on the pros and cons. So if you are thinking of setting up your own Album of the Month Club, here's a cut-out-and-keep guide of the Five Golden Rules of Album Clubs:

1.  **The main, slight drawback to offering an album every month to subscribers is that the entire concept is fundamentally flawed. (But don't worry, no-one seems to have noticed.)**

Sending out stuff to people that might not want it is intrinsically worse than sending out stuff to people that actually do want it. There are few things that annoy people more than being forced to buy something they don't want. It's bad enough at Christmas buying gifts. We've all seen people fake a smile upon opening an underwhelming present. That they haven't paid for. Now imagine if we had to pay for the gifts people gave us at Christmas. Which brings us neatly along to

**2. People don't really like surprises. Especially if they have paid for them. (Don't worry about this either. They'll get over it.)**

Even people who say they like surprises don't really. Think back to the last time someone threw you a surprise party. Oh, sure, you'll have happy memories now it's all over, but what about when it was actually happening to you? That unexpected sea of gurning, smug faces. Your feeling of utter horror. Then worrying you didn't look happy being ambushed. Despite the fact that nobody likes being ambushed. Ask General Custer.

When was the last time you saw anyone who didn't have to feign delight when a surprise party was organised? Let's be honest, anyone who has been the ~~victim~~ lucky recipient of a surprise party has had to fake the most stressed smile whilst all the while thinking "I'm not properly dressed for this, they've basically all lied to me for weeks, I've been mugged off, and it would have been nice to look forward to it, and organise it in the way that I would have done it". Most people's first reaction is the most honest: a horrified grimace at this real-life Jack in the Box filled with sixty giggling people already three sheets to the wind.

The next flaw in the model is this:

## 3. People don't like making decisions or saying "No". (Too bad: ignore this.)

Over the years one learns to spot the obvious traps and avoid dangerous questions. Questions such as "What do you think of this dress?" "How old would you say I look?" and "Do you know how fast you were driving?" All of these questions have one indirect intention: to incriminate the person being questioned.

An Album of the Month forces its members to incriminate themselves each month. What does their decision to not buy that album by Dr Dre say about themselves? Does this mean they are narrow-minded? Too old? Too young? And what if they do buy it? Mid-life crisis? Faking being hip? For the 90% of the population with a nervous disposition or chronic self-doubt these are awkward questions. At least when you flip past the album in a record shop you will know that when you 'Forgot About Dre' you weren't making a proactive decision.

The trouble is, the alternative is worse...

## 4.    No-one likes being lumbered with an album they don't want. (Whatever.)

Now that boffins have shrunk people's music collections onto something the size of a postage stamp, having records in your doubtless "carefully curated" collection that you are never going to listen to and which you overpaid for is just going to grate, especially when you try to file a much-loved album in your Kallax shelving and you tear the cover because everything is too tightly packed.

But perhaps the thing that the new breed of Record of the Month clubs are most guilty of is this...

## 5.    The Essential But Ludicrous Cross-Sell

We get it. You can't compete on price. So one way to differentiate your offer is to do something a bit (to use the parlance of commerce) "value-added". This quest for value-add allows you to charge a slightly higher price ("You're getting something in addition to the record!") and stand out from the crowd ("nowhere else will you receive this Peruvian poem!")

When done well, this can be genuinely welcome. Jack White's *Vault* offers an album, a single and an extra item. Some of these novelties are perhaps more crucial than others, ranging from USB sticks to photo books to tote bags and DVDs.

Other clubs' additional items appear to be less compelling. Like cocktail recipes, for example. One such Club is a wine merchant, who shall remain nameless because I'm about to be rude and it's someone's business and hey, good luck to them. Their bright idea is to increase sales of their wine business by sending out a vinyl LP with a matching bottle of wine in an admirable demonstration of ~~bandwagon-jumping~~ entrepreneurship.

The selection of LPs includes such obscurities as Prince's *Purple Rain,* Fleetwood Mac's *Rumours, Sticky Fingers* by the Rolling Stones and Bowie's *Hunky Dory.* There are no special editions. It's just the repressed album you can buy in the shops. Sure, you get wine. It's hard to knock such a compelling product. But... there appears to be a pretence that the wine somehow "goes" with the album in question. An Aussie Shiraz called 'Love Grass' with *Purple Rain.* A nice Tuscan red with *Sticky Fingers.* But why? What makes those wines go with music?

Now sure, wine labels are prone to a bit of exaggeration. In general, even the cheapest bottle of supermarket plonk will sport a label describing what food the wine best accompanies usually in very flowery language that has little resemblance to the sweetened tooth-dissolving paint stripper contained therein. But never have I seen a wine label that described the contents as "Hints of damsons and blackberry. Accompanies red meats, blue cheeses and *Rumours* by Fleetwood Mac."

There's some vague theory behind this, perhaps. Guns 'n' Roses' *Appetite For Destruction* probably wouldn't go with a 2005 Rioja quite so well as it might with three bottles of Thunderbird. James Bond noted with distaste when Red Grant ordered red wine with fish in *From Russia With Love.* But Bond's smoking out SMERSH agents by disapproving of their drinking a '58 Claret whilst listening to Dusty Springfield is notable by its absence in Ian Fleming's books.

Where will it end? Will there be a record club pairing clothing and vinyl? ("A leopard-skin pill box hat with every Dylan LP!") Or perhaps we could pair other items? Why not a subscription service that pairs a different album with various species of rodent? We'll call it "Vinyl and Vole Club". Or perhaps superhero costumes and cassettes? We'll name that one "Capes and Tapes". Or maybe kitchen appliances and CDs? Yup, that one's "Compact Discs and Handy Whisks"...

It's all very well my making snide comments of course, but none of this matters two hoots if, in fact, *Purple Rain* is demonstrably best listened to when drinking a bottle of Australian Shiraz. So I took it upon myself to 'match' Prince's *magnum opus* to various bottles of alcoholic beverages, purely in the interests of scientific research, you understand. I have come up with the following scientific conclusion: After the tenth glass of Shiraz, there's a real risk you might fall over, especially if dancing to 'Let's Go Crazy'.

## PART 3: I Put A Club To The Test

With 1980's Album of the Month Clubs such as Columbia House (USA) and The Britannia Music Club (UK) having gone the way of the Commodore 64, typewriter ribbons and Roland Rat you'd be forgiven for raising an eyebrow or three at the idea of a record subscription service revival. However, no matter how many eyebrows you might raise, there are still plenty of people out there who are looking to resurrect the idea.

At first glance this all seems rather strange. Album of the month clubs were a way to build an album collection quickly, hopefully cheaply and easily, with punters often taking "recommendations" from the club itself based on nothing more than ticking either "pop", "rock" or "classical" on a preference form. With YouTube and Spotify using algorithms based on your listening habits, "discovering music" through a generalist, remote, non-personalised service seems all a bit, well, 1985. You might as well ask Roland Rat to recommend his favourite albums to you.

Furthermore, no physical product can be as cheap as digital streaming, so there are no "Buy Four Albums for £1" style offers. Without price as a weapon, what angle can a budding music-loving entrepreneur use to encourage people to take up a new subscription? It's worth looking at a few of these clubs to see how some have, in different ways, found a model to be relevant in the 21st Century. To differentiate themselves in what might otherwise be a crowded marketplace, vinyl subscription services should have answers to the following questions:

1.  Is the subscription service providing something you can't buy in the shops?
2.  Is the subscriber forced to buy something they don't really want?
3.  Is it really a "club"? Does the subscriber get something beyond an album?
4.  Is it value for money? And of course...
5.  Does it come with a ludicrous cross-sell?

I put a well-known club to the test. The club produces exclusive editions, often in coloured vinyl. This is a big tick in the box. There's nothing quite like a potentially scarce record to catch the Magpie-like reflexes of the record collecting community. One recent album of the month was an exclusive reissue in grey vinyl of The National's *Boxer*. To accompany the album was an exclusive 7" single of two songs from the new album. As those old adverts used to say "This Is Not Available In The Shops!" So far so brilliant.

In only the second month I was confronted with a dilemma. On offer was Notorious B.I.G.'s classic *Ready To Die*. The issue I had with *Ready To Die* were the tracks 'Me And My B*tch' and '#!*@ Me (interlude)', the latter essentially a recording of Mr B.I.G. sh*gging his girlfriend whilst she describes him as a "fried-chicken-eating-gangster-mutha#!*@erf". I quickly realised if I was playing the track when my two young children popped into the room, I would feel relatively uncomfortable. My kids, on the other hand, would find it possibly hilarious, yet puzzling.

These are colourful phrases, and show a certain flair and imaginative use of the English language. I just think there are better ways to help kids with their English homework than teaching them phrases such as "Crack smoking, Oreo cookie eating, pickle juice drinking, fat greasy mutha". At least let's wait until they're in their teens, eh?

So how did the club's format cater for those of us who have got over our rebellious and misogynistic phase in life? There was no cancellation facility for long term subscribers (although there was a more expensive Month-by-Month option); however there was a "Swap" facility where the club has a back catalogue of exclusive vinyl that subscribers may exchange for the album of the month. The community 'club' aspect of the club was fostered through a series of emails and forums. The club newsletter *The Standard* was infinitely more interesting for music lovers than London's free newspaper of the same name. There was also a podcast and a Spotify playlist. As for value for money, that's rather in the eye of the beholder, but a three month package cost me around £27 per month.

But, I hear you ask, what about that final piece in the jigsaw? The ludicrous cross-sell? The club liked to bundle in a couple of extras to their monthly album. An art print, designed to appeal to that small niche of The National Fans who like limited edition vinyl and art prints. And then there was the cocktail recipe...

It's a mystery to me why someone has decided the biggest problem with listening to records – the one grumble they believe unites people who listen to music on vinyl – is a lack of decent cocktail recipes. I know a few record collectors and have never bumped into any of them in a cocktail bar. In the nicest possible way, it's not their normal habitat. It would be like finding a parrot in the North Pole, or Mariah Carey at a book club. Never mind cocktail bars, half the record collectors I bump into at record fairs would find themselves placed firmly outside the velvet rope of a Yates' Wine Lodge, what with their faint odour of charity shop dust, thermos flask boot-sale coffee and quiet despair. They'd probably start haggling with the bartender. "What's your best price if I buy two?" "Oh come on mate, that Gin Martini has seen better days, eh?" "Can I pay you next time?" I'm not saying this is a good thing or a bad thing, but it's definitely a thing.

So are Record Clubs treating collectors as a Pygmalionesque experiment, playing the role of Henry Higgins to the scruffy, unsophisticated Eliza Dolittles of the record collecting community worldwide? Is it dragging us record collecting plebs into the Hallowed Halls of Hipsterism where everyone drinks cocktails, craft beer and listens to coloured vinyl? And has had a wash. And, more to the point, does anyone actually put a record on and mix themselves half a pint of the finest premium rocket fuel in order to get the full experience? Does that experience make listening to records so much better? Well, there was only one way to find out.

I don't know if you have ever tried to make a cocktail yourself. It's generally more trouble than it's worth.

- First you fish down the back of the liquor cabinet amongst dusty old bottles of Campari that an aunt once brought to a family party.
- You pore through cupboards and cabinets to try to source the right sort of glass tumbler,
- Then you find you have run out of ice...
- You go to the off licence to seek the more obscure ingredients like Aperol and angostura bitters. They don't have them.
- You begin to wonder whether Jagermeister might serve for Aperol, whisky for mezcal and orange marmalade a decent substitute for angostura bitters...

By the time you have completed these various tasks still with no end in sight you are quite in need of a drink, and, what with the potential cost of all the various ingredients, a possible re-mortgage.

So now, I did what any self-respecting music blogger-about-town would do, and popped into the cocktail bar at Hawksmoor, chatted to the nice people behind the bar, and asked them to make me the club Cocktail of the Month. Bartenders like to try new recipes, I have found. They get a bit bored of making the same dozen cocktails. I didn't ask the bar staff at Hawksmoor – I'm sure they'd be too polite – but I imagine there are only so many times you can make a Pornstar Martini or hear "shaken, not stirred" from some idiot showing off in front of his mates before the initial flush of excitement begins to fade.

They told me 'The National + 29 Years' (not the snappiest name for a cocktail. Ian Fleming would have cut that out of his first draft, I suspect) was like a negroni but made with mescal. Which, if you are into cocktails, might mean something to you. It was very nice. The sweetness of the Aperol gave way to smoky mescal (hey, I don't write album reviews, but I can review a cocktail) and the enthusiastic bar staff then suggested we make another with Campari (not so sweet) instead of Aperol to see which one tasted best. They were both beautifully made and smelled delicious, enhanced no doubt by the forty stirs around the single ice cube mandated by the recipe, not to mention the expressed orange swath. Actually I couldn't find an expressed orange swath, so I just got them to twist some orange peel over the drink.

I left Hawksmoor significantly more cheerful (not to mention wobbly-legged) than I had arrived, but unsure as to whether listening to the National's dark, asymmetrical passageways and late-night, empty-city-street mood, and slightly menacing but mostly isolated vibe (description copyright: Pitchfork Magazine's review of *Boxer*) would have enhanced the experience.

# 10

## Two Vinyl Buying Guides: How to Buy Led Zeppelin and Nick Drake on Vinyl

### Led Zeppelin

The 2014 reissues of Led Zeppelin were a tremendous boon to record collectors. Because original copies of Led Zeppelin's back catalogue can prove quite expensive. But what's best: the original records, or the reissues? And why buy vinyl at all? For me, that's the easy bit. It's not just the sound: it's also for the fun bits. Not only do Led Zep have some great albums, they also have some of the greatest packaging. Let's have a look at the albums in turn:

First, the most fun record sleeve of all time. There's joy to be had in the spinning wheel on the cover of *Led Zeppelin III* that will transport you back to when you were two feet high and your best record player was made by Fisher Price. It's like a record and an activity set all in one. Ooh, look – a stripy ball, and wait: there's a butterfly – and a rhino wearing a nappy. Ooh – and there's a hairy, drunk mud shark-abuser ... Someone should make wrapping paper with the same design – it'll make millions. Well, I'd buy it anyway.

*Led Zeppelin II* is dull by comparison, a mere gatefold, whilst *Led Zeppelin IV* will remind you of your tenth birthday, but only because it has a gatefold sleeve and features a Gandalf look-a-like on the inside cover. Never mind. *Physical Graffiti* is much more fun. It has little holes in the windows of the town house on the cover. Depending upon whether you put the lyric sheet outermost or the printed inner sleeves, you can change the record's appearance. But why stop there? Why not have the house looking like a grotty council estate by drawing your own crack den on the sleeve, or hanging out washing from the windows? Or hang it on the wall and pretend to be James Stewart whilst acting out scenes from *Rear Window*? Or insert pictures of '70s Radio 1 DJs and pretend it's a great big prison. But all of this is for another time.

Led Zeppelin seemed to care more about the packaging than most bands do nowadays. *Houses Of The Holy*'s release was actually delayed not because the band had musical differences, but because they weren't happy with the way the sleeve looked. And not for a couple of days, or a week or so. Want to know how long? This is what Peter Grant said about the incident: "We were determined to ensure that nothing went out with our name on it until it was absolutely right. We delayed the release of the *Houses Of The Holy LP* for five months because the cover artwork wasn't right. You can imagine that Atlantic (who distributed Swan Song product) were going mad." Five months! I can only think it was very important to get the exact shade of orange shining over the naked children's bottoms (now there's a Google search term I don't want...)

Back to the albums; *Presence* had a gatefold Hipgnosis cover with mysterious *2001: A Space Odyssey* obelisks heavily featured. I think having Goscinny-and-Underzo-inspired-Obelix's might have been funnier, but you can't have everything. The inner sleeve also has some pretty odd Hipgnosis images. Meanwhile *In Through The Out Door* had six different potential covers wrapped in a brown paper bag, so you'd never know which of the six incredibly uninteresting covers you'd get until after you bought the album. Each photo is taken from the perspective of a different person in the photo. What's more, this album contains a colouring book! Honestly. If you paint the inner sleeve with a water filled brush, the ink bleeds (deliberately) and different colours are revealed. Amazing eh?

All this is fine and well. But what do the records actually sound like? Is there any benefit in buying the original UK records with the plum coloured label? It is received wisdom that the earliest Led Zeppelin UK pressings – with a plum and red label, rather than the later green and yellow label – are the ones to have. They therefore fetch the most money. But received wisdom, I have discovered, is not always correct.

When I first started building up my record collection again, my local record shop, Leigh Records, had a £40 UK plum labelled copy of *Led Zeppelin III* and a US pressing for £7.50 in the same condition. I plumped for the cheaper version. This wasn't because I have some sort of maverick vision or second sight as a record investor. It's because I could get *almost* the same thing for thirty-two pounds fifty less, and a penny saved is, as the saying goes, a penny earned. However, a bit of impromptu research from some audiophiles has revealed that in the majority of cases the US pressing actually sounds better than the UK one.

This is in contrast to the general rule of record collecting that if you buy an early pressing from the country of origin of the artist, you are most likely to be nearer the source tapes, and therefore the sound ought to be better. It seems Led Zep are an exception: they had such great success in the USA that this generally fairly reliable guideline doesn't hold true – after the first album at least. I didn't know it at the time, but my US pressing was pretty early and has excellent sound – probably better than an equivalent UK version.

Another thing you should know about buying Led Zeppelin vinyl is that their first couple of albums are very, very expensive. You shouldn't be prepared to look for first pressings unless you are fond of shouting "— Me!" whilst you suffer a heart attack from fright.

The first pressings of the first album *Led Zeppelin* are easily identifiable with turquoise lettering on the front cover. Oh, and by the £1,500 price tag in mint condition. No, I don't have one. Second pressings – still from the sixties and with orange lettering on the cover – are marginally less ridiculously priced, but may still set you back a few hundred quid if mint. No, I don't have one of those either. I found one for twenty-five quid a little while ago, but it jumped, so I didn't buy it.

*Led Zeppelin II* is less expensive, and there are a couple of things to look out for: Top money can be up to £250 for a mint first pressing – identifiable by a mis-credited 'Living Loving Wreck on the label. Still a first pressing, but without the mis-print is a £60 copy in mint condition which lists 'The Lemon Song', crediting the writers as Plant and Page on the label. Later copies are around £40 and call this same song 'Killing Floor' with a credit to Willie Dixon – which if you have ever heard Willie Dixon's song you will have some sympathy for. Look also for a light brown sleeve with a blurry green edge. However, whichever copy you look for, finding *Led Zeppelin II* in great condition is harder work than listening to Depeche Mode's third album.

This brings us to *Led Zeppelin III*; a terrific record all round. Ever tried to play 'That's The Way' on guitar? It's hellishly tricky – until you realise Page uses an alternative tuning (it's an open-G tuning, the same one that Keith Richards uses to play 'Rocks Off' or 'Start Me Up' - in fact pretty much all of his songs) and then you just learn a few basic chord shapes and Bob's your uncle (or should that be Jimmy's your uncle?) Once you've got that, it's actually pretty easy to play the basics. (Whilst we're on the subject, 'The Rain Song' from *Houses Of The Holy* is another not-as-tricky-as-you-think song to learn – with an alternative tuning from low to high DGCGCD – that just sounds beautiful as you play it).

*Led Zeppelin III* also (shock horror) has an inscription in the run off groove quoting that Scottish master of evil magick Alistair Campbell, sorry, Alastair Crowley. *"So Mote Be It"* and *"Do What Thou Wilt"*, which led to much apparently serious speculation as to whether Page, Plant, Bonham and Jones had sold their souls to the devil. It just goes to show how gullible people were in the seventies...

With all of these albums, you can buy cheaper copies by targeting the eighties reissues on green Atlantic labels. These can be bought for substantially less, albeit on lightweight eighties vinyl. And there's the rub; because the value in buying re-issues lies in the quality of the vinyl – especially for the first four albums. If you bought your Led Zep vinyl in the eighties, or if your old copy is crackly, then the newer versions ought to be better sounding copies – and that's a good reason to buy.

Buying the later (*Physical Graffiti* onwards) reissues on vinyl might not be so essential, because the original copies are still common and less expensive. The quality of the original vinyl is also very good: As Led Zep's manager Peter Grant revealed in a 1989 interview in *Raw* magazine, he got the idea for Swan Song after Atlantic apparently messed up the pressings for Led Zeppelin II. "They actually ran off 100,000 copies which jumped all over the place because they didn't follow Jimmy's precise instructions on the master tape. So we just decided that it was time for us to take control of our own situation and ensure that Led Zeppelin were presented in the best possible manner. We oversaw every aspect of record manufacture. I would go down to the pressing plant myself and make sure that everything ran smoothly. And I discovered some very interesting things. For instance, the records are dipped during the manufacturing process into vats of acid right? But for Rock/ Pop stuff these vats are only cleaned out every six months. However, for classical records there are separate vats which are cleaned out every ten days! So, I persuaded the powers that be to dip Zeppelin's albums into the classical vat, which is part of the reason why the sound quality on our albums was so good." However, even if better quality copies of Led Zep's later albums (*Physical Graffiti, Presence, In Through The Out Door*) are plentiful, the promise of extra tracks on the reissues may yet convince you to shell out the hard-earned cash.

## How to Buy Nick Drake on Vinyl

Chris Davidson was a bit pushy. He was also not the tallest boy. He wanted to join a band at school called the Perfumed Gardener. Rehearsals were in the school hall at the not very rock'n'roll time of first thing in the morning, in order to avoid unwanted attention from killjoy schoolmasters. But Master Davidson was out of luck. The Perfumed Gardeners didn't want him. He wasn't cool enough. He could have joined Sex, Love and Society. Or Les Blues en Noir. I suspect the ideal fit might have been the Four Squares. Even if they became the Five Squares. Such was life and band names at the elite fee-paying school that was Marlborough College in 1965.

And why would the Four Squares have been ideal for this short, pop-loving, unfashionable specimen? Because these are all traits that would never leave Chris Davidson, even when he later pursued a successful singing career and changed his name to Chris de Burgh. De Burgh might have had a big guitar, but the band he wanted to join were a year older than him, and it wasn't enough. He just didn't have the right image. What's more, De Burgh's pushiness got the back up of the leader of The Perfumed Gardener, a popular Marlborough sprinter who, as a result, rather cruelly wouldn't let him join in.

The sprinter was enjoying his life at Marlborough. He was well-liked, a bit of a late developer, but passed his A levels and went on to Cambridge University. He even went on to be House Captain by the time he left, and he possessed a sense of adventure, often hitch-hiking three hours to London overnight to watch Chris Farlowe and the Thunderbirds, Steve Winwood or the Moody Blues at The Marquee or The Flamingo in Wardour St, returning back in time for chapel. He'd even write a song one day, called 'Three Hours' about doing just that.

On his last day at school, as was customary for students who were leaving, he got spectacularly drunk and was found with a bottle of sweet white wine in hand, just outside the music block. He was, it appeared, quite the lad. And the name of this popular, outgoing, Chris De Burgh-baiting lad-athlete? Nick Drake.

It's odd that a man who was famously shy and uncomfortable onstage later in life began his days so full of confidence. The story of Nick Drake is ultimately a sad and strange one. Although he signed to Island Records, writing and recording three incredible, beautiful albums, those records did not sell well in his lifetime. He became despondent. He withdrew from his friends and struggled with depression, a state of affairs that ended in November 1974, when his parents found him dead at their home, having overdosed on antidepressants.

The music he left behind was rediscovered and reappraised over the next few decades to the extent his albums now regularly appear on "Best Album Ever" lists. In the U.K. interest in Drake was further boosted from a most unlikely source, when 'Fruit Tree' was played over a scene in popular 1990's Sunday night TV schmaltz-fest police drama *Heartbeat*. In the episode in question, Nick Berry's character, a village policeman, lost his wife to Leukaemia in front a quarter of the TV watching nation, many of whom were either blubbing uncontrollably or wishing Shazam had been invented so they could find out what the record was that was playing over the scene.

As Drake's reputation and the public's love of his music has risen, so has the price of the earliest copies of his albums. First pressings of Drake's LPs now regularly fetch £400-£500 for *Five Leaves Left* and upwards of £200-£300 for *Bryter Later* and *Pink Moon*.

Why? Because the original tapes of *Five Leaves Left* are damaged. If you want to hear the best possible version of Drake's first album, vinyl really is the closest you can get. Which is bad news for vinyl-loving fans of Drake's superb brand of folk rock. Well, sort of. First, there's only three (ish) albums, right? Perfect for completists short of time. And yes, you'd be forgiven for thinking at those prices, perhaps that's just as well.

But happily, decent copies of Drake's albums can be found for much less than the bankruptcy-and-divorce-threatening territories that a first edition will engender. For the vinyl lover and collector, here's a guide to your choices if you want to build a Nick Drake Vinyl Collection (Warning: it's going to get geeky from here):

### Choice 1: A First Edition. (Also known as the "millionaire's choice".)

**Pros**: lovely solid label on *Five Leaves Left*, pink Island rim labels on *Bryter Later* and *Pink Moon*. Heavy vinyl. True scarcity especially in great condition (only circa 5,000 of each sold). Absolute clarity of sound, straight off the freshest stampers. Widely considered the best by those fortunate to have heard them, especially in the upper echelons of the audiophile world (i.e. people who post comments on the Steve Hoffman forum on the internet).

**Cons**: Divorce, bankruptcy, awkward conversations with bank managers. Constant vexation that children might play the thing on their cheaply-purchased suitcase-style-turntables.

**Choice 2: A new copy: The "instant gratification" choice.**

**Pros**: Excellent value – you can get all three for £46. *Pink Moon* is currently only £10.99 on Amazon (although I'm sure you'd go to your local record shop first). The "right" versions sound great. The best value for money.

**Cons**: Choose your version wisely. There are counterfeits out there which don't sound so good. Other reissues are taken from digital sources and to some listeners don't do the album justice. The best sounding versions by many accounts are the 2012 'Back To Black' reissues.[7]

**Choice 3: The box set method.**

In 1986 a USA Box Set called *Fruit Tree: The Complete Recorded Works* was released, housing all three albums plus a further album of songs recorded by Nick Drake but not released in his lifetime.

**Pros**: Released on the US Hannibal label, these are excellent pressings from the original tapes. You also get an extra LP.

**Cons**: avoid the 1979 UK version – it squeezes the tracks onto 3 discs. Neither version comes with proper LP sleeves.

---

[7] The notes on these reissues explain why *Five Leaves Left* is going to remain scarce: "It is inevitable that when dealing with tapes that are now over 40 years old there will be some degradation in quality consequently we have not always been able to use the original first generation tapes. The sources are as follows:
*FIVE LEAVES LEFT* : The original tape was unusable and although there were tape copies the best source was using a 24bit digital file made from the original tape when re-mastered for CD some 12 years ago.
*BRYTER LAYTER* : Unfortunately the original Masters have been lost so I used my personal copy made at the time of the original mixes. (John Wood, Abbey Road Studios)
*PINK MOON* : This was cut from the original Masters.
All three albums were mastered at Abbey Road Studios, July 2012.

**Choice 4: The next best thing to a first pressing without incurring the threat of bankruptcy.**

Essentially, this means buying the 1976 Island blue and yellow label re-releases.

**Pros**: They can be found for a little over £30 each. More expensive than a new copy, but is definitely an all-analogue pressing from the original source, and might have investment potential as first pressings become more difficult to find in tip-top quality. Some of these second / third pressings of the albums still used the original stampers and so are as close as you can get to hearing a first pressing. The only difference for some is that vinyl quality and thickness in post oil-crisis seventies Britain was not quite as good as it had been in the sixties and early seventies.

**Cons**: More expensive than a new copy, but perhaps the best option for those who balk at spending £400 on an album (i.e. most of us).

It's also a much better option than building up a collection of Chris De Burgh albums.

# 11

## A Test, To Make Sure You Have Been Paying Attention ...

Having read through the articles above, you may be feeling more confident about your record collecting abilities. In which case you may be interested to learn Stax University is to offer a three-year degree course in Record Collecting. The degree course will examine pupils' understanding of grading the condition of records, why some records are more valuable than others, matrix numbers, stampings, the manufacturing process, mastering of vinyl and the weight bearing ratios of the IKEA *Kallax* range of shelving.

However, they won't just take anyone.

Keen to educate the public, yet also keen to exclude novices who might commit cardinal errors (trying to play a CD, banging on about the "warm sound") Stax University has produced an entry paper, which we are proud to exclusively reprint below.

Could you pass the entry test for the Record Collectors Degree Qualification? Find out on the next page ...

# Stax University Degree in Record Collecting, Entrance Exam.

Time allotted 30 mins.

**1**. If, in November, Adam has told his wife he paid "about a fiver" for the copy of a near mint pressing of Led Zeppelin's first album with turquoise lettering on the cover that he has just brought home, please state a) how much he really paid and b) how long the marriage will last if Adam has to pay for the family holiday in July.

**2**. Tony has just bought an original copy of Otis Redding's *You Left The Water Running* which was limited to just 500 copies, found in a charity shop for just £1. Express as a percentage how much of a damn Tony's girlfriend gives about that when they are a) late for dinner and b) at all.

**3**. Keith has spent the last forty years collating his record collection. It consists of mainly first pressings and has a full run of Stiff Records singles and over fifty Vertigo albums. It is valued at £70,000 on Discogs. Express in pounds how much Keith's widow will sell it for if she chooses any of the following methods of disposal.

a)     Keith's best mate, who has a shady past, secretly fancies Keith's widow and has been envious of the collection for many years.
b)     the local record dealer
c)     the skip

**4a.** Harry finds a VG copy of Pink Floyd's *Meddle* (1U matrix) and a NM copy of *More* (left facing). If VG is worth 1/2 a mint copy, which is more valuable? (10 marks. Show your workings, including the correct use of Pythagoras's theory of relative value).

**4b.** If the amount of brain power used to calculate this question was instead channelled towards solving the world's problems, how soon would world peace be achieved?

**5.** Alan has just sold his record collection as he thinks prices for vinyl are peaking. He paid £3,000 for his collection over twelve years and sells it for £10,000. If Alan spent six hours a week in record shops and boot sales instead of working, and is self-employed, earning £15 an hour on average, how much money has Alan really lost on his collection if you take into account the amount he could have earned working instead of hanging around wasting time in record shops?

**6.** Sarah likes to visit car boot sales on Sunday mornings to look for rare records and has been regularly visiting such sales every week for the last nine years, but only when it isn't raining. If it rains on average through the year one week in three, how many different copies of Paul Young's *No Parlez* would Sarah have ignored whilst trying to find something good?

Bonus point: How does the answer differ for the following albums: a) *The Sound Of Bread* b) Soundtrack to *Grease* c) Soundtrack to *Saturday Night Fever*?

**7.** Sophie has a mint condition first pressing of *Trout Mask Replica* by Captain Beefheart. It has never been played since she bought it in the early seventies. Explain how depreciation works by calculating how much the value of the album falls each time it is played on the following record players:

a)   a Rega 9 with top of the range cartridge
b)   a battered old Dansette player found in the loft
c)   a Fisher Price child's record player.

Bonus: Explain why answers b) and c) are the same.

Note: use your answer to calculate whether Sophie hasn't played the album because of the potential investment value, or because it is just a really difficult record to listen to.

**8.** Martin's teenage son has rifled through Martin's record collection and played his dad's NM condition copy of *Please Please Me* by the Beatles with a "Dick James" credit on the label on a cheaply-purchased suitcase-style turntable-with a badly adjusted ceramic cartridge. If Martin is of average health, how far above safe levels will his blood pressure be after he finds out?

**9.** John lives in a three bedroom semi-detached house and has two children. If he has a mid-life crisis and wants to start record collecting from scratch, how long will it take, on average, before John's collection is so large that he starts to talk about a "lack of space" or "moving somewhere bigger"?

    a)    ten years
    b)    two years
    c)    ten months

**10.** You see a new 180g remastered copy of *Born To Run* by Bruce Springsteen for £25 at the record shop. How many used copies of the album could you find in equally good condition for the same amount of money at your local record fair if you spent twenty minutes looking around?

    a)    five
    b)    six
    c)    eight, with a pound to spare.

**Bonus question.**

Geoff believes that vinyl has a superior sound whereas Andrea believes that digital music from CDs sound best.

If they raise the subject at a party, how long will it take before the last guest dies of boredom?

# 12

## The Story of *Wish You Were Here* by Pink Floyd

12 January 1968. Pink Floyd took to the stage as a five-piece band for the first time, at Birmingham's Aston University. Pink Floyd may have had a top ten charting single but not all was going well. Their main creative force, Syd Barrett, all rock-star-looks and the embodiment of a sixties hipster – which meant shaggy hair, black corduroy jacket and paisley shirt rather than the 2020 hipster uniform of beard, skinny jeans and a plate of pulled pork – appeared to be unravelling, not helped by his prodigious use of LSD. You'd be surprised how few doctors prescribe vast quantities of hallucinogenics to help patients with fragile mental health.

A new recruit, David Gilmour, had been recruited to help out alongside Syd. A U.S. tour and subsequent support slot for Jimi Hendrix at The Royal Albert Hall showed the progress Floyd were making, but the band were left frazzled by Barrett's behaviour. Syd had never been overly reliable, going back to when the band had been booked to play *Top Of The Pops* with single 'See Emily Play'. For most bands, a *Top Of The Pops* appearance was one of those moments you dreamt of, like scoring the winning goal in the cup final, or, if you are a parent of young children, having five minutes to sit down uninterrupted.

Not Syd. He was hugely reluctant to go on, and was so out of it for one show he couldn't stand up (they sat him on a cushion) and had to be dragged to the studio by the band. He refused a third appearance, and when Floyd was booked for the *Saturday Club* radio show, he simply walked out before it was the band's turn to go on.

Back in Birmingham in 1968, fresh faced, good looking new boy Dave Gilmour, drafted in to shore up Barrett's erratic playing, was not entirely comfortable. Barrett was not in mid-season form. Indeed, he seemed somewhat perturbed by Gilmour's presence onstage. Barrett stood so close to Gilmour as to be just an inch from his face. Gilmour's eyes cried out for help. Barrett continued to stand onstage right in front of Gilmour, seemingly oblivious to the fact that they were in the middle of playing a show. Barrett then began walking around Gilmour, his childhood friend, like a panther, "as if checking that Dave was a three-dimensional object" in the words of Floyd roadie Iain "Emo" Moore, checking "that he was real. It was as if Syd was thinking: Am I dreaming this?"

Imagine if you started a new job, doing whatever it is you do, and on the day you begin, the guy whose job it used to be prowls around, circling you, sometimes standing two inches from your face whilst you quietly get on with your job. You'd probably begin to feel at least mildly disconcerted. You have to give Gilmour a bit of credit for keeping calm there.

Gilmour had been incorporated into the band during three days of rehearsals in a West London school hall in January 1968. Syd spent a couple of hours teaching the band a new song, called 'Have You Got It Yet'. Each time the song reached the chorus, Syd would change the song, so the band could never get it. As a piece of performance art or comedy, it was rather clever. But it also confirmed to the rest of Pink Floyd that they were right to draft in another guitar player alongside Syd. "Alongside" soon became "instead of".

Syd left Pink Floyd on the night of 26th January 1968. I say he left. What actually happened is that the other members of the band decided not to pick him up on the way to a gig at Southampton University. The gig went so well, they didn't call for him the next night either.

This caused a few issues for keyboardist Richard Wright, because he was still sharing a flat with Barrett. Wright would tell Barrett that he was going to nip out for a packet of cigarettes and then nip away, play the show, and come back the next day. It says a lot about Barrett's situation that he was slow to catch on.

There was one gig on that UK tour however when Barrett did turn up, according to roadie Emo. He was already there when the band set up the gear onstage. Barrett sat at the side, waiting for the show to begin. It wasn't until Floyd took the stage without him that it sunk in that there was someone else playing his part. Barrett's departure was officially announced on 6 April 1968. His mental health had declined and he withdrew from public life.

Fast forward seven years, to 5th June 1975. Pink Floyd are recording the follow up to the gazillion selling *Dark Side Of The Moon*, an album called *Wish You Were Here*. At its heart is a tribute to Syd Barrett called 'Shine On You Crazy Diamond'. You possibly know the rest ...

Floyd were doing the vocals for the title track of the album. During a playback each of the band noticed a bald, sixteen stone man in an old tan rain mac, carrying a plastic shopping bag, lurking in the studio. He had shaved his eyebrows off, and every now and then he would hold a toothbrush still to his teeth and jump up and down to brush them. At first, none of them recognised this man. After forty-five minutes, Gilmour realised it was Syd Barrett. "A huge shock," said Gilmour. "I hadn't seen him for about six years". Roger Waters had tears in his eyes. It was terribly sad to see what had become of the sixties hipster with the Byronic good looks and boundless enthusiasm.

After seven years' absence from being a member of Pink Floyd, Syd had returned, on the very day Floyd were doing a song about him. Keyboards player Rick Wright later told an interviewer: "I saw this guy sitting at the back of the studio ... and I didn't recognise him. I said, 'Who's that guy behind you?' 'That's Syd'. And I just cracked up, I couldn't believe it ... he had shaven all his hair off... I mean, his eyebrows, everything... he was jumping up and down brushing his teeth, it was awful...

"Roger [Waters] was in tears, I think I was; we were both in tears. It was very shocking... seven years of no contact and then to walk in while we're actually doing that particular track. I don't know – coincidence, karma, fate, who knows? But it was very, very, very powerful."

Barrett meanwhile appeared oblivious to the seven-year gap. His next question had echoes of that night seven years previously, when he had stood at the side of the stage before the band played without him.

"Right, when do I put my guitar on?" asked Syd. Waters gently told him the guitar part was all done.

The band and Syd all went down to the canteen, shared a cup of tea and talked for a while, and after some time had passed Syd left the studio. "It couldn't have happened without him" Waters later reflected. "On the other hand, it couldn't have gone on with him. I wanted 'Shine On You Crazy Diamond' to get as close as possible to what I felt. That undefinable, inevitable melancholy about the disappearance of Syd. Because he's left, withdrawn so far away that, as far as we're concerned, he's no longer there ... Syd wore out his welcome with random precision".

## The Story of Mercury Rev's All Is Dream

"Invention ... does not consist in creating out of void but out of chaos." Mary Shelley.

"We just knew [chords] E to A. It was a maelstrom." Jonathan Donahue, Mercury Rev.

It's funny how the most chaotic of circumstances can give rise to the most beautiful of things. Like the music of Jonathan Donahue and Sean "Grasshopper" Mackowiak, the two founder members of Mercury Rev. You might never suspect they have a past so turbulent it makes the last days of Rome appear positively civilised. Mercury Rev formed in the late 1980s in Buffalo, New York. Like the Replacements a decade before them, they thrived on being the most shambolic version of themselves. They took pride in never rehearsing and constantly argued, particularly lead vocalist Dave Baker who by all accounts could start an argument in an empty room. Their first gig was in front of seventy people. Their second was in support of Bob Dylan, in front of considerably more.

Imagine that. Your second ever gig and you are supporting Bob Dylan, and not only that, but you can see Dylan at the side of the stage watching you, and presumably tutting and wondering how the hell you managed to get yourself on his bill.

Just how shambolic was shambolic?

Well, when band member (and later, producer) Dave Fridmann, who subsequently left to work with the Flaming Lips, secured Mercury Rev's record contract, he spent part of the advance sending his mother to Bermuda on holiday. You can picture how that sort of conversation might have gone down with the rest of the band:

Dave Fridmann: "Great news! We've signed a record deal!"

The rest of Mercury Rev: "Yay! How much is the advance?"

Dave Fridmann: (shifts uncomfortably in his seat) "Er...well, there's good news and bad news..."

The rest of Mercury Rev: "Okaaay, what's the good news..?"

Dave Fridmann: "Um, I've got this lovely postcard from mom, she says the weather's lovely...."

Somehow, Jonathan Donahue's persistence and songwriting talent, not to mention work ethic, secured a record deal that gave birth to debut album *Yerself Is Steam*, featuring 'Frittering'. Out of chaos, beauty.

Meanwhile, the band continued to fracture. Donahue reminisces, tactfully describing David Baker, as "eccentric" adding "with David...you never knew when he'd sing the song or when he'd go to the bar", something that actually did occur mid-set during an early UK tour. "That's what led to *See You On The Other Side* because you never knew what would happen. Sometimes he would drop the mic ... and you would see the crowd part." I guess it's thirsty work being a front man.

And as for those early shows? "We didn't know how to play. A great solo would qualify if you just walked closer to the amp. Especially if you didn't smash the guitar afterwards. Career move? The jury's still out." It wasn't all bad. A year later and Mercury Rev were on the bill at Reading Festival in front of 20,000 people. They were still arguing and refusing to practice.

By 1995 Baker had left, after another band argument on an aeroplane ended in an attempt to gouge out Grasshopper's eye with a spoon.[8] It failed, but it's a really rubbish way to settle an argument. Let's face it, Baker was always on borrowed time after that: I don't know about you, but I'd probably have brought it up quite a bit if he'd done it to me and we were still arguing.

"Absolutely no-one" bought the 1995 album *See You On The Other Side* according to Donahue, which was a tremendous pity, as in hindsight it's a remarkable album, showing early signs of the shape of things to come. Things took a distinct Spinal Tap-esque turn when the band played at a "little theatre somewhere in Britain called the Penny Whistle. It seated 80 people. There was a puppet show on before us, and only four people showed up." The band split up. Grasshopper did what any other self-respecting rock guitarist on hiatus would have done, and booked himself into a Spanish Jesuit Monastery for six months. Well, we've all thought about it. Donahue meanwhile reportedly shook off the effects of either a nervous breakdown, a heroin addiction, or both.

Batteries recharged in 1998, Mercury Rev signed to V2 Records and retired to the Catskills Mountains to make another record. They teamed up with Levon Helm and Garth Hudson of the Band. *Deserters Songs* was the result, and it was one of the best albums by any band of the nineties. If there has been as impressive a resurrection anywhere outside of religious texts, I have yet to hear about it. It was quite some turnaround from this shambolic, argumentative bunch of stragglers.

The making of the follow up, *All Is Dream* also came from chaos. The record was due to be produced by Jack Nitzsche, but he died a week before they were due to start. Grasshopper was mugged in New Orleans and had to play the solo to 'Little Rhymes' with his arm in a sling. To top it all, the album was released on September 11th 2001. As Donahue says. "It was freaky seeing the posters saying '*All Is Dream* – released 9/11', up there on the walls in New York City, covered with World Trade Centre dust. You couldn't really get around the association."

Now Mercury Rev has new kinds of chaos to deal with, including touring, and for Grasshopper the challenges of fatherhood, but that's a good kind of chaos, and many years after their shambolic second ever gig, opening for Bob Dylan, it looks like it is doing them no harm at all.

---

[8] Interestingly, reports vary as to whether Baker or Donahue was the spoon-wielder. If the latter, it speaks well of Grasshopper's tolerance levels

# How Carole King Became a Headline Performer

The story of how Carole King transformed from back-room songwriter to headline performer is a fascinating one, especially as it came about after she was thrust into the limelight one night by James Taylor …

Carole King's *Tapestry* is officially the thirty-sixth greatest album of all time, according to the two-hundred odd members of Rolling Stone Magazine's voting panel. And it's not just a few muso-types saying that either. Lennon and McCartney were early fans of Carole King and her songwriting partnership with Gerry Goffin. It's worth reminding ourselves of the songs that the Goffin-King partnership was responsible for writing: 'The Loco-motion' (Little Eva), 'Up On The Roof' (the Drifters), 'Will You Love Me Tomorrow' (the Shirelles), 'Take Good Care Of My Baby' (Bobby Vee), 'I'm Into Something Good' (Herman's Hermits), 'Pleasant Valley Sunday' (The Monkees) … An impressive canon. As Mark Lewisohn says in his book *All These Years Vol 1: Tune In* "to John and Paul, especially, the composer credit Goffin-King would become nothing less than a trademark of quality, sufficient in itself to make them listen to or buy a record, and rarely were they disappointed."

Early Beatles sets included many Goffin-King covers including 'Chains', 'Keep Your Hands Off My Baby', 'The Loco-Motion', 'Don't Ever Change', 'Sharing You', 'Take Good Care Of My Baby', and there are even witnesses who say John performed 'Will You Love Me Tomorrow' with Paul and George on backing vocals. John Lennon summed things up neatly when, in 1971, he told The Trinidadian Express "When Paul and I first got together, we wanted to be the British Goffin and King".

Goffin and King were part of the Brill Building network of songwriters in New York's 'Tin Pan Alley'. And, it appeared, King was happy to remain out of the limelight. Simon Napier-Bell went to the Brill Building as an aspiring songwriter in 1966. He saw "a floor on which every door had a six-inch square window… like prison cells." Napier-Bell wondered who "agrees to sit in a little sweatbox and slog away at writing songs in such an atmosphere?" His guide opened a door to reveal Neil Sedaka, and then another nearby to reveal Carole King. "It was unbelievable that the reward for having [written 'Will You Love Me Tomorrow'] was to be imprisoned eight hours a day," reflected Napier-Bell. "It can be a bit of a nightmare sometimes" Carole admitted at the time.

However, my favourite story about Carole King tells the tale of the first time she sang one of her songs live before an audience and is described in her memoir. It was all because of James Taylor, who was convinced King could be a solo performer and did what he could to make it happen. King moved to Laurel Canyon in 1968, and met James Taylor for the first time at Peter Asher's house[9]. Asher was preparing for the production of sessions for Taylor's 1969 LP *Sweet Baby James*. Asher asked King to play piano on the album and King and Taylor became friends. A year later, Asher asked King to join Taylor's touring band for a handful of weekend shows.

One night on the tour, Taylor put the Drifter's song 'Up On The Roof' on his set list which Carole had, of course, co-written. Just before the show Taylor leaned across to King and said "I'd like you to sing lead on 'Up On The Roof' tonight". King was just part of the band and had no desire to perform solo. "Don't make me sing lead in front of all those people!" she protested and confessed: "I was terrified". But Taylor appeared to have planned the whole thing. "We'll do it in your key" he whispered.

The moment came. Taylor introduced his band and then his piano player by telling the audience some of the songs she had co-written, to no little applause from the impressed audience. Taylor then declared "Ladies and Gentlemen: Carole King!" King played the opening chord of 'Up On The Roof', to a rapt and astonished audience. No audience had ever heard King perform onstage before. Yet there she was singing one of popular music's most well-known and well-loved songs, that she had written.

King describes how she looked up mid-song to see her bandmates smiling as she performed. The audience began to sing along to the last bridge and Carole King found she had unlocked something within her. "When the song ended the audience clapped and cheered and wouldn't stop". A magical moment.

King was still a reluctant performer, but agreed to open for James Taylor at the 300 capacity Troubadour club for a week in November 1970, prior to the release of *Tapestry*. It was then just a small step to her very first headline appearance in front of thousands at New York's Carnegie Hall – which was preserved forever on the live album *Carole King: The Carnegie Hall Concert*.

---

[9] There had been a brief "hello" when Taylor had been too shy to speak with King a year or so earlier, but this was their first proper meeting. Peter Asher was the brother of actress Jane Asher – whose boyfriend in the '60s was Paul McCartney.

# 13

## Elton John

The Vinyl Revival continues apace, sucking up the cash of Millennials faster than a pop-up craft-beer-and-smashed-avocado stall at a box park. With new LPs often costing £20 or more, vinyl-loving Millennials are reportedly struggling to save for a deposit on a flat. Some of us find it tricky enough to save for a deposit on a flat white.

So now the sockless beardies of East London are forced to swarm like famished locusts to the charity shops of Hoxton in an attempt to save money by buying "thrift store" vinyl (let's use those Americanisms: if we're all going to live in penniless gig-economy squalor we might as well pretend we're on the set of *Girls*). The thrill of finding a record for as little as the cost of a gourmet halloumi wrap from a streetfood stall sadly lasting only as long as it takes to discover Jim Reeves was not, in fact, any good. And neither were those old *Top Of The Pops* albums.

As everyone agrees, except people who look at facts, the reason Millennials are unable to buy property is because they are squandering all their money on smashed avocado brunches, negronis, man-buns and moustache wax. With their apparently insatiable appetite for avocados forming an insurmountable barrier to saving a 10% deposit on a studio flat in a part of town even Bear Grylls wouldn't survive a night walking through, Millennials must find other ways to save money.

Avocados are non-negotiable by all accounts, so the answer must be to find cheaper records. But how to find such records that are actually any good? Charity shops selling decent records for a pound died out at roughly the same time as the dodo, or at least the release of the debut CD by Dido, whichever of those two ancient events happened most recently. CDs are boring, and void of hipster-cred, even if they are wonderfully cheap in charity shops. If you like Hard-Fi, JLS and B*Witched.

But there is an answer. Happily, the sound made by some of the most popular bands of the indie loving fraternity is distinctly familiar. The War On Drugs have clearly been listening to their parents' Dire Straits, Springsteen and John Waite LPs, and Father John Misty might be unfairly described as a chorus-free babbling stream of consciousness trying to find his favourite Elton John song.

So the answer to those trying to scrape together the impossible dream of a house deposit while hooked on vinyl? Save Father John Misty for your Spotify account. Listen to Elton John on vinyl. Why? Because Elton is your saviour. He was a record collector himself. He gets vinyl. His early records – before the cocaine kicked in – are fun, and interesting. They are stuffed full of inserts, photos, lyrics, posters and even comic strips. There are loads of them. Although Elton is known for his hits, they are also loaded with good album tracks you may not have heard on the radio. Not only that, but Elton actually sounds better on vinyl. Those early recordings were beautifully produced and orchestrated. The instruments have room to breathe on vinyl, something lost slightly on MP3.

And, most importantly, because they sold in their millions, they're cheap! At least, original copies are. You can buy a five or more original Elton Johns for the price of a single Father John. Granted, you won't find wry non-sequiturs about existentialism and the irony of modern day love and life on Elton's records, but on the plus side, you won't have to listen to wry non-sequiturs about existentialism and the irony of modern day love and life. Swings and roundabouts.

So, let's look at Elton John's records. It's been a glittering rise, from answering an NME advert and covertly sneaking into recording studios at midnight, to worldwide stardom and dancing with Miss Piggy. It doesn't get any better than performing with the Muppets. Ask the Scissor Sisters. The origins of Elton John can be neatly catalogued into a series of events which, thankfully for archivists all over the world, were preserved in the annals of the specialist history magazine Jackie in the seventies, at a time when a teenage female historian was yet to discover the seeds of her crush on Elton were likely to fall on stony ground.

For those of us unable to immediately lay a hand on a complete run of Jackie comics, the entire strip is reprinted in one of the booklets included in 1975 LP *Captain Fantastic And The Brown Dirt Cowboy*, one of many reasons to buy that particular album on vinyl.

## The Lost Letter

17th June 1967. The joining together of one of the century's most successful songwriting partnerships comes down, in the end, to one person. That person is Bernie Taupin's mum. If not for her fastidiousness in cleaning her front room, Elton and Bernie may never have met. As with so many rock stories, it all began with an advert in the NME.

Reg Dwight, a piano-playing child prodigy, had joined Long John Baldry's band, releasing a single and backing the likes of Doris Troy and Solomon Burke in the U.K. But, having seen Little Richard send a crowd wild with excitement through the judicious kicking of his piano stool, Elton aspired to be a star. It says much about how boring Britain was back then that standing up at the piano and kicking back your piano stool drew an apoplectic response from onlookers.

It's not the same now. It's okay when Little Richard does it, but apparently kicking back your chair at work is now "unacceptable behaviour" and will earn you strange looks and a visit from HR. It did me, anyway. Back to Elton: the NME's advert – from talent / A&R agency Liberty – caught his eye. "Liberty wants talent. Artistes/Composers, Singers-Musicians to form new group." The nineteen-year-old Reg went to Liberty's offices to audition. But with little room to kick back his piano stool, he didn't impress. What now?

Meanwhile, 17-year old Bernie Taupin, a Lincolnshire-based villager and budding poet, had seen the same NME advert. He had written a letter, complete with samples of his lyrics, but then lost it. At this point the odds on a Taupin/Dwight union appeared as remote as the prospect of a contestant on *Love Island* having something intelligent to say about Brexit. One had lost his letter, the other failed the audition. And yet, we know how the story ends. So what was that about Bernie's mum?

This sainted lady found Bernie's letter two weeks later hidden behind a clock. She posted it for him. Reg was called back to Liberty's offices a few weeks later and told of his failed audition by the author of the NME advert, Ray Williams. As Williams relayed the bad news – and perhaps realising the limitations of the office when it came to kicking piano stools – he gave Reg a lifeline. Would Reg possibly be interested in seeing some lyrics Williams had just received from a bloke in Lincolnshire?

## Reg Becomes Elton

As 1968 got underway, Reg and Bernie had put together some songs they hoped to sell to publishers for other people to record. But Reg's demo vocals were so good, he was offered a record deal in his own right. One problem remained: Reg felt his name lacked, as the French would say, a certain *I don't know what*. According to Jackie's story he specifically thought it was a name a window cleaner would have. (Incidentally, the exact same issue would affect a certain Rita Crudgington a decade later before she changed her name to Cheryl Baker and joined Bucks Fizz. Cheryl/Rita wins the "least glamorous real name of a pop star" competition every time, with Reg/Elton a close second).

At the time, Reg was playing with Long John Baldry, and in the band was a saxophone player called Elton Dean. Reg wondered if he could simply have Elton Dean's name? Understandably Mr Dean wasn't entirely comfortable with the request, so Reg took the 'John' from his band leader's name and the name Elton John was born, much to the disgust of Rowan Atkinson in a famous *Comic Relief* sketch. Elton's name, apparently, was also a source of similar fun for Groucho Marx who would tease Elton about it whenever they met.

# But what about the vinyl?

I was on the lookout for original vinyl pressings of Elton's early albums. It wasn't the trickiest task, as record fairs and used record shops are rammed to the back teeth with them. You can't move for Elton John's albums in these places. The reason is that Elton sold in the millions during the seventies and early eighties, and right now he is a little under-appreciated, so there's lots of 'em around.

If there is a criticism of vinyl (and there are people, as shocking as it sounds, who aren't entirely taken in by the marketing) it is, as the New Yorker cartoon famously put it, the expense and inconvenience. If we were to add a sub-category to the inconvenience bucket, it's the storage aspect. You may be aware that aside from infidelity and money issues, the biggest cause of marital disgruntlement in Britain (and has been since SatNavs eliminated "map reading on journeys in the car" as a cause) is the storage of records. So although Elton's albums are plentiful and, best of all, dirt cheap, there may be only room in your collection for a few select items.

To put this into context, if you live in the London borough of Kensington and Chelsea, as I like to imagine most of my readers do, and you rent at the average of £41 per square foot, it costs 75p per year to store a single LP assuming you can fit fifty-five LPs in a square foot of space. Owning and storing ten Elton John albums in your flat therefore costs you £7.50 a year, which is more than it would cost you to buy a decent copy of *Honky Chateau*. Store more than 165 records and, frankly, you are better off having a Spotify account and moving somewhere three square feet smaller.

Therefore, let's keep costs to a minimum, and find the four or five Elton LPs that will give you the most joy. Although we might all have a stab at naming Elton John's best albums, in these times of Spotify, there sometimes needs to be a reason why a particular record should be bought on vinyl.

Happily in Elton's case there are several reasons. Firstly, his records are often beautifully packaged, with posters and lyrics sheets. Second, they can be found in used condition for pennies – there's frequently little difference between the cost of Elton on (used) vinyl and (used) CD. Third, those early analogue albums often sound better on vinyl than MP3 or CD – they were well produced and vinyl allows them room to breathe. But first, here's some early Elton John recordings you can find cheaply, but might be better off avoiding ...

## Elton: The Early Top Of The Pops Recordings.

It is a truth, universally acknowledged, that a singer with a small income is in need of additional work. As Elton John recorded his first two albums, *Empty Sky* and *Elton John*, he worked as a session musician, honing his craft on a popular series of albums of cover versions of the day, entitled *Top*

*Of The Pops.* Difficult to imagine as it may be, these were an even worse version of the modern day *Now!* compilations, as none featured the original artists.

For a budget price, the undiscerning or impoverished record buyer could buy ten or so cover versions of current hits (these things were often released monthly) recorded professionally, but, naturally, with all the magic that made the original records special taken out. If you want to hear the Rolling Stones' 'Street Fighting Man' with all the spit and venom removed, this is the place to come. A limper and less inspired version of 'Spirit In The Sky' you will be hard pushed to come across even if you were to scan the entire studio recordings of Doctor and the Medics. Lest we be accused of being mean, let's say in some cases the covers are equally as dubious as the middle of the road pap of the originals.

What is notable about these records is that some are early examples of Elton John's vocals, as he sang lead on such classics as 'Bridge Over Troubled Water'. That these records were produced before, during and after the recording of Elton's first two albums is fascinating. Because this workmanlike fluff was coming off the production line just as Elton was knocking out some solid gold on his own records.

The self-titled second of Elton's records is the first of his classic LPs to be worth picking up on vinyl. It contains 'Border Song', a song so good that Aretha Franklin covered it on her album *Young, Gifted and Black.* Other classic but less well known songs on the album include 'The Cage' and 'Take Me To The Pilot'. (For vinyl hounds who want to dig a bit deeper, the b-side to the single release of 'Border Song' was a song that only otherwise appeared on the live album *17-11-70,* the superb 'Bad Side of the Moon'. There is a RSD 2017 extended version of *17-11-70* out there, but originals can be picked up cheaply.)

For the *Elton John* album, look for one with a gatefold matte textured sleeve. You should be able to find this for around £5 or less in very good condition. There's not much point picking up anything that is too damaged. These aren't rare, and you can afford to wait until you find one in good nick – there will be plenty about.

Later in 1970 came *Tumbleweed Connection*, an LP with strong American / Americana influences and the next vital slab of Elton vinyl for your collection. *Tumbleweed Connection* has a lovely sepia-tinged gatefold cover depicting a none-more-Old-American railway station – that is, until you notice the Daily Telegraph advert and you realise it was shot at the Sheffield Park railway station on the Bluebell line in Sussex – and none of the songs were huge hits, so for people only acquainted with the radio friendly canon, it's a chance to discover an album of unfamiliar songs.

And what songs! 'Son of your Father', 'Amoreena', 'Burn Down The Mission' and 'Where To Now St. Peter' all extraordinary and not overplayed on radio. 'Country Comfort' was later covered by Rod

Stewart, and is a perfect slice of life in early-century America. Except for one small detail... Taupin writes eloquently: the local Deacon preparing his sermon, of fixing barns and of Clay, a man who prefers horse drawn machinery to the new-fangled variety. It's the Penny Lane of Americana, written by the Band. And then he writes about cooking and eating hedgehogs and suddenly there are questions. Not least of which is "Where did they find hedgehogs? Were these flying, migrating hedgehogs? Had the hedgehogs been wily enough to fashion a raft and sail across from Europe yet stupid enough to be caught between bricks on a fire once they got there?"

I guess all we can say in Taupin's defence is a) he isn't David bloody Attenborough and b) this was the seventies, and Google hadn't yet been invented. The other thing to say about *Tumbleweed Connection* is the packaging – gatefold sleeve, illustrated pages of lyrics – superb stuff.

Elton followed this up in 1971 with *Madman Across The Water*, another gatefold-sleeved package with illustrated lyrics. As with many of Elton John's early '70's records, you may find your LP is a "red" colour when you shine a strong light through it. Many of Elton's early albums have this quality, due to the type of vinyl used at the Pye pressing plant used for Elton's LPs. They aren't worth any more than regular copies, but it's fun.

*Madman Across The Water* features 'Levon' – a US hit - and 'Tiny Dancer'; the latter never a huge hit (number 41 in USA, never released in U.K.), and almost forgotten until it cropped up in Cameron Crowe's movie *Almost Famous*, since when it has gained a life of its own, having been name checked on Ed Sheeran and Lana Del Ray songs and, at the time of writing, has been streamed on Spotify over 126 million times. Just as good is the title track, a slow building, orchestrated epic, and 'All The Nasties', another epic song embellished with a choir and a rolling, climactic choral chant.

Next for your collection is *Honky Chateau*. Jousting for the title of "best Elton album" with *Tumbleweed Connection,* the record was recorded at the eponymous Chateau d'Hérouville in France, as had become *de riguer* thanks to the Rolling Stones and the UK Government's grasping approach to collecting taxes at the rate of 75p in the pound. The studio was later used by David Bowie to record *Pin Ups* and *Low*. If *Tumbleweed Connection* is an Americana album, and *Elton John* and *Madman Across The Water* have orchestration aplenty, *Honky Chateau* is the album that ditches the styling and strings and focuses on the band.

The packaging is innovative, with the LP nestling in a fold-over sleeve with a tab. In terms of familiar songs *Honky Chateau* has 'Rocket Man', 'I Think I'm Going To Kill Myself' and 'Honky Cat', but it's the non-hits that make this one of his best. 'Mona Lisas And Mad Hatters' is a standout track, written by Taupin after arriving in New York and being scared witless by a police shooting outside the hotel in which he was staying.

*Don't Shoot Me, I'm Only The Piano Player* is next on the list, worth buying on vinyl for the gatefold sleeve and inner pages again. More of a rock 'n' roll album than *Honky Chateau*, there are loads of unfamiliar Stones-style swampy rock tunes – see 'Midnight Creeper' – but the real gold aside from the single 'Daniel' is found in a couple of hidden gems: 'Teacher I Need You' is catchy pop, but rides roughshod over Ofsted guidelines whereas 'I'm Going To Be A Teenage Idol' slows the pace down and is a 'Honky Cat'- style groover with horns and the kind of percussive piano we associate Elton John with. 'High Flying Bird' slows down even further and is a prototype mix of 'Sacrifice' and 'Don't Let The Sun Go Down On Me', and is a terrific ballad.

Elton's next album was *Goodbye Yellow Brick Road*. If you read those "1,000 albums to hear before you die" or "Top 500 Albums ever" lists, this is the one that will always feature, and for good reason – it is Elton's most expansive record and has more than its fair share of hits: 'Candle In The Wind', the title track, 'Saturday Night's Alright (For Fighting)' and 'Bennie And The Jets'. But I'm going to break with tradition and say don't buy this one. Or at least buy this last. Like many double albums, it's too rich for one sitting. It's no place to start. What I will recommend is to search for the yellow vinyl version.

If there was ever an album meant to be pressed in yellow vinyl, it is *Goodbye Yellow Brick Road*. This was a limited edition released a year after the black vinyl versions and is still decent value – I picked mine up for just £13. Of the lesser known tracks, 'Grey Seal' is an older track, given a spruce up for the album and is all the better for it.

Skipping past *Caribou* (vaguely dull packaging, slightly below par album, therefore stick to online streaming), the final Elton album to recommend is 1975's *Captain Fantastic And The Brown Dirt Cowboy*. Available in black and the translucent red vinyl, this was lavishly packaged in a gatefold sleeve with a poster, a 'Scraps' book – which includes that Jackie comic strip of Elton's early career, and a 'Lyrics' book. A concept album about Elton and Bernie's career so far, this has one well known hit, the often overlooked 'Someone Saved My Life Tonight', and a bunch of less familiar tunes all worth getting to know. Stand-outs include the closing ballad 'Curtains' and 'Bitter Fingers', a song about Elton's Tin Pan Alley days.

There is a brown vinyl version of this album – 2,000 copies were released in the USA personally signed by Elton and Bernie. The price for these copies varies dramatically – perhaps more than anything I have ever seen on the Discogs wesbite: whilst the cheapest copy may have sold at £3.04 and the median price at the time of writing was £7.60, the highest price paid for the album was a staggering £1520.02.

And so, finally a word on price for all of these records. I picked up *Captain Fantastic And The Brown Dirt Cowboy* for £5 in near mint condition. To put that into context, that's just £1.75 more than it cost when it came out in 1975. (If you had bought the same amount of gold, you would have £22 more today). No-one is saying Elton's albums are good financial investments, but it's a great time to buy used copies now: *Tumbleweed Connection*, *Madman Across The Water* and *Honky Chateau* cost me £3 each, while *Elton John* and *Don't Shoot Me I'm Only The Piano Player* were £5 (and in especially good condition). That's six LPs for £25, less than what you might pay for just one of Elton's records new. Oh, and while I was looking for these, I also found a copy of *Greatest Hits 2* – with the booklet inside – for £1, and for that price (and some claim GHV2 is Elton's best album) it would have been silly not to.

Taking into account the songs, the packaging and the price, if you target these records, there may not be a better value artist – or one with such a deep and rewarding back catalogue – to buy right now on vinyl.

# 14

## Record Maintenance: How I Deep Clean My Vinyl Records With Wood Glue …

There are a number of ways to clean and maintain your record collection in pristine condition. An occasional wipe with vinyl friendly cleaning solution using a microfibre cloth will do the trick in most cases if you don't want to splash out for a vacuum style record cleaning machine. Keeping the LPs in good inner sleeves is a good way to ensure they stay cleaner than Mother Theresa's driving licence. But what about those really grotty records? You know, the ones that are dirtier than the 1966 Uruguayan World Cup squad and grimier than Dizzee Rascal running a Tough Mudder?

When I heard about a method for cleaning vinyl using wood glue I was rather sceptical. It doesn't intuitively sound like a good idea in the same way that leaving King Herod in charge of the babysitting doesn't intuitively sound like a good idea. In fact, I was struggling to think of things that might be less appropriate.

I say that, I actually found ten things that are less appropriate than wood glue. They are:

- The Dishwasher
- Toothpaste (good for teeth, less good for vinyl).
- Wire wool
- The iron
- The fuel-soaked cotton bud thing that Turkish barbers use to burn away ear hair.
- The washing machine, even on a delicate setting.
- Inexpensive aftershave (can't speak for the expensive stuff – I don't have any)
- Nail polish remover
- Your Dyson hand held vacuum cleaner
- Cillit Bang: "Bang! And your record is gone!"

But when I found a copy of Yeah Yeah Yeah's second LP upon which it appeared the previous owner had apparently spilled 'Um Bongo' or some other similar sugary drink, and then attempted to clean up the mess using one of the methods listed above, I knew there was little to lose, and I thought I would (metaphorically) roll my sleeves up, and give it a go. Sadly the record's lacquer had already been damaged beyond repair, so the results were inconclusive. I therefore waited for another, less damaged LP to try. This time, the result was noticeably improved. The glue seeped into every pore and groove, lifting all the dirt embedded within. There was a noticeable improvement and less crackle. The method was simple....

I laid the LP flat on a piece of card, then squeezed wood glue over the vinyl and used another piece of card to smooth it around so it covered the whole of the grooves. "Don't leave any gaps. Avoid the label in the middle. You don't need to cover the run off groove in glue." I reminded myself. Some people suggested applying the glue is easier to do if you have the LP on a spinning turntable, but trust me: applying glue to moving objects is not the easy option.

Cover the record in wood glue

Overnight, the wood glue dries

I then waited overnight for the glue to dry. (If you were to ever try this method - at your own risk of course - try to keep the record away from your cat at this stage. As a general rule of thumb, records become more difficult to play when animals are attached to them.) As the glue dried, it became transparent. Once dried, I could then lift the film of glue from the LP leaving the pristine, clean vinyl. That's about it. It was cheaper than buying an expensive vacuum record cleaner (a device that uses liquid to clean the LP and then vacuums off the dirty fluid instantly), and a useful way to improve the quality of the dodgier end of my record collection.

## How I Fixed Scratches In My Records ... With A Toothpick

Mending a broken record is the holy grail for many record collectors. It also gives you a tremendous feeling of satisfaction when you succeed. When I say "broken" I mean an old record in one piece that nevertheless skips or jumps, presumably because of dirt or a scratch, or both.

A couple of years ago, I found a copy of the Rolling Stones' first 'Hits' compilation *High Tide And Green Grass* in a bargain bin at a record fair. It was priced at a *steep* £1, but the cover was glossy (albeit creased), with a large six-page booklet of photos. Furthermore it was an unboxed green Decca label, dating it to when the record was first released. Even if the record was scratched, I reasoned, trying to justify the lavish expenditure to myself, it was still worth it for the cover.

Sure enough, as I took it home and played the thing it took about thirty seconds into opening track 'Have You Seen Your Mother Baby (Standing In The Shadows)?' for the record to skip (the rest of the record was fine). I sighed a resigned sigh, accepting the old adage that when something looks too good to be true, that's usually because it is.

And that was that, until I heard about a method of mending scratched records using a toothpick. "Surely that wouldn't work?" I mused sceptically, as I do most things, but given that I had nothing to lose except the pound I had spent on my jumping copy of *High Tide And Green Grass* I decided to give it a go. Against all reasonable odds and expectations, I found it worked. For me; don't blame me if you try it with less success.

I sourced a wooden toothpick. I found one in a restaurant and pocketed it. (NB. Don't use it for its intended purpose first. That's unpleasant.) Back home, I located the area on the record that jumped. This was trickier than it sounds because it the record was spinning quickly and black vinyl is deceptively featureless, but I found a method that helped me: as the record spun on the turntable, it skipped in the affected area. As it did so, I look at the label in the centre to see which bit was pointing to the needle as the record jumps. It took me eight unsuccessful tries before I found this somewhat elementary method, which probably says more about me than anything else…

I took the record off the turntable and inserted the end of the toothpick in the grooves where I reckoned the skipping occurred. This felt odd, as we are always advised never to touch the surface of a record, especially with a pointy stick, but it was okay. I moved the pick back and forth within the groove in the area where the record was affected. In my case there was an area of ingrained dirt that was blocking the needle, causing it to jump and skip. The toothpick dislodged a fairly long streak of dirt that resembled a scratch and all was well. The toothpick wood was soft enough to not unduly damage the record and sufficiently hard to remove the dirt.

As a further caution, don't try this on CDs. Or cassettes. Or rare paintings, furniture, other people's faces, pets, cars etc. My army of lawyers have also asked me to point out I won't be held responsible for damages should you further maim your priceless (yet presumably scratched) copy of *No Parlez*.

Naturally, I played the record to see if I had been successful. If not, my plan was to try steps 1-3 again. (You can bend the vinyl slightly to open the grooves a little.) Ultimately, it worked for me. I then gave the rest of the record a clean. When I buy an old record which is a bit grim, (cleanliness-wise I mean. I don't mean "when I buy something by Morrissey") I clean it with a micro-fibre cloth.

# 15

## The Stories Of Three More Classic Albums

### The Story of Dexy's Midnight Runners' *Don't Stand Me Down*

In March 1985, Kevin Rowland, lead singer and songwriter of Dexy's Midnight Runners was facing total ruin. *Don't Stand Me Down*, his labour of love and an album he had spent two years of his life writing, recording and mixing, might just have been burned in a fire at the record label's office in New York, and lost forever. Two years' work, and possibly the best album of the eighties might just have gone up in smoke...

This news came just a few weeks after he had failed in an attempt to steal the tape back from the studio he was mixing it in after an unpaid bill meant it was being held to ransom. But both of these incidents were just two of a long line of setbacks in recording the follow up to the three million selling *Too-Rye-Ay*. The attempted theft happened, according to record producer Alan Winstanley when Kevin and the band "allegedly grabbed the tapes, ran through the Electric Lady studio, straight through reception ... got to the car, and the chauffeur had gone off for a cup of coffee ... the door was locked! A studio employee foiled the getaway."

And the fire? After the tapes were released they were stored at the record company office in New York. The office below suffered a fire and for a week no one could enter Phonogram's offices to see whether the tape had survived. We can only imagine Rowland's state of mind for that week. The tape survived, as it happens. And although the album that resulted was, by all commercial measures, a failure it remains an artistic triumph and one of the most important albums of the eighties.

Some 29 years later, I was at a record fair thumbing through some Gerry Rafferty and Linda Ronstadt LPs with gloom in my soul when my heart leapt. There it was: the purple cover of *Don't Stand Me Down*. It's a record rich in Beach Boy harmonies, a *Blonde On Blonde* vibe and Van Morrison-esque soul which has barely dated since its release in 1985, but which was born out of tremendously difficult circumstances and, as I hinted earlier, on release was almost entirely ignored by the general public.

I should probably pause for breath at this point as you may find yourself in one of three camps:

1. Those who know and love *Don't Stand Me Down*.
2. Those who thought Dexy's split up after 'Come On Eileen'.
3. Anyone under the age of (roughly) forty, the vast majority of which will never have heard of Dexy's Midnight Runners. (This is a strange fact but one I have tested on many occasions. Whilst most people born in the eighties will generally be aware of Wham!, Boy George and Adam Ant, very few in comparison will know Dexy's Midnight Runners, despite how huge they were, particularly in the UK).

I told the dealer I bought the record from how pleased I was to find it. "Well, it's only one of the best albums ever made" he said, as though this was received wisdom, akin to "The Beatles were a good band" or "never eat yellow snow". Yet, like many people, this is an album I came to quite late.

Let's start from the beginning. In April 1983 'Come On Eileen' reached the top of the Billboard charts, knocking off Michael Jackson's 'Billie Jean'. The album sold millions. Yet whilst band leader Kevin Rowland had experienced success, it left him feeling unfulfilled. His reaction to this feeling was encapsulated in the making of *Don't Stand Me Down*, which began as a vision of Rowland's socio-political view of Ireland but ended up being a far more personal record. After nine months of writing, demos were made in the spring of 1984 featuring a band which included Atomic Rooster keyboardist Vincent Crane and ex-Spider from Mars Mick "Woody" Woodmansey. These songs were recorded, dumped, and re-recorded.

Three weeks in the studio became six months. Two hundred boxes of tape reels revealed the lengths perfectionist Rowland was going to. There were tales of 120 versions of 'This Is What She's Like'. Eight months into recording, only two songs had been completed and the record company were getting a little nervous. Strangely, the turning point appeared to be when Al Green's drummer Tim Dancy replaced Woodmansey. A flurry of songs were recorded by September 1984 and then Rowland began mixing the album – in New York. This took another two months, the release date was scheduled for spring 1985.

Yet still Kevin Rowland wasn't happy, and he spent another two weeks mixing the tapes at Electric Lady studio. The record company refused to pay the bills, and Electric Lady reputedly threatened to withhold the master tapes, leading to the incident that began this story.

But what about the music? It is perhaps the twelve and a half minute suite 'This Is What She's Like' that most separates *Don't Stand Me Down* from the foot-stomping rag-wearing cartoon version of Dexy's that has been the traditional floor-filling staple of every party ever held since 1983. What a tune this is! Two minutes of studio chatter gives way to a killer first phase, which fades to a gorgeous *a cappella Pet Sounds*-style harmony, which builds across a killer finale that knocks 'Come On Eileen' into a cocked hat. Listen also to the 'Satellite Of Love' feel to the reflective 'My National Pride'. Or even the absolute outright thievery of the excellent 'One Of Those Things', a song which Kevin Rowland belatedly gave Warren Zevon songwriting credit to (it is a terrific song, but a complete lift of the latter's 'Werewolves Of London') saying in the liner notes to a later re-issue he was "embarrassed" he hadn't credited Zevon before. There's also the hit-single-that-never-was of 'I Love You (Listen To This)'. Meanwhile the eight minute closing track 'The Waltz' might have sat comfortably on *Tupelo Honey* without ever feeling like it had gate-crashed an Ambassador's reception.

This was an album released in 1985, which, to remind ourselves, was also the year of *No Jacket Required*, *Songs From The Big Chair* and Wham!'s *Make It Big*. *Don't Stand Me Down* entered the UK charts at a lowly 22, three years after the release of *Too-Rye-Ay*. It would take many years before it was recognised as being one of the greatest albums of the eighties. The 'Director's Cut' edition of this album adds a track or two and can be found on CD with a little searching. It's worth the effort. Especially after what Kevin Rowland went through to make it ...

## The Story of Muddy Waters' *Live At Newport*

I'm going to start this piece about Muddy Waters and the history of the blues by talking about the Sex Pistols and Bob Dylan, so bear with me.

The Sex Pistols 1976 gig at the Manchester Free Trade Hall was one of the most influential of all time, not because of a vast crowd – there were only 42 people there – but because, as legend has it (and as articulately explained by Steve Coogan in the film *24 Hour Party People*) everyone who was there went out and formed a band, including members of Joy Division, the Fall, the Smiths, New Order, Buzzcocks, Magazine and the writer Paul Morley. Oh, and Mick Hucknall.

Bob Dylan caused consternation in 1965 at the Newport Folk Festival when he went "electric". It was, some thought, a betrayal of the "pure" folk music and political songwriting Dylan had become known for. However, before both these incidents, one man achieved similar influence and controversy. That man was Muddy Waters.

Muddy Waters and his band may not have invented electric blues, but they made the biggest impact of any of their contemporaries: transforming the perception of blues as a mainly acoustic regional folk music to that of amplified Delta blues – a style which became known as Chicago blues. After the Mississippi Delta, Chicago became an important breeding ground for the blues for a very good reason. Robert Palmer's *Deep Blues* history says as much:

"Even before the end of the century the Delta was acting as a kind of funnel for blacks. On the one hand they were being drawn into the area from the South and East. On the other hand many of them were already leaving and heading North. Most of those who left took the Illinois Central Railroad, which ran ... from New Orleans up through the Delta to Chicago in just 24 hours.

People became economic migrants and in return gained a measure of independence. In Chicago they wouldn't have to wait until the cotton harvest each year to find out how much their crop was worth, how much debt they'd accumulated at the plantation store and whether he'd come out in the red or in the black."

Time Magazine estimated that since the beginning of the decade and 1944, 50,000 black people had left Mississippi for the North.

The electric guitar first appeared on records in the late 1930's. Muddy Waters bought his first one in 1944. He formed a band with Little Walter Jacobs on harp, Baby Face Leroy on drums and Jimmy Rogers on guitar and began playing gigs and making records for Aristocrat, soon to be re-named Chess Records.

Before Muddy Waters, there was Delta blues, but his 1950's recordings for the Chess label transformed this music into one with popular appeal and laid the foundations for rock 'n' roll. He did this by his use of amplification which didn't just make the music louder, it made it – and the message it carried – more urgent. When he toured the UK in 1958 he caused a stir in the folk and skiffle loving community just as Bob Dylan would do seven years later. As Charles Shaar Murray put it in his excellent "Boogie Man" "The notion that "Chicago Blues" – the rumbustious calamitous soundtrack of the urban world of Delta migrants transplanted to the big cities – had cultural value equivalent to that of the downhome rural forms was an entirely new one, and not entirely free from controversy."

"Screaming guitar and howling piano" said the next morning's UK newspaper headlines. Muddy Waters told Melody Maker, "Cause, see, I'd been playin' here in Chicago with these people who turned [their amplifiers] up. Now I know that the people in England like soft guitar and the old blues, next time I come I'll learn some old songs first".

"Until Muddy arrived in England all the black bluesmen who'd performed there – Broonzy, Josh White, Terry and McGhee – had played acoustic music in a style the skiffle fans could easily relate to. Muddy, innocent of this audience's expectations, cranked up his amplifier, hit a crashing bottleneck run, and began hollering his blues."

Or as Bob Stanley describes in Yeah Yeah Yeah, Muddy "shocked the beatnik purists at St Pancras Town Hall by playing electric guitar. Some booed."

Two years later came Muddy's performance at the Newport Jazz Festival. The festival was almost cancelled after ten thousand teenagers broke in and a riot ensued, but the Sunday afternoon blues show was allowed to take place, and Muddy brought his whole band. Chess recorded the performance and the record was a critical success. It remains in Rolling Stone Magazine's Top 500 Albums list.

Muddy Waters' *Live At Newport* was the most influential blues record in the UK, because – just like the Sex Pistols gig at the Manchester Free Trade Hall twenty five years later – it inspired people to go out and form a band. Specifically in this case (according to Charles Shaar Murray) it inspired harmonica player Cyril Davies and guitarist Alexis Korner to form, in Blues Incorporated, possibly the first white electric blues band in the world. Korner would himself become the most influential British bluesman, starting a club that would eventually give the Rolling Stones their first real platform.

But the record's influence isn't just what makes it great. It remains a fun and compelling document of a great live performance and performer – and it is also a record that will have you jumping around, tapping your feet or whatever else you might feel like doing in your living room as you play it. Listen to the original version of 'I Can't Be Satisfied' for the catchiest, nay *jauntiest* slide guitar riff you could ever wish for. It's wearing its hat on the side of its head and is whistling cheerfully in time to the chugging-train beat.

And Muddy isn't all about one album. 'I Want To Be Loved' was a Willie Dixon penned song re-recorded by Muddy on his *Hard Again* LP released in 1977. *Hard Again* was produced by Jonny Winter and represented a successful "comeback" after Waters left Chess Records and features three songs that Muddy had recorded previously, including the two aforementioned songs.

The harmonica riff on 'I Want To Be Loved' is infectious and Muddy's delivery is so self-assured. The Rolling Stones covered the song in their early years but their version, although charming, is a pale imitation. 'Mannish Boy' (co-written by Bo Diddley and Mel London – who also wrote 'Poison Ivy') is another cast iron classic. "I'm a man!" declares Waters, fighting back against that racial slur of 'Boy'. Indeed, *Hard Again* is a great album, additionally featuring strong originals such as 'Little Girl', and 'Walking Through The Park'.

Although they are worlds apart perhaps the comparison between blues and punk isn't as crazy as it sounds. After all, both punk and blues began as forms of music made by society's poorest, most persecuted and disaffected. However, *Live At Newport* doesn't want sympathy. It just wants to make you move your feet, and although it was recorded more than fifty years ago, it doesn't sound as though it will ever get old. No future? *Live At Newport* has many more years left in it ...

# The Long and Winding Road: How Cher Found Her Mojo On Jackson Highway

It is 1965, and the nineteen-year-old Cher is about to perform in front of Princess Margaret, in what will be the worst performance of her life. Riding high in the charts with "I Got You Babe", Sonny and Cher are asked to perform at a charity ball, compered by Bob Hope, in front of an audience of not only British, but Hollywood royalty: Doris Day, Rock Hudson, Zsa Zsa Gabor. Cher tries to ignore the imposing sea of famous faces as she sings Dylan's "All I Really Want To Do". But she's too loud for delicate royal ears. Princess Margaret motions to an aide to turn down the volume. The sound technician cuts Cher's microphone by accident, then Sonny can't hear his monitors.

Sonny tries a rather unfortunate joke: "We do, in a way, represent the young people... But it's nice to perform for you." This does not go over well. As he starts singing again, a heckler shouts "That's gotta be the worst thing I ever heard!" and the entire theatre erupts with laughter. The crestfallen couple close with "I Got You Babe" and withdraw hastily, with Cher in tears and Sonny furious. Life, for Sonny and Cher, was always a struggle.

The story of Cher is a fascinating one. Her life was surprisingly tough, right from the moment her mum Jackie had got as far as sitting in the abortion clinic before deciding not to go through with the operation, and to have her baby daughter Cherylin. How tough was her childhood? Tough enough to make Monty Python's Four Yorkshire men doff their flat caps out of respect.

She grew up poor and her father was often absent, thanks to the somewhat rigid, one-sided terms and conditions he had to accept when staying at San Quentin's prison on drugs charges. Having an often absent father was a double edged sword. On the plus side, when he was around, they would bond for a while, but on a less positive note, he would then pawn her mother's jewellery and set the house on fire while high on drugs. Not ideal.

Being poor manifested itself in different ways, but you can imagine the grief Cher received when she went to school with her shoes strapped with elastic bands to stop them falling apart. Her mum made ends meet by singing in saloons for a dollar a night. That meant travelling around: Cher went to as many as fifteen schools, and was, perhaps, called "rubber band shoe girl" in each one. To compound the transient, unsettled upbringing, Cher found school difficult, as she is dyslexic.

Cher would deal with her tough upbringing by dreaming of being rich and famous. She once fantasised about finding the cure for polio. "I was really pissed off when Salk beat me to it. I really was" she said later.

She met Sonny Bono when she was sixteen, and he was twenty seven. He was more interested in her next door neighbour and moved close by. Cher found this older man hugely exciting, and saw an opportunity to be independent of her mother. Sonny had all the romance of an air conditioning unit - Cher moved in after he told her he didn't find her attractive but if she cooked and cleaned for him she could stay. Which you have to admire as one of the least appealing chat up lines ever. It doesn't say much about Cher's sense of self-worth at the time to note that she accepted.

Sonny Bono was looking for a career in the music industry, had written 'She Said Yeah' for Larry Williams (a song the Rolling Stones later covered) and soon found himself working for the renowned humanitarian Phil Spector. Bono learned a lot from Spector, not least about how to treat wives who sang pop songs. With the benefit of hindsight, and from a pop-song-singing-wife's perspective, if there is one person you don't want your husband to be taking relationship advice from, it's Phil Spector.

One day, Spector asked Cher to sing backing vocals on a song and noted her lower register, which added a solid brick to that famed wall of sound. The song was by the Crystals and was called 'Da Do Ron Ron'. It was a massive hit, and suddenly Cher was singing backing vocals on all the Ronettes singles.

Two months later Sonny wrote 'Needles And Pins' for Jackie DeShannon (and later the Searchers, Tom Petty, the Ramones) and they were up and running. Cher's first record, in February 1964, was a tribute to the best drummer in the Beatles, 'Ringo I Love You' and recorded under the name of Bonnie Jo Mason. Cher's low voice confused people, who wondered whether it was a man's voice serenading Ringo. The song flopped, Sonny suspected Spector of deliberate sabotage, and the two men parted ways.

What happened next is unusual: Cher signed to two different record companies. Sonny sorted all the paperwork. She signed with Imperial Records to record solo material, and Atlantic Records as a duo with Sonny. Cher's five solo albums on Imperial have much to recommend them. All cover versions, the song selections - often folk tunes - are impeccable and Cher's voice suits the Dylan covers in particular.

The real success, however, came with the Sonny and Cher records, and 'I Got You Babe' in particular, which went to the top of the US charts. By the end of 1965 Sonny and Cher had five top twenty hits. In 1966 another Sonny Bono composition, 'Bang Bang (My Baby Shot Me Down)' was Cher's first solo hit record, reaching number two, and in 1967 Sonny wrote another classic, 'The Beat Goes On'. Yet even success failed to win them respect, either when singing in front of royalty, or when their unusual dress still got them refused tables at restaurants: Sonny's solo hit 'Laugh At Me' was written after they were asked to leave Martoni's restaurant in LA on the grounds of their hippie-like appearance. It sold 700,000 copies, and Sonny pointedly sent one of those to the restaurant manager.

But by 1968 Cher was 22 and her career appeared over. Four dud singles and two flop movies, *Good Times* and *Chastity* had seen to that. So Cher decided to make her first album not produced by Sonny, gradually finding her independence. The album title was *3614 Jackson Highway*. If that sounds familiar, that's because this is the address of the Muscle Shoals recording studio in Sheffield, Alabama.

The album cover captures the producer Jerry Wexler (who produced Aretha Franklin) and the Muscle Shoals house band, horn section and backing singers, plus Sonny. *3614 Jackson Highway* was a terrific album - effectively Cher's equivalent of *Dusty in Memphis*, with a move from pure pop to more earthy Southern soul sounds, and deserved to be a hit. Sadly, as with many things in Cher's life at that time, it didn't go so well from a commercial perspective. The LP, and the singles from it, failed to make the top 100. By the end of the year Cher faced a huge tax bill and possible ruin. Her childhood struggles and financial worries had yet to recede.

But Sonny and Cher were nothing if not determined and hard working. They developed a nightclub comedy routine, the two of them trading witty barbs, and this was picked up for a TV show, which became a huge success just as the song 'Gypsys, Tramps and Thieves' (again, not produced by Bono) became a big hit. As Cher's success grew, so did a further desire for independence from Sonny Bono.

Her instinct was right. Just how one-sided the relationship had become was revealed during a very public divorce in 1974. It turned out Cher was an employee of a company called Cher Enterprises, which Sonny Bono owned. As an employee, she was entitled to three weeks holiday a year. Cher had trusted Sonny with her business affairs and didn't even own a fair share of the company that collected their joint earnings. Sonny denied he treated her badly, and Cher sued, claiming involuntary servitude. Revealingly, he said "the shock to men in divorce is to find out that you don't own what you thought you owned".

In the end Sonny Bono, along with Cher's own talent and determination may have made Cher a star, but he never treated her as an equal. And it was that struggle for equality in an overwhelmingly male-dominated music industry and society, even more than the poverty and the tough childhood that has driven Cher and her career. Or as Cher put it some time later, "this business is tough ... if you're a woman it's harder ... because women aren't supposed to stand up for what they want. If you're nice you'll get your ass walked all over; if you stand up for something you're a bitch." *3614 Jackson Highway* was Cher's first big step towards independence, her first album without Sonny. We hear a more confident voice than in those earlier recordings, and in songs like 'I Walk On Guilded Splinters' some of the best recordings of her career.

# 16

## An Idiots Guide To The First Six Albums By The Rolling Stones

### *Or, a quest to discover whether it's worth buying those early Stones albums on vinyl ...*

We were in the pub. The conversation, a couple of hours in, had turned to how the skeleton of a dinosaur would no longer be displayed in the Natural History Museum. I know what you're thinking. Some of our discussions can be pretty scintillating, nay, sparkling at times.

Chris said, "They effectively expired years ago. They might have dominated the whole planet, lumbering across the globe, but they've had their day. No-one really cares." I nodded agreement. "And it's all because of punk, in my view."

To be honest, I'd just come back from the Gents. I reasoned I must have missed something, but couldn't grasp what. "Punk rock killed off Diplodocus? What are you on about?"

My friends rolled their eyes. "We've moved on to the Rolling Stones..." Chris explained patiently.

"But how did the conversation move from..." I stopped myself. Even Watson on an off-day would have deduced that one. "Ah. Yes. Quite."

Chris isn't a big fan of The Rolling Stones. "They've effectively released four good albums and a few singles, and nothing much good since 1972" he ventured.

I looked pained. Disgraceful views. I knew what he meant though. Those four albums: *Beggars Banquet, Let It Bleed, Sticky Fingers* and *Exile On Main Street* were stone cold classics. Aside from a couple of best-ofs, those were the only four Stones albums I actually owned, at least on vinyl. But when was the last time I played any of their early albums? Maybe never? I tried to smoke him out.

"What about those early R&B albums? They're classics too!"

"Really? Have you even heard them? When was the last time you played any of them?!" challenged Chris "The early albums were all Chuck Berry covers, and then they did a couple of dodgy psychedelic albums that no-one ever listens to".

"That can't be true," I reasoned. "The Rolling Stones were one of the two biggest bands on the planet in the sixties. They didn't get there by being just a singles band."

A quick straw poll found that none of us had actually listened to many of the Rolling Stones' first six albums more than once, and some not at all.

"OK then, I think we have a new challenge for you then," smiled Chris. "We'll take it as read that you can find all the albums for, say, less than a hundred quid. That's one part. The other, more difficult part, is to find reasons why anyone should bother. Find the albums, listen to them, and then come back here and tell us why they aren't just full of rubbish Chuck Berry covers."

"OK. But as it's your challenge, you have to pay a forfeit if you're wrong."

"And you do too..."

"No. If the albums are rubbish, then my forfeit is that I'll have spent a lot of money on six terrible albums. Your forfeit if they turn out to be good, is that you'll have to write a letter of apology to the band, and post it to them." Well, it seemed a good idea at the time.

So off I went to some record fairs. I found the records. And I listened to The Rolling Stones with fresh ears. This was a band whose early records I hadn't, until now, paid much attention to. And I discovered some interesting things about those first six UK albums. Have you ever checked the Rare Record Price Guide ("RRPG") prices of the Rolling Stones' first six LPs? They made me wince like I'd just smelled Keith Richards' breath in his heyday.

- *The Rolling Stones:* 1st pressing £1,000.
- *The Rolling Stones No. 2:* £130
- *Out Of Our Heads:* £110
- *Aftermath:* £110
- *Between The Buttons:* £150 mono
- *Their Satanic Majesties Request:* £200 mono

£1,000 for the first LP? Aside from the slight problem of not having that much cash, it did make me wonder: why bother? They're all on internet streaming sites. Not only might they be highly underwhelming, but wasn't it all a bit pointless buying original copies? Perhaps Chris was right?

Like the chap Thomas in the Bible, I get these minor doubts pop up in my head from time to time. To resolve them, I pop down Spitalfields Record Fair. I can't help thinking large parts of the New Testament might have had a happier spin if Thomas and a few of his friends had done the same. It never fails to energise the senses, as that unmistakable smell of musty old record collectors fills the nostrils.

It turns out that you can buy copies of these records in very good condition for much less than £1,000. Five out of six of the albums were secured over the course of three visits to Spitalfields and Southend Record Fairs. Total amount spent: a not-insignificant £80, but all were early / "first" pressings. This left me with £20 to find *Their Satanic Majesties Request,* which was admittedly a problem: I couldn't find a copy anywhere for less than £40, which was ironic considering my preconception was that it was the Rolling Stones' worst album of the sixties.

But buying the records was not the biggest task. I was reminded of my friend's challenge: "Find the albums, listen to them, and then come back here and tell us why they aren't just full of rubbish Chuck Berry covers."

Here are five reasons why you should possess the Rolling Stones' first album on vinyl:

1.  **The copy in your loft might be worth £1,000.** As we now know, record collectors value the very first pressings of records above all, because the fresher the "stampers" are that actually press the vinyl, the fresher the sound. "First" pressings of the UK release are all on a red/silver Decca "ear" label. There are, however, some differences between first pressings. The very first issue, which is the one that fetches big money plays a different version of that first Jagger/Richards composition 'Tell Me' with a running time of 2:52. This edition is recognizable by the matrix number (printed between the label and where the grooves end) of side B: XARL 6272-1A. All later issues (with varying matrix numbers) play a different version of 'Tell Me' with a running time of 4.06. Unhelpfully there are five label variations and four cover variations in existence, making for twenty-one different versions of a "first pressing". Check out that running time and matrix number whenever you see a copy of the record. Sleeves that credit the 4th track on side A as 'Mona' (RRPG: £250 mint) rather than 'I Need You Baby' (£130 mint) are also more highly valued amongst the cognoscenti, for no discernible reason other than it's a slightly earlier pressing. Needless to say my copy was the latter, and although not mint, sounds great. Still later pressings have a "boxed" Decca logo on top of the label, these are considered second pressings, and are therefore a good option for those on

tighter budgets. The concept of paying £900 extra to hear a shorter version of a song may appear odd to you. If it does, congratulations. It means you are normal.

2.   **The songs aren't all Chuck Berry covers.** Although there is a great version of 'Carol', technically 'Route 66' is a Bobby Troup song originally recorded by Nat King Cole. The two best songs are, in fact, covers of Muddy Waters and Slim Harpo songs. "Would you let your daughter go with a Rolling Stone?" asked Andrew Loog Oldham's famously provocative editorial. You can just imagine the consternation amongst Britain's parents hearing the Stones' version of the Muddy Waters/Willie Dixon classic 'I Just Want To Make Love To You'. The Rolling Stones' version isn't as good as Muddy's original, but gallops along at a good pace nevertheless. Slim Harpo's 'I'm a King Bee', however, is perhaps the best song on the album - with a licentious vocal from Jagger that leaves the listener no doubt what Jagger had in mind when he sang of "buzzin' round your hive". The other stand out is 'Can I Get A Witness', the Holland-Dozier-Holland classic originally recorded by Marvin Gaye. The Stones don't come within a million miles of Gaye's version, but their faster paced version still rocks, and it's a great song. The cover of Jimmy Reed's 'Honest I Do' is less laid back and, dare I say it, more bluesy than the original, more countrified version with some great harmonica playing. 'Mona' stands up well to the original too, with Brian Jones embellishing the Bo Diddley sound with some style. On Solomon Burke's 'You Can Make If You Try' Jagger's vocal merely pales into comparison, although the band deserve huge credit for unearthing such a great b-side!

3.   **The front cover breaks new ground.** On the cover, there's no clue as to the name of the band. Think that Led Zeppelin were first to do this? Oh no. The Rolling Stones were the first pop group to omit the name of the band from the cover. Their faces are cast in shadow, in a move reminiscent of the cover of *With The Beatles*. On the reverse, Oldham's sleeve notes tell us that "The Rolling Stones are more than a group. They are a way of life..."

4.   **The story behind the first Jagger/Richards composition.** Stones manager Andrew Loog Oldham knew the Beatles through having done some PR work for Brian Epstein. In late 1963, during a frustrating recording session at Studio 51 in Soho, when a follow up single to debut 'Come On' was proving hard work, Oldham went for a walk in Jermyn Street, near Piccadilly. By chance, out of a taxi jumped Lennon and McCartney, on their way home from a Variety Club lunch. The boys asked Oldham why he was looking thoughtful. "Oh, I'm fed up. The Stones can't find a song to record." They replied: "Oh, we've got a song we've almost written. The Stones can record that if you like". The song was 'I Wanna Be Your Man'. John and Paul went back with Oldham to the studio where the Rolling Stones were still arguing, finished writing the song, and the Stones had their first top twenty hit. The ability of Lennon and McCartney to write a song at the drop of a hat was not lost on Jagger and Richards. However, it took further "encouragement" before the songwriting came naturally. Needing material for their first album, Andrew Loog Oldham locked Jagger and Richards in the kitchen of their Willesden basement "and threatened not to let them out until they had written a song," says Philip Norman

in his biography. "Tell Me" was the result – not the greatest song you'll ever hear, to be frank, but it was the only Jagger/Richards song that made it onto the first LP.

5.   **The album best captures the early Stones R&B sound.** The album, released in April 1964, sold 100,000 advance copies, knocking *With The Beatles* off top spot (in fairness, the Beatles album had been released in the previous November). It stayed at number one for twelve weeks. This is the best document of why the Rolling Stones became so popular. We are effectively listening to the R&B set that they played at The Crawdaddy Club in their earliest days. It also gives us a window into the R&B songs the band themselves admired. The LP was released in the USA six weeks later, on 30th May 1964, and in a different form, as was customary at the time. The USA LP was titled *England's Newest Hit Makers* and included third UK single 'Not Fade Away' instead of 'Mona'.

I reported back to Chris. One album down, and some great reasons why a) this is a great album and b) why it's worth getting on vinyl: it's a potential goldmine, it has great songs, a great cover, there's a great story behind it and it's a brilliant historical document. One down, five to go…

Whilst a mint copy of the Rolling Stones' imaginatively titled second album *The Rolling Stones No. 2* is valued at £130 in my copy of the Rare Record Price Guide, most copies cluttering up the record fairs and car boot sales of the nation are as minty as a discarded piece of chewing gum, and therefore fetch half that price, or less. I secured a copy at Spitalfields Record Fair for what I considered to be a pretty fair price of £20. The cover was in great condition except for a sticker over the top right hand corner on the reverse, which someone had tried to remove, unsuccessfully. Why would someone place a sticker on the record? All would be revealed…

The record was a first pressing, in maroon, with the unboxed Decca label. As with the debut, *The Rolling Stones No. 2* was released in the USA in a different form, taking the cover of *12×5* but sharing songs with *The Rolling Stones…Now!* with seven tracks taken from the UK version surviving on the latter LP. But again the big question is why bother? Why buy this album on vinyl? Why buy it at all? Here are five reasons:

1.   **This is the best value David Bailey photo you will ever find.** The cover of *The Rolling Stones No. 2* was taken by the young up and coming photographer David Bailey, who happened to work with Jean Shrimpton, whose sister Chrissie was dating Jagger at the time. Just like the first album, the Rolling Stones chose not to have their name on the cover, so you get to just enjoy the mugs of Jagger, Jones, Richards et al in all their glory. To get a 12" by 12" photo by Bailey anywhere else for £20? Not gonna happen…

2.   **Sleeve Note Controversy!** The Rolling Stones' then manager Andrew Loog Oldham created some shudders down the spines of the establishment with his sleeve notes on the reverse of the cover. The notes, written in the style of *A Clockwork Orange,* jokingly

encouraged fans to knock over blind men and steal their wallets to get the cash to buy the record: "If you don't have bread, see that blind man knock him on the head, steal his wallet and lo and behold you have the loot", states the sleeve. A month after the January 1965 release, a Mrs Gwen Matthews, secretary of the Bournemouth Blind Aid Association, rather took offence to the suggestion that the blind might be a ready source of income for impoverished Stones fans who needed to raise cash to buy the album. Mrs Matthews was quoted in the press saying "They're horrible. It's putting ideas into people's heads. I'm writing to Decca to ask them to change the cover."

The subject was even raised in the House of Lords – Lord Conesford asked the Director of Public Prosecutions whether the sleeve constituted "a deliberate incitement to criminal action". Sir Edward Lewis, Chairman of Decca Records played dumb. "I am told that this inscription was meant to be humorous, but I'm afraid this jargon does not make sense to me." he said, and recalled the offending album sleeves, or – judging by my own copy – on some arranged for a sticker to be placed over the offending paragraph. I like the fact that my copy demonstrates this story, showing clear evidence of Decca's censorship before they could re-press the sleeve. There is no record of any blind people being mugged for their copies of Rolling Stones No 2.

3.   **Chuck Berry quota: only one and a half songs.** My ears were still stinging from Chris' rebuke/accusation that Stones albums are "just full of rubbish Chuck Berry covers". Although cover versions do dominate the track listing (as they do on the band's debut album), only one song – 'You Can't Catch Me' – is written by Chuck Berry, although he did cover 'Down The Road A Piece' himself, and the Rolling Stones almost certainly copied Berry's version, rather than earlier recordings by other artists, given that Berry was present at the recording.

4.   **The cover versions are better than on the debut album.** The Rolling Stones and Loog Oldham had become more sophisticated in their search for new material, seeking R'n'B obscurities to cover. Said Oldham in his *Stoned* biography about a visit to Liberty Records to search for new material: "Up came a white-labelled Imperial 45 bearing the artist's name, Irma Thomas, and her devastating recording... of 'Time is on My Side.' Yes, it was my good fortune to hear God two times on this first tour: once when the Valentinos literally jumped out of the grooves and into our path with 'It's All Over Now', and twice when Irma beamed 'Time is on My Side' my way." Oldham also had a say in the cover of another lesser known song, after the song's writer had mocked the Rolling Stones' perceived lack of skill; Jerry Leiber suggested the Rolling Stones cover Alvin Robinson's 'Down Home Girl' instead, in a not-so-subtle dig at their R'n'B profiency.

Oldham's response was similarly unsubtle: the Rolling Stones covered the song. For some reason, 'Down Home Girl', was not a commercial success for Alvin Robinson and might otherwise have languished in obscurity. The Rolling Stones' version is a snaking piece of R'n'B with Jagger's harmonica interlinking with Brian Jones' bluesy descending lick and Wyman's insistent bass-line. It's a great cover of a great song and up there with the Alvin Robinson original, which has a nice horn section. 'I Can't Be Satisfied' doesn't match up to Muddy Waters' original, but Brian Jones has a good attempt at the catchy slide riff.

Aside from these cover versions, we also have evidence of a new songwriting partnership. Two strong Jagger/ Richards album tracks are present with the best being 'Off The Hook', which had me trying to find out who did the original, only to discover it was not a cover. The other is 'What A Shame' – a decent blues number which appeared on the B-side of single 'Heart of Stone'. The album does have a couple of dodgy moments. The plodding 'Everybody Needs Somebody To Love' isn't even as good as the Blues Brothers version, never mind Wilson Pickett's or Solomon Burke's, whilst the cover of the Drifters' 'Under The Boardwalk' sounds so lacklustre that even Bruce Willis might claim to have made a better effort.

5.  **The Stones become Blues legends:** Some of the songs were taken from sessions recorded at the Rolling Stones' first visit to Chess Records Studio in Chicago. At these sessions, Keith maintains he saw Muddy Waters painting the ceiling, whilst Bill Wyman recalls Waters helping them with their bags. Andrew Loog Oldham describes the Chess Records sessions in hushed tones: "2120 South Michigan Avenue housed the Chess…studio. In two days the group put down some thirteen tracks – their most relaxed and inspired session to date – moved, no doubt, by our new-found ability to sell coals to Newcastle. Who would have thought that a bunch of English kids could produce black R&B in the States?

    "Nothing sensational happened at Chess except the music. For those two days, the Stones were finally true blues artists".

I reported these findings back to Chris, who queried the Chuck Berry quota in particular. "That's one in six songs by Chuck Berry on *The Rolling Stones No.2* and if you count 'Route 66' and 'Walkin' The Dog', which I'm sure Chuck Berry also did, that's more than twenty percent of the first two albums that are Chuck Berry covers! "He's good with numbers, is Chris. He's less good with his rock n roll knowledge. For the record, Chuck Berry never recorded 'Walkin' The Dog'.

With two parts of the quest complete, my friend Chris was on the warpath, one eye no doubt fixed on avoiding having to write a grovelling letter of apology (and I'd make it pretty grovelling) to Mick and Keith. "So I was right about the Chuck Berry covers," he maintained.

I countered, "You have to admit the first two albums are pretty good. And if I hadn't bought them on vinyl, we probably wouldn't have bothered listening to them." Chris still looked fairly confident. It was a slightly unsettling feeling.

"This is all very well, but we both know that you don't have a copy of *Their Satanic Majesties Request* – which costs a fortune – and even if you did get one, which looks unlikely, it's well known as being a dodgy album. Even if it is free of Chuck Berry covers," he added, somewhat needlessly. "Oh, and I listened to *Between The Buttons* on Spotify for the first time this morning," added Chris, rolling his eyes, then mock-whispering in a conspiratorial manner, "It's a bit of a stinker. Good luck with that one..."

He was right about *Their Satanic Majesties Request*'s reputation of course. But that was for another time. First, there was the Rolling Stones' third UK album, *Out Of Our Heads*. Remember, the challenge was to find the albums, listen to them, and then explain why they aren't just full of rubbish Chuck Berry covers.

1. **The best Rolling Stones song you've never heard.** With '(I Can't Get No) Satisfaction' being played – by law, it seems – at every school disco I ever went to, it is hard to conjure up the feeling of how new and exciting the Rolling Stones must have been to the teenagers of the sixties. How can we get that surge of fresh excitement now music has moved on and every song the Rolling Stones ever recorded can be downloaded or streamed in an instant?

   *Out Of Our Heads*, with its blistering opening track, a cover of Larry William's' 'She Said Yeah' gives us the chance to hear the Rolling Stones with fresh ears. It's sufficiently obscure to fit the bill (at least it was to me) and certainly hasn't been overplayed on radio. What a track this is! Richards and Jones wrestling with feedback (in 1965!), Jagger the gleeful rock star and perhaps the world's first proto-punk tune.

2. **It's Two Albums In One!** The only one of the Stones' first five U.S. albums to share a title with its UK counterpart, you can find both UK and U.S. versions on vinyl, with the U.S. version having a different cover and only six shared songs, adding '(I Can't Get No) Satisfaction' but losing 'She Said Yeah' and 'I'm Free'. Not only that, for the final time on a Rolling Stones LP, there's still a great bunch of R'n'B classics to re-discover, or discover in their original form for the first time. The band doing 'Hitch Hike' sounds great, until you hear Marvin Gaye singing it. Never mind 'Heard It On The Grapevine', here's a side to Gaye that doesn't get played on the radio, and is all the more refreshing for it.

3. **Jagger/Richards song-writing starts to gain momentum.** Another less-often-heard track, 'The Under Assistant West Coast Promo Man' is a genuine highlight, with its catchy-as-heck riff played on guitar and harmonica. The song itself satirised the band's

actual West Coast promotional man, George Sherlock, described fondly by Andrew Loog Oldham as "all tan, B-movie houndstooth suits, Dane-Clark-meets-Kramer in Seinfeld." As for other Jagger/ Richards songs, on the U.S. version of the album we hear 'The Last Time', which has a great lick/riff, (and was released as a single) and – of course – '(I Can't Get No) Satisfaction' itself.

4.   **The 'Baggy Scene' of the nineties gets its first anthem.** Twenty five years later, the Soup Dragons will take a (ahem) souped-up version of another Jagger/Richards composition 'I'm Free' into the Top Five.

5.   **The Rolling Stones begin to re-interpret the R'n'B songs rather than simply cover them.** This is the last Stones album to contain a majority of R'n'B cover songs, and rather than simply copy them the Stones are, in the parlance of Simon Cowell "owning the songs" and "making the songs their own". Thankfully, Cowell isn't there telling Jagger he has a great "recording voice", telling him he sounds "really current" or getting him to ditch the piano player. 'She Said Yeah' is the best example of this development, being better than the original – but listen also to the much-changed Chuck Berry cover 'Talkin' About You' which is slowed right down, and is all the better for it. Whilst Jagger is no match for Solomon Burke's imperial vocal on 'Cry To Me', he still sounds authentic rather than a mimic. Released in the UK on 24 September 1965, and the U.S. a few months earlier on 30th July, *Out Of Our Heads* became the Rolling Stones' first number one U.S. album. It entered the U.K. charts at number three and stayed in the top ten for eighteen weeks, peaking at number two.

The photo for the English cover was shot by Gered Mankowitz. According to Oldham, Mankowitz got the gig because of "some nice snaps of Marianne Faithfull, being a nice guy, and being the son of Wolf Mankowitz. David Bailey was globetrotting for *Vogue* and Gered became our man." The cover was used in the U.S. on the next release over there, *December's Children* which also used songs omitted from the U.S. release including 'She Said Yeah', 'I'm Free' and 'Talkin' About You'.

So far, as good, with *Aftermath* to come next. But with Chris' warning about the quality of *Between The Buttons*, not to mention not being able to find a copy of *Their Satanic Majesties Request*, I was a little thoughtful about my prospects.

*Aftermath* was the most difficult album to find on vinyl at a decent price – most copies were on sale for £30-£40 upwards, so when I found a nice copy for £20 I snapped it up. The reason it fetches a high price? Probably because of all the early Stones LPs, *Aftermath* has the strongest reputation. Here's why:

1. **_Aftermath_ is all about the songs.** From opener 'Mother's Little Helper' to the soul groove of 'Under My Thumb', the underrated ballad 'I Am Waiting' and hit single for Chris Farlowe 'Out Of Time"' it's the songs that make _Aftermath_ a great album. The U.S. version even had 'Paint It, Black', taking Brian Jones' sitar to number one in the charts. Even the more straightforward R'n'B numbers have nice flourishes. For example, 'Flight 505' has a great heavy bass line and there's a playful piano introduction that knocks out the riff to '(I Can't Get No) Satisfaction'.

2. **More sexist than a Whitesnake/Kiss collaboration (not that sexism is good)!** Jagger appeared to use _Aftermath_ as a series of not-so-subtle messages to (soon to be ex-) fiancée Chrissie Shrimpton. His one-man tirade against women on this album begins with 'Stupid Girl', which is less than flattering to the opposite sex in the same way that The Death Star was less than flattering to Alderaan. Next is 'Under My Thumb', a victorious brag about a girl who has "changed her ways" thanks presumably to Jagger's sheer wonderfulness: _"It's down to me, yes it is / The way she does just what she's told"_ he tells us. It is, even now, quite breathtakingly misogynistic.

   No better is 'Out Of Time' (_"you're obsolete baby"_ – always the way to a girl's heart, I find), and it was a wonder that the next song on the album wasn't titled 'Welcome To Dumpsville, Population: You'. But perhaps that might have been too subtle. Either way Ms Shrimpton's days were numbered, and history will tell us she may have had a lucky escape. Ironically one of the last songs on the album, "It's Not Easy" bemoans how hard it is living on your own. Work that one out if you can...

3. **Classic marimba action.** Aside from Jagger's chronic misogyny, the album is notable for Brian Jones' creativity on a number of exotic instruments, including a ferociously picked sitar on 'Mother's Little Helper', dulcimer on the stately 'Lady Jane' and the lovely 'I Am Waiting', plus most notably of all, the marimba on 'Out Of Time' and 'Under My Thumb'. As Bill Wyman said about the latter: "Well. Without the marimba part, it's not really a song, is it?" 'Under My Thumb' is still an extraordinary record. Jagger's lyrics are rather ungentlemanly, but it's one of the Rolling Stones best tunes.

   The story of how Jones came to be playing the marimba was pure chance: The Baja Marimba band, a Mexican novelty group, had left their instruments – including a marimba – in a corner of the RCA studio where the Rolling Stones were recording. Brian Jones spotted the instruments, went over, started experimenting and the rest is history.

4. **An eleven minute Blues epic!** At eleven minutes long, 'Goin' Home' was a true rarity, or as Andrew Loog Oldham put it, "By 1965 only Dylan, the Stones, and Marty Robbins had defied the three-minute law – and kicked open the doors to the future." However,

the reason how it became such an epic – and a forerunner of classic Stones track 'Midnight Rambler' – is more prosaic. The truth is, no-one had worked out how the song would end. Bill Wyman remembers "While we were playing it, we awaited a signal to stop but no one signalled. There is a gap in the drumming at one point when Keith picked up his coat and threw it at Charlie, but that didn't stop him for long."

Oldham breathlessly recalls the session in *Rolling Stoned*: "at the five-minute line ... Mick's vocal was over and he crossed his arms without missing a beat. Keith curled into his guitar ... not allowing anybody to catch his eye. As we crossed into six minutes, it was still the one, still the take, but if something didn't happen and if somebody didn't take charge and find an ending, we could be derailed." He describes the track minute by minute until "The Stones ... allowed themselves to descend to a last après skasmic crawl. Eleven minutes-plus on the slopes and spent; thank God we'd had enough tape between reels. The group fell about, as well they should, exhilarated. They laughed, hugged each other, and collapsed on the floor."

5. **No Chuck Berry covers!** *Aftermath* is the first album by the Rolling Stones not to feature any cover versions. No doubt the band felt pretty confident on the back of a string of three major singles '(I Can't Get No) Satisfaction', 'Get Off Of My Cloud' and '19th Nervous Breakdown'. These strong songs, all written by Jagger/Richards, paved the way for this, their first all-originals album. The growing song-writing bond between Jagger and Richards coincided with Brian Jones' estrangement from his band members.

*Aftermath* sees the band in the early stages of breaking apart, seen in Jagger's increasing frustration with Jones' erratic behaviour, as described by Denny Bruce, who shared a flat with keyboard player Jack Nitzsche: "There was one session where Jack, the next day, said, "you know Mick and Keith can be really nasty, man. Last night Brian just wasn't allowed to contribute on a song they were working on. He had a harp part he thought would work out. And they went "alright, go out in the studio." They made him do it five or six times, where he had blood on both sides of his mouth from wailing so hard on the harp. But they hadn't even rolled the tape."

The earliest copies of *Aftermath* had a purple shadow behind the white lettering of the title. If your copy has this, congratulations. That might be worth twice the regular price. Mine doesn't, sadly. A 'regular' mint copy of Aftermath may still fetch over £100. Also, the album is the only place to find the original five minute-plus version of 'Out Of Time'. The later version on U.S. album *Flowers* is a 3:41 minute edit, and the *Metamorphosis* version released in 1975 takes Jagger's vocals and adds them to Chris Farlowe's backing track. With *Aftermath* proving to be a strong album, that was the first four Rolling Stones albums done. Plenty to enjoy, and not too many dodgy Chuck Berry covers.

Next? Well, six months after *Aftermath*'s release, The Beatles released *Revolver* and the first waft of psychedelia found its way to the UK. The Rolling Stones were listening, and *Between The Buttons* was the result.

Having risen to a challenge to listen to The Rolling Stones' first six albums and, if appropriate, find some good reasons to like them, I could have done without any negativity from within the Stones own camp. As King Minos of Crete discovered when his daughter Ariadne deftly palmed the handsome Theseus a ball of string and a sword before he was shoved into the hungry Minotaur's labyrinth, it doesn't help your cause if your allies turn against you. I had some idea as to how the Cretan King might have felt upon seeing a sword poking out of the cake his daughter baked for Theseus "for the journey" when I assembled my defence of *Between The Buttons*, the Rolling Stones' fifth UK album. It transpires that Mick Jagger talks about the album as he might describe an especially out-of-favour ex-girlfriend to whom he has just lost a paternity suit.

"I was really disappointed with it," says Jagger, seemingly oblivious of my task of wanting to talk the album up. "I don't know, it just isn't any good. 'Back Street Girl' is about the only one I like," he continued, twisting the knife slowly but firmly, going on to describe the album as "more or less rubbish." So here we have poor old *Between The Buttons*, with a face even its mother doesn't love.

And yet it's really rather good.

Bill Wyman: "*Between The Buttons* was the result of the first studio session at which we concentrated on an album as a finished product." Rather than a collection of recording sessions packaged together, The Stones set to work on a cohesive whole. To put the album in context, it was released in January 1967, five months after the Beatles' *Revolver*, and was preceded by the singles 'Have You Seen Your Mother, Baby, Standing In The Shadows?' in September 1966 and the double A-side 'Let's Spend The Night Together'/'Ruby Tuesday' released contemporaneously. Here are five reasons why *Between The Buttons* deserves space on your record shelf:

1. **Brian Jones' weird expression on the cover photo.** Gered Mankowitz took the famous cover photo on Primrose Hill after an all-night recording session. To achieve the hazy effect around the edges, Mankowitz used an ingenious DIY method – he smeared Vaseline on a piece of glass and took the shot through the glass. In the middle of the shot is a strange looking Brian Jones. Mankowitz explained why: "We endlessly found ourselves working in spite of Brian. During the *Between The Buttons* session he continuously tried to screw the pictures up: he was hiding behind his collar; he'd bought himself a newspaper and buried himself in it; he was just not cooperating." The reverse of the sleeve, on the other hand, reveals drummer Charlie Watts' artistic talents, with a cartoon and accompanying poem: "To understand this little rhyme / You must tap your foot in time / Then the buttons come much nearer / And the Stones you see more clearer."

2.  **Scary tunes!** 'My Obsession', recorded at RCA studios in Hollywood saw the Beach Boys' Brian Wilson pop by the studio to witness the Rolling Stones recording the track. Wilson thought it so scary, he had to leave the studio. He still describes it as one of his favourite Stones tracks, though.

3.  **More shockingly bad attitudes towards women!** 'Yesterday's Papers' likens a relationship to a girl with the throwing out of the newspapers, which is pretty cold – and may refer to Jagger's relationship with Chrissie Shrimpton: their relationship ended in December 1966. However, it is the pure cynicism of Jagger's favourite song 'Back Street Girl' that mixes a beautiful melody with the most breathtakingly unpleasant lyric addressed to Jagger's lowly mistress, "Please don't be part of my life / just keep yourself to yourself / please don't you bother my wife / that way you won't get no help / don't try to ride on my horse / you're rather common and coarse, anyway / don't want you out in my world / just you be my back street girl…" Well, what right minded girl could resist?

4.  **Back to Mono!** All reissues of the album since 1968 have been in stereo; at the time of the challenge the album's mono mix had yet to see an official CD release, so buying the original album was the only way you could hear the album's mono mix. Unless you unplug one of your speakers.[10]

5.  **Side Two is a belter!** There are plenty good tracks on the first side, including 'Connection' and 'My Obsession', but Side Two is the most eclectic and interesting mix of Rolling Stones songs on any Stones album so far: 'All Sold Out' sounds like an outtake from *Revolver*. The band blend R&B with a pop sensibility and infectious backing vocals. 'Please Go Home' has a bluesy, feedback-drenched chugging guitar to accompany the Bo Diddley beat, and some striking vocal echo effects. 'Who's Been Sleeping Here' is a Dylan-influenced tune in a folk rock style. Very catchy and one of the best tracks on the album. 'She's Complicated' has a fuzzy bass line mixed with some organ flourishes and some insistent drumming from Charlie Watts. 'Miss Amanda Jones' is a great R'n'B track that could have appeared on *Exile On Main Street* without sounding too out of place. 'Something Happened To Me Yesterday' sees Jagger and Richards sharing lead vocals – Keith Richards sings the chorus – and [alongside 'Cool Calm and Collected' which features dulcimer and a solo played on a kazoo] is the most vaudevillian track on the album, very much in the style of The Kinks. There's a tuba in there, a Dixieland Jazz band, and a valediction from Jagger at the end which mimics the policeman in popular TV show *Dixon Of Dock Green*. The song is apparently about an LSD trip.

The U.S. version of the album is arguably stronger, omitting 'Back Street Girl' and inserting the superior (and less insulting) 'Ruby Tuesday' plus leaving out the Bo Diddley-esque charms of

---

[10] The Rolling Stones have since re-issued their albums in mono

'Please Go Home' but kicking off the album with 'Let's Spend The Night Together'. Producer Andrew Loog Oldham tells a good story about recording the latter song and how he averted a disastrous drugs-bust a few months before the famous one that left Keith and Mick (briefly) incarcerated. Whilst the band were "smoking" in the control room during the sessions for 'Let's Spend The Night Together', Oldham spotted eight policemen heading into the studio, intent on causing the band a little difficulty. He ran out of the control room and stopped the first two.

"Quick, Have you got truncheons?" Oldham asked. "Right, now hit them together". The policemen obliged. "That's perfect. Just what we need on the track. Could you sit down here and do it when we record?" Oldham said "They sat down dead chuffed – forgetting all about trying to bust us – and we recorded two of them, hitting their truncheons together. It even stayed on the finished track, I think."

In reporting back to Chris on a fifth successful album ticked off the list, he seemed happy. "I was expecting you to be a little more concerned by this stage" I remarked.

"Concerned? Nah. You were always going to find something. The real contest was not about those albums. The real bet is you finding a miraculously cheap copy of the *Satanic Majesties* album, and then somehow finding something to like in what is universally acknowledged to be one of the worst albums of all time! You still don't have a copy do you?"

I bluffed. "Um, it's all in hand..."

Sensing my discomfort, Chris laughed. "Of course it is!" I think this was sarcasm. "So, what is it? £20 and three days left? Good luck with that..."

Trying to buy an original copy on vinyl of *Their Satanic Majesties Request* for twenty quid is like breeding pandas. An awful lot of effort without much hope of success, and it just ends in disappointment for everyone involved. I trawled Spitalfields Record Fair and looked in every crate marked "Rolling Stones", but to no avail. I even found a Black Sabbath bootleg called *Their Satanic Majesties Return*. Then, just as I was about to give up, I somewhat unexpectedly found what must have been the only copy in the place, just tucked away behind some hen's teeth. The only trouble was, it was £30, and a second pressing at that, without the lenticular cover. It's odd. What many people regard as the Rolling Stones' worst album is also the rarest and most expensive.

I wasn't going to pay £30, and with the end of a lunch-hour looming like a big, looming thingy, I had to give up. This was a bitter blow. If there's one thing I dislike more than paying £30 for one record, it's losing a bet to one of my friends. I may be able to find a good deal like Joey Essex can find Things He Doesn't Know Yet, but there is a limit even to my powers of discovery and negotiation. To get an idea of how I felt, picture the inner turmoil, angst and frustration of Dostoyevsky when his wifi signal started playing up.

But just when I was working out how to review an album I didn't own (there's always the internet, I thought) I found myself near Bond St. tube station. I passed by the HMV. "I don't suppose..." I thought to myself...

Sure enough, there it was! It's a bit of a cheat, but you can buy the album for just under £18 if you are prepared to slum it and buy a brand spanking new copy on 180g vinyl. It's a bit daft, this record collecting lark sometimes. I was £2.01 under budget. But what of the album? My task was not just to buy it, but also to praise it, if at all possible.

**1. The world's first 3D cover!** The cover is lenticular, or at least early copies are. Said Keith Richards, "That was acid. We made that set ourselves. We went to New York, put ourselves in the hands of this Japanese bloke with the only camera in the world that could do the 3D. Bits of paint and saws, bits of styrofoam." Sadly the reissue is not lenticular, so I have to imagine the excitement.

**2. Think it's a wacky title? You should hear what they were going to call it...** The first title for *Their Satanic Majesties Request* was going to be *The Rolling Stones' Cosmic Christmas*. The Stones also recorded several tracks that weren't released, including potential classics such as 'Bathroom/Toilet' and 'Gold Painted Fingernails'. As a sense of how good these tracks were, a recording of Wyman snoring on the settee in the control room did make the final cut.

**3. Four of the songs.** Okay, it's time to come clean. I don't have five good things to say about the album as a whole. There are four really good songs on this LP, two okay ones (one of which was covered by Kiss of all people) and four absolute shockers. I decided to make a few notes on a first listen. Here's selected "highlights" of what I wrote:

Track 1: 'Sing All This Together'. *There's a junior school music lesson going on in the background. With triangles: traditionally the instruments left in the music box at pre-school after all the tambourines and drums have gone. This stinks the place up like leaving a kipper under the bonnet of a Ford Cortina for a month. I hope the rest of the album isn't like this.*

Track 5: 'Sing This All Together (See What Happens)'. *See What Happens? Sod all. Genuinely terrible. Like we are three hours into a particularly interminable junior school music lesson which is interrupted by one of those Hari Krishna bands that used to bang their tambourines around Oxford St. Just when you think it couldn't get any worse, some jazz flute pops up. Possibly the worst song ever committed to vinyl.*

Track 8: 'Gomper'. *Another shocker. The sort of track that even Tony Blackburn wouldn't play if he were the DJ at your local Indian restaurant.*

Track 10: 'On With The Show'. *Oh dear. Utter tripe. A museum piece, if the museum was The Museum of Awfulness, in Awful Town, Awful Land.*

However, it's not all bad news.

There are some good songs on *Their Satanic Majesties Request.* I really like 'The Lantern'. It sounds to me like a prototype of 'Shine A Light' on *Exile On Main St.* 'Citadel' is good, 'She's A Rainbow' is all chorus – a great pop song that I am familiar with through The World of Twist's cover (I prefer the Rolling Stones' original version) and '2,000 Light Years From Home' is a terrific song, although it really belongs on a Pink Floyd album next to 'Astronomy Domine'.

Overall, *Their Satanic Majesties Request* demonstrates that some albums are best heard on a format other than vinyl: some albums need the skip button. The highs are great, but the lows are really terrible. It's not really a surprise. Bill Wyman: "It was one of the three times we came really close to splitting up". Keith Richards: "It ended up as a real patchwork. All a bit of flim-flam for me. None of us wanted to make it, but it was time for another Stones album, and *Sgt. Pepper's* was coming out, so we thought basically we were doing a put-on."

To be fair, when making *Sgt. Pepper' Lonely Hearts Club Band*, the Beatles had quit the road, had George Martin as producer and were settled and happy. For the Rolling Stones, their relationship with producer Andrew Loog Oldham was about to end, both Mick and Keith were on bail pending appeal for drugs charges which might have seen them spend a year in jail, and Brian Jones was having residential psychiatric treatment.

I reported back to Chris. "You're right" I told him. "*Satanic Majesties* is 40% stinker, 20% average and 40% excellent." He looked vindicated. But we got one thing wrong. Taken as a body of work, the first six records are amazing. They aren't all dodgy Chuck Berry covers at all. There's loads to enjoy, and they are a great introduction not only to the Rolling Stones, but also to American R'n'B, even now, some fifty years after '(I Can't Get No) Satisfaction' first hit the airwaves.

# 17

## FINAL THOUGHTS AND WARNINGS ON COLLECTING RECORDS, YOUR HIFI, SOME USEFUL VINYL ACCESSORIES AND TIPS FOR YOUR SOCIAL MEDIA PROFILE

In a world where people consume music through pre-determined streaming service playlists with grim titles such as 'Cinematic Chillout', 'Music for Concentration' and 'Songs for Sleeping', is the album still relevant to the zombified masses? Masses moreover, who willingly listen to playlists entitled 'Indie Sleeping Pill' or 'Music for When You Are Tired' which are presumably full of bland, beige sub-Claydermanesque waltzes – or perhaps Razorlight ballads – and for which half the music industry is writing songs in order to earn their way on to that particular money-train. What next? 'Music to listen to while you stare into the void of your unhappy and ultimately meaningless existence'? How long before we see a playlist with the title 'Songs Written by a Faceless Corporation's Algorithm You Are 80% Likely to Quite Like'? It could all get very depressing.

Under such provocation, it is remarkable that bands – presumably not in existence merely to help people "chill" or "sleep" – can still inspire people to actually listen to a whole album. And, what's more, that people still wish to hear the music on vinyl, one of life's least convenient formats. You can gauge how vinyl has grown in popularity over the last few years by how often it crops up in films and TV. For years, actors in bad TV dramas have been shoving Hootie and the Blowfish and other CDs into pretend car stereos whenever the director needs some music - but now it's vinyl's turn.

First it was Harvey Specter in *Suits,* the hot shot lawyer who solves every case with nonchalant ease, despite the obvious distraction offered by having the Duchess of Sussex working in the same office. To celebrate solving an especially complex case Harvey relaxes in his voluminous corner office by pulling cool jazz records from a well-stocked shelf of LPs onto an expensive looking turntable. Specter put the needle on a record once and I used the internet to identify the song he was playing. Instead of delighting in the discovery of a rather breezy Charles Bradley track, I was silently appalled to find I was listening to the last track on side one while the record onscreen was clearly playing the first one. And that is everything you need to know about record collecting right there.

I tell you this as a warning. Rather than revelling in the "Magic of Television", this is what you may become. The unwary music lover may, instead of being transported into the heavens by Van

Morrison's *Astral Weeks*, find themselves looking at the label in the middle of the record to see if it is green (an original), a later "Burbank" one which has a pretty picture of the WB studios in Burbank, California, or a less interesting eighties white "Warner Bros" one, quite forgetting to appreciate Van's sublime Celtic vibes. There appear to be some more militant vinyl lovers who imagine a hollowness of the soul when they hear Beatles songs coming from a disc with a silver Parlophone label from the 1970s, rather than the original sixties labels.

I therefore feel I should share the reality of record collecting with you before you get too involved. Because once you are in, there may be no way out.

## Sage Advice Part 1: Being sensitive around other record collectors.

They are a funny lot, record collectors. Personally, I find it distasteful to brag about the rare records I have, such as a Mofi pressing of Beck's *Sea Change*, an original aperture sleeve of Pulp's *Different Class*, or a clear vinyl copy of Bowie's *Blackstar*. You won't find me banging on about those, or my 2012 Record Store Day 'Starman' Bowie picture disc. I tend not to mention my signed copy of Brian Eno's *Another Green World* in conversation. It's best not to. If I had a signed copy of Suede's *Bloodsports* (and I do), the last thing I would do is mention it at any opportunity. I'm far too discreet to do that.

People are sensitive, and easily upset. They feel envious towards people who have done well. They can't be happy for them. Personally, I'm always delighted to hear of a fellow record collector who has found a rare first pressing worth a small fortune in a car boot sale for a pound. One can only feel pleased they have finally found a reward for the hundreds and possibly thousands of lost weekend mornings drinking bad tea, losing never-to-be-reclaimed beauty sleep leafing through countless damaged copies of Ted Heath and James Last LPs, probably contracting sciatica and lumbago in the process. I know that others are perhaps less generous in their outlook but one should always be thoughtful of other people. I have known people to fall out over the width of the spine on a copy of *Sgt. Pepper's Lonely Hearts Club Band* (the wider ones are prized, apparently). It's unseemly.

Record collectors can have unattractive characteristics hidden beneath the surface. For example, if a friend finds a nice copy of something I already have, the first, most polite instinct is to ask how they came across it and let them tell you the story. Very often this will result in their telling you how much they paid. At that point, it only seems fair to share how you found your copy (often, it turns out, in better condition for half the price five years ago) purely to help inform them of relative value of things over the years, and to give some overall perspective on how well they have done, to stop them getting carried away.

166

You would have thought a friend would be delighted in this new information, and perhaps pleased for your good fortune, however I have found a weakness in some people who appear to take the news badly. I once patiently explained something along those lines to a friend who, frankly, had paid about the going rate for something but thought it was a tremendous bargain, and he got in quite a dark mood and began muttering things under his breath. Very odd. Conversely, I have known friends who struggle to show more than a passing interest in my own miraculous finds, many of which were genuine bargains. There is always someone who will insist on telling you how they "used to see those all the time for fifty pence ten years ago. They couldn't give them away." It seems such a mean-spirited, joy-crushing thing to say.

## Sage Advice Part 2: The best time to buy records.

The best time to have been collecting records is always the same, in the same way the best time to buy a house is always the same, namely twenty years ago. It was cheaper, there was more of them, those were halcyon days. I sometimes wonder what those days were like, when everyone was chucking away their records and the vinyl-heads were swooping in and picking them all up at boot fairs. As lovely as it must have been, the fundamental problem would have still remained, namely most people's taste in music is dreadful.

Well, it isn't, but it's usually different from everybody else's, and the top selling records must have come up all the time, so even twenty years ago, you had to work pretty hard to find anything of interest. You can probably approximate what it was like by trying to buy CDs in a charity shop or boot fair now. Substitute those Spice Girls, JLS, Dido, Take That and BoyZone CDs for *No Parlez*, *Alf*, and the best of Rod Stewart, Bread, The Carpenters and Phil Collins on LP and you have just skipped a generation in a time machine.

## Sage Advice Part 3: Social media, or How to Attract Thousands Of Instagram Followers For Your Vinyl Blog - A Beginner's Guide

Whether we prefer to use Social Media as a way to keep in touch with old friends, to post videos of the funny things our pets do when confronted with green vegetables, or simply for 3am rants about the FBI and the fake news media while sitting on the toilet, we are all becoming increasingly adept with these useful tools. Instagram's visual strengths have solved the issue that many record collectors face, namely how to square the owner's pride in their collection and wish to shout about it from the rooftops, with the rest of the world's total and profound disinterest in anyone else's record collection. It does this by providing a platform for people to post pictures of their record collections, which combines brilliantly with a function to allow the viewer to swipe swiftly past dull pictures of people's record collections.

The more persistent or perhaps insecure record collector therefore has to find ways to make their record collection more interesting. Self-worth on social media is measured by "likes", and therefore the most determined record collector must find ways to (as social media strategists put it) engage their audience, or to put it another way, secure these confirmations that yes, someone out there gives a flying flip that you once had the money and inclination to buy a purple vinyl pressing of Morbid Angel's third LP.

The more enterprising Instagrammers must therefore find new and interesting ways to display their records, so the following is a comprehensive guide to allow you to emulate these brilliant and inventive minds, and engage your own audience in new and exciting ways.

**1. The intimidating record collection.** Why not put people in their place straight away by showing off just how enormous your intimidatingly large record collection is? If you don't have an enormous record collection, take a photo of someone else's and pass it off as your own. No-one will check. Then, why not take exactly the same photo, only with different records? Fascinating! Nothing engages your audience better than the promise of another three hundred almost identical shots of records. People love seeing and hearing the same old thing over and over again. I mean they must do, right? Westlife were huge.

**2. It's a visual medium: don't be too interesting - it's hard work.** Some try a little harder, with some information about the record. This is great, although you may find it hard work copying, pasting and subtly editing the Wikipedia entry every time.

**3. It's All About Capturing The Moment.** Others go for a "lifestyle" vibe, perhaps depicting an attractive millennial or hipster, just caught in the act of pulling out a record from his heaving, pristine Ikea Kallax shelving. This is a classic take. I do admire the photographer's instinct in these shots, because they invariably have found the exact moment where the sleeve is most prominently displayed, but just before it is completely removed from the shelf.

**4. Capturing The Moment (part 2).** Sometimes the camera catches the exact moment the record is pulled three quarters from the sleeve, although usually the inner sleeve is nowhere in sight. It must be quite a skill to have such reflexes, and to also frame the shot so the turntable is just visible in the background.

**5. Capturing more impromptu moments.** It's a great on-the-hoof skill, I'm sure, capturing the moment when the instagrammer is gently adjusting the volume knob on their amplifier. Note how they always adjust their amplifier from the side. Never from the front, despite that position being possibly an easier one to adjust your amp from. It's photographer's luck, some might say, to capture both the finely-tuned adjustment as well as a clear shot of the amplifier and knob-twiddler themselves, but I think you make your own luck in this game.

**6. The Rodin shot: the thinking record collector.** Another shot we can learn from is seeing the poster sitting on their wooden floor, quiet in contemplation, looking at a particular album cover, especially if the artist in question has recently passed away. Why not look forlornly at Prince's records in order to pull greatly at your readers' heart strings. What greater tribute could the great man wish for than for you to be photographed looking mawkishly at his records? Nothing like capturing a private and intimate moment of contemplation and bare, naked grief.

Sometimes they have been doing this all afternoon, and have carelessly strewn a number of records on the floor, all captured in the shot. I do worry they will be spending most of the afternoon tidying up, but I guess we must all suffer for our art. At my age I can only envy their ability to get up from that cold floor without a) stiffening up the joints and b) accidentally treading on one of the records.

**7. Sex sells.** The "Half-a-bum-cheek" shot is a bit of a classic. In this, the poster will have selected the chosen LP, but will be holding it by their fingertips (seldom the most comfortable way of holding a record but bear with me), cover facing back towards the photographer, down by their side with their back to the camera. To be clear, the strict rules around nudity on social media mean they are fully clothed, before you get the wrong idea. The patience the photographer has to show in capturing these moments is remarkable, because that awkward way of holding an LP, especially with the cover so prominently displayed, can't happen too often, yet the moment is captured quite magnificently, and quite frequently. If the photographer was at my house, I can't help feeling they would have their work cut out. For some reason I tend to carry the LP with both hands, and in front of me, so these magic moments must be more difficult to capture.

**8. Why not tell people about stuff you like?** It's remarkable to see how often the posters with large numbers of followers have new equipment that they really like, and which they are pleased to photograph - and endorse apropos of nothing I would imagine - just from the kindness of their hearts. This must therefore be really popular with audiences. Sometimes they carry the hashtag #ad but I'm not sure what that stands for. Oh well.

**9. Definitely don't own a cat.** Despite most vinyl-lovers owning cats, 100% of Instagram vinyl lovers definitely do not. I have worked this fact out by counting the number of times such folk have dust covers over their record players. I once played a record without the dust cover on when my cat was in the room. Never again. First, it spent a few seconds wobbling its head round and round. Then, it decided to pounce onto the deck. Although my cat had not anticipated the surface it had jumped on would revolve, it recovered remarkably quickly, leaping off with a triple salko having revolved a full 180 degrees in the meantime - quite a difficult technique. But in the cat's haste to pull the trick off he wasn't quite quick enough to prevent the tone arm being knocked significantly off-course and ploughing a large furrow through my Style Council LP. An ignominious end to an old LP, similar to the reaction that many fans of the Jam gave the same record nearly forty years before.

**10. Don't forget your street cred.** Instagram posters who own hip hop albums tend to store them near their trainers. It isn't clear why.

**And another thing...** Instagram record finds often come with a comment telling the viewer how little the buyer paid for them. This may come with a little detail about how they were found in a bric-a-brac shop in a twee village in the middle of nowhere, nestled under a Gucci coat no doubt, in one of these mythical shops that sell rare goods for pennies. It's amazing how often people find rare records in mint condition in charity shops, I find.

Social media is full of people discovering priceless LPs three times a day in shops raising money for the British Heart Foundation, yet if I ever found anything of interest in one of those shops, the shock would be so great I'd need their support. The only things I have ever found in charity shops have been battered copies of Jim Reeves, Cliff Richard and James Last LPs amongst the broken teapots and Franklin Mint. It's almost a relief when Paul Young's *No Parlez* crops up. In such barren plains it's like a flower in the desert. Far be it for me to suggest these priceless finds are either in terrible condition or the instagram poster has lied about the real price they paid and where they found them.

## Gear: In Search of The Cheapest Decent Hifi

To most people, there are few things less likely to brighten someone's day than hearing someone bang on about the quality of their hifi. It's up there with People Who Bang On About Their Cars, People Who Bang On About Golf and People Who Bang On About People Who Bang On About Things. Ah, yes, well, let's move on. Suffice to say, when Lech Walesa, the Leader of the Polish Solidarity Movement helped to bring about the end of one-party Communist rule, he didn't win the hearts and minds of his people by telling them about his new stereo.

So, in order to prevent seeing copies of this book thrown into the street from sheer boredom, this section will be mercifully brief, hopefully giving the reader two or three new things to think about, but strategically placed towards the end just in case.

Firstly, the secret to gaining happiness from vinyl is simple: Don't let it bankrupt you, and don't let it lead to a breakdown in your relationships with people. The second one represents deep waters, so let's stick to the first. How can we make vinyl work when a record costs twenty quid and streaming is so much cheaper? (i.e. £9.99 per month to hear almost anything). On the face of it, picking vinyl for your preferred format to listen to music if you are short of a few bob is like choosing doughnuts as your first choice method of dieting.

And yet ... Firstly, old records can be cheap. And there are millions out there. As long as you are patient, and can sniff out the cheaper places to buy, and keep costs down, buying most of the stuff for a fiver or less. As a bonus, buying records of this kind drives you away from the musical motorways, and down the less-well-trodden paths. Not that you have to listen to Mantovani and Jim Reeves albums. Be selective.

Which leads us to what to play the records on. You need three things: a record player, and amplifier and a set of speakers. The simplest solution is something new, plus a new amplifier, and a couple of new speakers. Plug and play, and very simple. But with all that you are looking at perhaps £400-£500. Wouldn't it be nice to pay £150 or less and get something that sounds just as good or better?

I have always been somewhat sceptical of spending money on hifi. It seems to me that you can spend any amount of money on a system and most people will struggle to know the difference. And for most people, the quality of a person's stereo is seldom something they will even notice. Few people, after going to someone's house for dinner will remark, "well the food was nice, wine decent, the conversation sparkled, but good grief, can you believe how the background music's soundstage seemed so flat and one-dimensional, particularly in the mid-ranges? I wonder if he's using a cheaper cartridge and stylus than would do justice to the tone arm?"

For those of us who are slightly impecunious, therefore, buying second hand equipment is the answer. Because vinyl's heyday was in the seventies, the equipment made back then was excellent, and it still works, and sounds great.

For a cheap, reliable and decent sounding record player for a starter system – one that will beat one of those suitcase players all hands down, my advice is to look for a Kenwood KD 1033. Search on local websites. I bought one down the road from me last year for £27, and as I write this there's one near me for £40. It's a belt-drive and there is very little that can go wrong with it. However, by now the original belt will most likely have perished and unless the seller knows what to do they will sell it as "spares or repairs".

This is an opportunity - a better one if the buyer wants collection only (always a good idea to prevent damage of a heavy item in the post) because that limits the number of buyers. All you need to do is buy a new belt (£8 online), take the platter off and remove the old, perished belt (will require scraping off with isopropyl/alcohol - a very easy job), put on the new one and fit a new cartridge (buy an AT95e for £34 - a brilliant cartridge that sounds better than others at twice the price - or for £10 more the even better AT95ex). That's a proper hifi deck with a brand-new cartridge for less than £100. You'll also feel very pleased with yourself for being a) environmentally kind and b) frugal. You will also surprise yourself just how handy you are with a small screwdriver when you have the right motivation.

Alternative record players that might be found for similar money and which are worth looking for include the Pioneer PL12D and the Dual 505. Both can be found for below £50 (with patience), given new belts and spruced up. For those who are willing to be a little more handy, and for just over £100 there is much fun to be had with a Lenco L75 and the online forums that tell you how to spruce up these classic old machines.

There were two events in my life that destroyed my cynical view that one stereo system sounded very much like any other. The first was when my local hifi shop played me something on a hifi that cost over £100,000. It was amazing. I'll give them that much. But at that price, so it should be. The second was when I bought an old amplifier built in the 1970s called an A&R A60 for £75 online and compared it with a brand-new amplifier I had bought a couple of years ago for twice the price.

It turns out because amplifiers in the 1970s were built around the phono stage (the bit the record player is plugged into), they spent a lot of time making the phono stage sounding great. In 2018, for budget amps, the phono stage is more an afterthought at the budget end of things, with the focus being on the CD player or streaming inputs. The difference in sound between the new amplifier and the old one was like night and day. The old one sounded so much better, with its superb phono stage. I even compared the A60 against a far more expensive modern amplifier combined with an external specialist phono stage and there was very little to choose between the two. It truly is a budget marvel. For the hipsters, or for those with half an eye on interior design amongst you, it also sports a fetching oak casing. I later tried out a Trio KA2000A amplifier for £50 as it had two phono stages so you can plug in two record players into one amplifier. This too sounded fantastic, a hefty bass that the modern amp simply lacked. Two amplifiers from the 1970s which both out-gunned a more modern amplifier.

At this age, it's worth hearing them before you buy to make sure they don't pop and crackle when you turn the dials - if they do, you might need to clean them with a contact spray (Servisol), or find a friendly electronic repair shop locally who can service them, perhaps replace a few components. These things can usually be fixed by someone who knows what they are doing, and are worth the effort to preserve them.

Finally, the speakers. It's worth considering the following before splashing out on speakers: new speakers cost many hundreds of pounds. Generally speaking, speakers last for decades. Especially passive ones (ie not plugged into a mains supply) where, assuming you don't have small, poking-sort-of-children and/or climbing-sort-of-pets there's not much to go wrong. Many people think speakers are ugly looking, especially (if we may generalise for a moment) the partners of folk who buy speakers without prior consultation or thought about whether the speakers match the general decor of the room.

Newer multi room speaker systems like Sonos and Bluesound, Apple HomePod, Google, Amazon Echo are being installed everywhere, and are less ugly. They are also mains-driven and there is more to go wrong with them. Therefore, we are in a happy position where there are loads of used passive speakers being sold, as people "upgrade" their home hifi to all-in-one solutions allowing the turntable/amp/speakers enthusiast to pick up these old relics (the speakers, not the people selling them) for very little money. It won't take you long to find a pair online for about £20. I found such a pair for a friend a few months ago. They were by Mission, and they sounded fine. The owner had owned them for more than a decade and was upgrading.

Very often, the uglier or bigger the speaker, the more difficult they are to shift, so as long as you don't object, that's a decent route to go down. If having two sound-producing gargoyles in the house doesn't appeal, and you are handy with Annie Sloan paint, you can give them a Blue Peter-esque make-over. Ugly black speaker cloth can be replaced with colourful/tasteful eBay-sourced speaker cloth that will match your home decor.

## Don't Panic: how to best navigate Record Store Day

Although RSD sounds like it should be some form of communicable disease, it is actually one of the most anticipated days of the year for hipsters, music obsessives and general nerdlings throughout the land. It's right up there with the Bridlington Annual Star-Trek convention in terms of sheer adrenaline-packed excitement.

It is a day when we step back and think about how our High Streets look, and we ask deep and meaningful questions, such as "Since when did our 'record shops' become 'stores'?", and "Why are loads of scruffy excited-looking middle aged men lining up in the high street? Is a new Wetherspoons offering free beer?" and (if you are under eighteen) "What's a 'Record'? Is that, like, Spotify for old people or something?"

It is also a great day for seeing long queues of (predominantly) men lining up overnight to buy different versions of things they already have, whilst moaning, apparently without irony, about how their wives have bought yet another pair of shoes.

Every year, the Record Store Day release list of releases is er, released and the first tents spring up outside the entrance to one of London's finest independent Record Stores, Rough Trade East, ever earlier as the keenest vinyl hoarders look to be first in line for that limited edition box set of Ringo Starr 7" singles. The keenest record buyers thus learn the practicalities of camping by seeing their tents blow away in a gust of wind – because it's hellishly difficult to stick tent pegs into concrete, those at least that haven't been removed by Brick Lane police in the mistaken belief that they are the return of the "Occupy London" protesters. ("They certainly look like a bunch of protesters" said one policeman, "just look at their beards").

It is also the one day a year when the plight of an ageing group of people who have been the backbone of the music industry for years, supporting it with little financial reward or acclaim, is deservedly highlighted. That's right – even the Rolling Stones re-release their records.

There are, of course, irritating things about RSD. There are the eBay flippers who get up early and buy up everything just to make a profit. This is irritating because a) no-one should have to wake up early to buy records – waking up early is about as rock'n'roll as a JLS CD; b) it stops me from doing it (just kidding); and c) it lessens my (admittedly very slight) chance of buying a record that might increase in value.

An interesting dilemma that RSD brings is whether to buy re-issues of your favourite records, instead of the originals. For example, in 2011 a lovely two record set (and booklet) of Iggy Pop's *Raw Power* was released – with both the Bowie mix and the Iggy mix – for about £40, which is about the same price as a mint copy of the 1973 original, and £25 more than later re-issues. Tom Petty saw some nice coloured vinyl re-releases a year later, but £30 for *Damn The Torpedoes* is about £25 more than you'd pay for the original, black vinyl version. On the other hand, The Kinks saw *Village Green, Something Else* and *Face To Face* re-issued in coloured vinyl double sets (a mono and stereo version in one package). Any of these would cost about £100 less than the originals, so they were great value.

So what should the clued-up vinyl collector do? The first thing is to recognise this is a day for the store, rather than the collector. Go to the shop, and support them with your presence. And don't panic! Those "hot" new Record Store Day releases may not be as essential as you think. It is useful to look at the value of those previous Record Store Day purchases you may have made fortunes from. After all, everyone knows buying these rare records is like printing money, right? That Vaccines single must be worth hundreds of pounds by now, surely?

How should we be investing our hard-earned cash? Everyone knows that past performance is no guide to the future, but what can we learn from previous years? First, the good news for anyone who invested their money wisely or perhaps fortunately in, say, 2012's Arctic Monkeys' 'RU Mine' 7″ purple vinyl or David Bowie's 7″ picture disc of 'Starman': congratulations, you hit the jackpot. Both are now regularly fetching silly money on Discogs and eBay: 'Starman' has averaged £228 over the last ten trades and is only currently available at £195 whereas 'RU Mine' has averaged £70 over the last few years which is roughly an 8-10x return on your cash. With those investing skills, a career in private equity awaits.

Should we jump on the bandwagon and buy more Bowie or Arctic Monkeys? Well, not necessarily. If you bought Bowie's 'Drive In Saturday' picture disc on Record Store Day 2013 with similar expectations as 2012, you'll be feeling like the guy who invested in Alan Sugar's Emailer phone when everyone else piled into Blackberry, or a Blackberry investor at a time of iPhones. The average sale price for that one is £35. Not bad, but hardly a goldmine, and the picture disc of *The*

*Man Who Sold The World* released in 2016 has lost money for owners – it is currently averaging just seventeen pounds per transaction. Similarly, Arctic Monkeys' 'Don't Sit Down' 7" single released on Record Store Day 2011, has failed to make money for anyone, being consistently available for a bargain £6. Other well-known artists have also failed to set the world alight. Radiohead are a good example (a 2011 release of 'Supercollider' is available for £15) and so on. It's difficult to say why those particular Arctic Monkeys and Bowie discs were so valuable.

If it isn't the artist, what makes a record appreciate in value? Is it a limited run? Possibly, but that doesn't explain why 'RU Mine' had a run of 1,750 copies and has rocketed, whereas Elbow's single 'McGreggor' had an even more limited run of 500, but is still available for £3. Is it 7" singles? Not if you look at the value of the Beatles 2012 box set – which has fallen from £50 (which was steep, to be fair) to a more sensible £30. To try to get to the bottom of all this, by way of research I took a basket of twenty five "hot" releases of RSD 2012 and tracked their prices. These releases included records by Kate Bush, Coldplay, The Sex Pistols, The Kinks, The White Stripes, The Vaccines, Flaming Lips, Noel Gallagher, The Beatles, Abba and Arcade Fire. All blue-chip names with excellent investment potential. I left out those releases by Bowie and Arctic Monkeys because they skew the results hugely and would give an otherwise misleading picture.

The result? With the exception of those two 7" singles by Bowie and Arctic Monkeys the prices are little more than what they were on the 19th April 2012. By comparison, two years after RSD 2012, £100 invested in Gold was worth £77, if you had bought £100 of shares on the FTSE100 index, then you would be sitting on £117, whilst the RSD2012/25 merely stayed the same. Mind you, had you spurned the independent record stores and invested in HMV shares, your £100 would be worth precisely zero. Compared with those alternatives, buying records doesn't look like such a bad investment after all.

But the really good news is that if you miss out getting that record you want on the day, (and remember it's always better to support the shop itself, but let's take that as read), the chances are you'll be able to pick up what you want a bit later. Avoid the rush on the internet. It'll all be double the price for a few weeks, and then tends to settle back as buyers dry up and potential sellers realise no-one else really wants that Bathory picture disc. As for it being an investment, well – even if their value dips a bit, it's still the only investment you could have made and still heard Mastodon's cover of Flaming Lips' 'Spoonful Weighs A Ton'.

## Five Essential Vinyl Accessories:

Let's look at some useful accessories for the vinyl enthusiast...

**1. Digital scales to measure the tracking force of your stylus.** These are freely available online for £8. Essential for checking your stylus is tracking at the correct weight, which is usually around

2 grams, (but you can check online for the manufacturer's recommendation). One of the reasons those suitcase-style record players are viewed with such suspicion by some people isn't just the tremendously disappointing sound coming from the poor internal speakers, and it isn't just having to avoid the disapproval of hoards of hifi snobs on the Internet when you post a picture of the thing on Instagram, but rather it's the thought that the weight of the stylus, sometimes well over 5 grams, which cannot be adjusted manually, is going to place unnecessary force on the records you play, and damage them by ploughing a deep, irreparable furrow through the grooves like a particularly large-billed heron digging for sand worms. Groove damage caused by a heavy stylus can transform the magic, velvety tone of Adele's singing voice into rough, harsh sandpaper-like noises rather similar in effect to the difference between Adele singing, and talking. These digital scales will make sure you set the counterbalance correctly, and not have too much, or indeed too little (just as bad), downforce.

**2. A Plastic Bottle (£1) with Atomiser (Spray) capability to fill with Cleaning Fluid for Records (£5-£30), and a Micro-Fibre Cloth (£1).** It is hard to completely agree with those people who say they like hearing crackles and pops as they listen to their records. I mean, sure, there are some records - let's use Westlife as an example - where you would wish to hear far more crackles, to the point where they might completely, say, obliterate the actual record, but on balance, if you listen to Dusty Springfield, you would surely rather hear Dusty's voice unaffected by the background sound of a wet log in a fire unless you can absolutely help it.

You don't need to be a zealot about this. There are some deep feelings of nostalgia in a love of extraneous noise, and there's nothing wrong per se with hearing a record that crackles from time to time, just to remind us we are human. As John Peel put it, "Life has surface noise" and such sentiments are particularly acceptable when the record in question has been rescued from a box marked "Singles: 25 pence each", but it is not something to be specifically targeted. In short, if you can spend a minute cleaning the thing to make it sound better, then why wouldn't you?

Before you go down the route of buying a £400 Okki Nokki record cleaner clean your records by spraying with cleaning fluid and wiping clean with a micro-fibre cloth. Your ears, records and your stylus will all thank you - records don't have to be crackly all the time).

**3. A Super Exstatic carbon fibre and velvet disc cleaning pad/brush (£15).** Once you have cleaned the record, you only then need to brush any new dust off with a brush before playing. I have tried a few brushes over the years. Brushes solely made of carbon fibre bristles are excellent for moving dust on the record one way or another, and collecting it in a neat line. If that is the effect you are looking for, then go no further. It means that all the clicks come thirty three and a third times per minute at regular intervals, rather than at random times all the way through. However, for those of us who set our sights slightly higher, and wish to then remove the dust from the disc, you will need the velvet pad part of the brush to lift this off.

**4. Magic Eraser Sponge (£1).** Not the most obvious addition to the kit bag this one, but a doozy. These are used for keeping your stylus clean. It's a piece of soft putty / plastic material that you lower the stylus onto. The putty then grips the dirt as you lift the stylus off. Do this a few times and your stylus is lovely and clean, picking up every detail in the record rather than sounds being muffled by embedded dust stuck on to the needle. A much cheaper solution than the "dust buster" (£21) solution which does exactly the same job but is sold by specialist hifi suppliers.

**5. Plastic-lined inner sleeves.** There are few things that attract dust and dirt more than records it seems. I could cover myself in glue and bounce through a coal mine while eating crisps with mittens on my hands and end up with less dust and fewer crumbs than the mere act of taking a record from its sleeve and placing it onto a turntable appears to do. It's quite uncanny. As a result, the most observant reader will have noticed much of this paraphernalia is about keeping stuff dust-free. After cleaning your records, nothing says "I'm only doing this half-heartedly" by shoving the clean record back into the original dirty inner sleeve. Keep the old sleeve as it is part of the original package, especially if printed, but buying fresh poly-lined sleeves will allow you to maintain your freshly-cleaned LP in the best possible condition.

And that's it. Let's not make things too complicated. There are many other things that hifi dealers, internet forums and other various experts will tell you are needed to get the most out of your record collection, but it's surely best to spend the money on the records.

## How many is too many records?

There are many answers to this question of course, largely dependent upon whether a) you are a record collector (where the answer tends to be very much of the open-ended variety) or b) their long-suffering partner (where the answer tends to be not quite so open-ended). You should then factor in c) the size of your living space, d) the prohibitive cost and inconvenience of external storage facilities and e) the attitude of your work place to your leaving stacks of records lying around despite their "clear desk" policy.

The collector may begin with honourable intentions. Perhaps they begin with an initial expectation of curating a discrete collection of fifty LPs to while away the cold winter nights. Very soon, they will likely find themselves with a collection that has overshot that initial underestimate many, many times, with few signs of slowing down. The problem appears to be that the more musical and vinyl-related knowledge that is built up, the more opportunity presents itself to vary the soundtrack on those cold winter nights. Then there is the need to ensure the afternoons and mornings in winter have a tune to accompany them, and let's not forget spring, summer and autumn, because who wants to listen to music only at Christmas? (Everyone says they like hearing Christmas carols, but if that were really true, we'd be singing them all year round wouldn't we?)

Then there is something else - the same in-built need, buried somewhere deep inside that propels us to buy clothes only in a sale. That sense of finding a bargain. The feeling that you are winning in a harsh, cruel world where earning and subsequently holding onto every penny is a struggle. Winning by wearing clothes that, by any reasonable definition, are the ones the shop had left over because no-one else wanted them.

'How many is too many?' is maybe the wrong question: a collection of a dozen Ariana Grande picture discs in an eleven year old's bedroom is as valid - and will likely be as prized to the owner - as an attic stuffed with a thousand-strong-none-more-John-Peel LPs.

Do records make you happy? Put it this way: the world's biggest record collection is owned by a guy in South America called Zero Freitas. He has six million records, most of which are stacked haphazardly in boxes in a 25,000-square-foot former candle factory in São Paulo, Brazil. I'm not envious of Mr Freitas' collection. I have seen photos of it, and front and centre was an LP featuring duets between Placido Domingo and John Denver. He is welcome to that one, and if the other 5,999,999 records are of a similar ilk, he's welcome to them.

What's more, how long does he spend listening to his records? With six million records, that's five hundred and thirteen years' worth of music. His "to listen to" pile is 18km high and must be giving him stress headaches (I worked it out - and that's assuming each record is stacked flat on top of each other, which every vinyl-head will know is the best way to warp a record). Every time he listens to a record, he must glance over and get a nagging feeling of being behind schedule. This is not the secret to happiness. Perhaps not surprisingly, he reportedly mostly listens to the radio. If that is what happens when you have the world's biggest collection, count me out...

So if record collecting isn't about quantity, what is it about? Quality?

The Ultimate Judge of everyone's record collection is, alas, the proprietor of your local second-hand-record shop to whom, tradition dictates, those that survive you lug your record collection upon your death - and that esteemed arbiter will confirm their judgement with cold, hard cash. For those of us who might worry about such things, you might want your loved ones to at least be comforted by a not-too-tricky negotiation followed with the crisp feel of fifty pound notes on your passing, rather than a stern look and a further trip to drag your apparently worthless and, frankly embarrassing, collection to the charity shop or local dump.

So, what is the best way to amass an exquisitely chosen collection of vinyl that might actually be worth more than the music that it contains and which makes you happy? Is there a way to enjoy music and also, if not make a profit, at least have an opportunity to recoup some of your hard-earned cash?

We have already established quantity is not a road to happiness. Neither is throwing money at the problem. If a friend has a beautiful record collection but they look like Steve Lamaq after an especially heavy cider-drinking session, clearly skipping meals to fund their collection/addiction, this risks taking the shine off it somehow.

"Give it a few years" you think "and he'll be in hospital with an incurable kidney condition, and all I need to do is slip a few quid to the house clearance company". If you are going to have a great record collection at least have the decency to be in good enough health to bore people with it in person.

If record collecting is going to be a profitable enterprise, the best people to buy records from are those who will sell you stuff cheap. The clueless and the desperate. Sadly, these people are rare in record collecting. It's quite the puzzle, because wherever I go I see swathes of apparently hopeless specimens, and you'd think by the law of averages there'd be one or two lurking about who you could rely upon to sell you a record or two. The comments section of online publications are crammed with barely literate thoughts from people who are quite clearly clueless. Why don't any of these people own large record collections?

Driving around I see people manifestly incompetent. People who pull out at junctions when they shouldn't, or hog middle lanes of motorways. People unable, apparently, to use their indicators. People whose spatial awareness leads them to drive two feet behind a car travelling at seventy miles an hour, but then take up two car parking spaces. Why aren't they at a boot fair selling original Island pressings of Nick Drake's debut for a pound? They're stupid enough, surely?

There are people who jump on crowded trains before letting people off first, conduct conference calls on the quiet carriage on a train, or conversations in a doorway. There are some who stop dead for no reason in the middle of a busy pavement, and who play music on their phones on public transport without headphones. The world is jam-packed with people who are, by any rational measure, idiots. Where are their records for sale?

It's not the fault of the record shop owners. You don't get to be one of the few hundred remaining record shops in the country, surviving recessions, a global financial crisis, offshore VAT loopholes and internet competition by being clueless. The second hand record shop owners of 2020 are the hardy survivors of natural selection - the velociraptors of the prehistoric retail / music industry, having out-lasted the diplodocuses and pteranodons of the record world through their cunning, ferocity and ability to spot a first-press Vertigo label at a hundred paces.

Record collecting is, in its purest form, a contest of knowledge. Like a City Trader in the Thatcher years, every time you go to a new record shop you are looking for a deal, only without your having to wear a striped jacket, obnoxiously drinking champagne. In fact, the shop owner might be tempted to charge you more if he thinks you have a few bob. Given enough money, anyone can go online, buy all the records they want, and sit back like a smug so and so, listening to them all. But where's the fun in that? And who has that sort of money? As Lemmy from Motörhead once sung (probably not about collecting records), "the thrill of the chase is better than the catch".

For those of us who don't bathe in ass's milk more than once a week the best way to build a collection is to buy records for less than they normally sell for, finding arbitrage between what is fair value, and what price the seller wants. We still spend our money, but there is something comforting or even thrilling in knowing we weren't a mug when doing so. Which gets us back to the record shop owners and their exhaustive knowledge of how much their stock is worth, and their determination to extract every last penny of value from it.

Modern day record shopping can be seen as a gladiatorial battle of wits. The task of the record buyer is to spot the chink in the armour of the shop owner. They may have the sort of knowledge of English progressive rock from the late sixties that would win an entire series of *Mastermind* and have prices to reflect that knowledge, but do they know the difference between The Beautiful South's 'Welcome to the Beautiful South' (average price: £9) and The Beautiful South's 'Greatest Hits' (average price £120 because it was released in the nineties when everyone bought CDs and there aren't many of them)?

But do we always want a gladiatorial battle? Why can't we just drop in to a record shop, have a nice chat and a cup of tea, talk about music and records without worrying about what tactics you should deploy in a record shop? How do you stay on the right side of polite in a polarised, angry world? How do you stop a harmless hobby from becoming all-consuming and miserable?

Etiquette in general is a complicated thing. A hundred years ago, if you wanted to blend in to the general throb of your friends at Downton Abbey, you would just need to learn which knife and fork to use, dish out a few withering put downs and find the best way of moving a Turkish diplomat's corpse from one room to another in order to prevent a sex scandal. Life was so much simpler back then. Now technology has introduced new and interesting questions of etiquette: when is it okay to leave a WhatsApp group, for example, or de-friend someone on Facebook?

In a record shop, owners tend to roll their eyes at certain behaviour, so if you want to judge where you stand in their eyes, take the following questionnaire...

Q1.

You are in a record shop and see an interesting record in good condition. You don't know whether it is worth the £25 asking price. Should you:

a) Brazenly take your phone from your pocket, smile at the record shop owner and say "Just checking whether you are trying to rip me off. I know what you're like!"

b) Nonchalantly take a phone and tap or scan in every record you look at, and admonish the store owner should he attempt to charge fifty pence above the lowest available internet price for anything in store.

c) Try to check your phone without being noticed, perhaps pretending to answer a phone call so you can nip outside the shop, and then check the price on Discogs.

d) Buy the record without checking the value on Discogs, and then inwardly massively agonise over whether you have grossly overpaid until you leave and can check.

Q2. You spot a record in a shop that has been on your wants list for four years. It is underpriced, but in a rack that someone else is leafing through slowly. What do you do?

a) Barge the Dithering Leafer out of the way, with a firm "Come on, mate, there are other people in the shop", dig out the coveted LP and hold it aloft, exclaiming with a cackle "Ha! She's mine, all mine!!!"

b) Distract the Dithering Leafer by pointing to the other side of the shop and exclaiming "Wow! Is that a turquoise 'Led Zep 1' for just a tenner?", and grab the coveted LP while they look away.

c) Stand over the D. L. so they can feel your breath on the back of their neck. Tut regularly, and tap your watch, shaking your head and muttering.

d) Stand aside politely, with your heart in your mouth. If you can, stand just close enough to psychologically block other would-be diggers of that particular crate, waiting patiently for the person to finish.

Q3) Follow-up Question: The person in front of you picks up the underpriced record that has been in your wants list for four years. What should you do?

a) Shout "Fire!", set off the shop's alarm, get everyone out of the shop, and then once the confusion dies down, make sure you are first back in the shop to pick up the LP.

b) Immediately say "Ugh! That's such an awful record isn't it? Embarrassing...." Then stare aggressively hard at the person, shaking your head in disgust until they put it back.

c) If they take the record from its sleeve, point out minor imperfections as though they were fatal flaws. Say, "Oof, considering how warped and scratched it is, that's a very toppy price..."

d) Smile, and congratulate the other person for finding it first, saying "I think you have found a real bargain there - well done!" Leave the shop before showing any tears.

Q4. You see a record you want to buy, but want a discount. You strike up a friendly conversation with the store owner, but when you ask for their best price, the store owner rolls their eyes skywards and points out the price sticker. What do you do?

a) Look hugely irritated, pull out your phone and show how a poor condition copy on sale in Greece is going for half the price, (except postage, ignore that) pointing out that should be a fair price for the really nice copy in your hand.

b) Throw the record on the counter, saying "You can keep your stinking records" and flounce out of the shop, shouting abuse.

c) If the shop owner refuses to drop their price sufficiently, stare at them like Paddington Bear, and start writing a furious and nasty trip advisor review in front of them, mouthing words such as "arrogant", "unfriendly" and "rip-off" until they crumble.

d) Find a couple more records you like and see if the shop owner will offer a discount for buying a few at a time.

Q5. You see a well known record that the store owner has completely mispriced. It's a rare first edition worth a hundred pounds on sale for £5. It must be a mistake. What do you do?

a) Take the record, but add it to a small pile of other records you want to buy in the hope that adding it to a pile will draw attention away from it and make it less likely the shop owner will spot his mistake.

b) Double down. Ask for a further discount.

c) Take it to the counter guiltily, and in silence. If the proprietor spots it, try to confuse them by playing dumb. Pretend you are unfamiliar with the album by saying "Not my normal cup of tea, but maybe it's worth a punt, eh...?"

d) Flag the error with the shop keeper in the hope they will thank you and perhaps offer a small discount on items in the future.

Q6. You have no money and no intention of buying anything, but find yourself in a record shop. How should you behave?

a) Monopolise the time of the proprietor by sharing your Patrick Bateman-esque thoughts on the careers of Phil Collins and Huey Lewis & The News while he tries to serve customers who actually want to buy something.

b) Launch into an awkward diatribe to the whole shop about how rap isn't really music.

c) Ask the proprietor to play records on the shop stereo that you already like and own and have no intention of re-purchasing.

d) Go home and do something useful.

Q7. Another customer comes in to the shop to sell a record collection. How should you react?

a) Stand over their shoulder as they go through the records on the counter. Look pained, and tell them in minute detail why their records are actually the sort of records liked by people who don't like music.

b) Wait until the shop owner makes an offer, then say "Is that all? They're worth twice that!"

c) Wait until the shop owner makes an offer, then discreetly gesture to the person that you will offer ten pounds more than the shop owner.

d) View from a distance, and once the person has left, discretely ask the shop owner when the records are likely to go on sale so you can have a proper look.

Q8. You find a rare, but expensive LP in the rack. You can't afford it until next payday. What do you do?

a) Take the record from the alphabetised section, and place it in the "Foreign Soundtracks" section underneath the main area, perhaps hidden in between a gatefold sleeve, in the hope it stays undiscovered for a few weeks.

b) Carefully place the record in between a gatefold sleeve of a record you are going to buy, and feign complete surprise if the shop owner discovers you trying to steal it.

c) Wrap the record in a paper sleeve you have felt-tipped in bold letters DO NOT TOUCH!, and place back in the rack

d) Ask the owner if he will accept a deposit, and put it aside for you.

Q9. You travel to a record shop new to you. All the stock appears dreadfully over-priced. How should you react?

a) Walk up to the counter, and ask furiously "Twelve pounds for a copy of 'No Parlez'? Are you having a chuffing laugh?"

b) Ask the owner in a sarcastic manner "Have you made a mistake on the pricing? Only it looks like you want twelve pounds for a copy of 'No Parlez'? That's a joke, right?"

c) Discreetly take a photo of the copy of 'No Parlez' for £12 and tweet it to @NoParlezClub and @VinylStupidity.

d) Sigh, and keep looking, just in case there is something vaguely of interest, properly priced, somewhere. Later, write a harsh but fair review on Google to warn off fellow crate diggers who might otherwise waste a long trip.

Q10. Another record collector arrives at a record shop at the same time as you. What is the protocol?

a) Wait for them to choose a crate, then go to the one immediately next to them and work slightly faster so, with the exception of that first crate, they are always looking at a crate you have already looked through.

b) Push past them to get to the "New Arrivals" crate first. Only look at crates they haven't seen.

c) Ask a few questions to ascertain whether they are looking for the same type of records as you. Relax a little. Swap Instagram accounts so you can bore each other with posts of your purchases (and make sure they're not misleading you).

d) Politely wave them in front of you, and follow them as you both work your way around the shop. Compliment them when they dig out a particularly interesting record.

How Did You Do?

Mostly As: You're an idiot. You probably film entire gigs from the front of the crowd with an iPad.

Mostly Bs: You're an idiot, and sometimes a thief.

Mostly Cs: You have a nice record collection, but what price your soul? Perhaps dial it down? There may be some overly devious traits in you that are unattractive, and pushing the boundaries of Record Store Etiquette.

Mostly Ds: You are a very nice person, and nicer than me.

If record collecting is not about quantity, and not about quality, what is it about? At this point, we can learn from (where else?) the government of Bhutan.

Bhutan looks rather differently at the world. While the rest of us are slogging our guts out, busy producing and consuming and generally judging our success from a Gross National Product perspective, the Bhutan government looks at a different measure: one of Gross National Happiness. This is measured using an index, measuring nine "domains" including psychological well-being, health, time use, education, cultural diversity and resilience, good governance, community vitality, ecological diversity and resilience, and living standards. That all seems a bit complicated for the simple act of buying a record and filing it on a shelf with others in alphabetical order. But bear with me. I think we can measure Record Happiness with two measures.

1. The Marie Kondo question: of each item in your home ask, does it spark joy? Kondo goes on to suggest if it doesn't, you should get rid of it. Clearly this Kondo person is the arch-enemy of any collector of things, and the idea of getting rid of records is hugely unsettling. You may not wish to go so far, but there's something healthy in asking whether the collection is bringing you joy, and selectively pruning a collection (in order to make room for other things) can be refreshing.

2. Relative value. By dispensing with an overall volume or value measure, we can consider how much the collection is worth in relation to how much we paid for it. The question then becomes whether the records in the collection are the right ones, and did we buy well? Example: why buy a new copy of an old record for £20 if the original is available for £5. Equally, when, if ever, should you pay £30 for an original pressing of a record you could buy new for £20? We examined such matters earlier in the chapters about Bowie, Nick Drake and The Beatles.

And finally, (and most of all) for goodness sake don't be like our friend in Brazil, Mr Zero Freitas, and sit on a big pile of vinyl and not play the things.

Because records are there to be played, and to spark joy.

After all, every record tells a story, don't it?

## … And Finally…

If by some miracle, you have enjoyed the contents of this book and would like to read more (really? Was this not enough?), you may also enjoy the online content found at www.everyrecordtellsastory.com.

There you will find further record-buying exploits and various other unlikely tales featuring your favourite musicians.

Every Record Tells A Story can also be found on social media; Facebook, Twitter (@EveryRecord) and, naturally, Instagram (@Everyrecordtellsastory) for all those braggy record-buying show-off posts…

All that is left for me to do is to thank you for supporting / buying / reading this book and reaching the end without, I hope, sending abusive emails to me.

Steve Carr

# SELECTED BIBLIOGRAPHY

**Blues All Around Me:** B.B.King - The Autobiography by B. B. King
**Deep Blues** by Robert Palmer
**Symptom of the Universe** by Mick Wall
**I Am Ozzy** by Ozzy Osborne and Chris Ayres
**Re-make/Re-model** by Michael Bracewell
**Milton Nascimento and the Clube da Esquina: popular music, politics and fraternity during Brazil's military dictatorship (1964-85)** by Holly L. Holmes (http://hdl.handle.net/2142/97330)
**Freddie Mercury: The Definitive Biography** by Leslie Ann Jones
**Diamond Star Halo** by Tiffany Murray
**The 3rd Mojo Collection**
**Is This The Real Life** by Mark Blake
**Truth and Beauty: The Story Of Pulp** by Mark Sturdy
**Pulp** by Martin Aston
**The Last Party** by John Harris
**The Life Of Aretha Franklin** by David Ritz
**Making Tracks - The Story Of Atlantic Records** by Charlie Gillett
**Sweet Soul Music** by Peter Guralnick
**Respect Yourself: Stax Records and the Soul Explosion** by Robert Gordon
**Staring At Sound: The Story Of Oklahoma's Fabulous Flaming Lips** by Jim DeRogatis
**The White Stripes and the Sound Of Mutant Blues** by Everett True
**No-One Knows: The Queens Of the Stone Age Story** by Joel McIver
**Neil Young** by Johnny Rogan
**Shakey** by Jimmy McDonough
**Waging Heavy Peace** by Neil Young
**Through Gypsy Eyes** by Kathy Etchingham
**Jimi Hendrix: The Man, The Magic, The Truth** by Sharon Lawrence
**God Save The Kinks** by Rob Jovanovic
**You Really Got Me** by Nick Hastead
**Ray Davies: A Complicated Life** by Johnny Rogan
**Kink** by Dave Davies
**Nick Drake: Remembered for a While**, compiled and edited by Carly Cameron and Gabrielle Drake.
**Pigs Might Fly: The Inside Story Of Pink Floyd** by Mark Blake
**Inside Out: A Personal History Of Pink Floyd** by Nick Mason
**Embryo: A Pink Floyd Chronology** by Nick Hodges and Jan Preston
**Syd Barrett & Pink Floyd** by Julian Palacios
**All These Years** by Mark Lewisohn
**Ta-ra-ra-boom-de-ay** by Simon Napier Bell
**A Natural Woman** by Carole King
**Captain Fantastic: Elton John's Stellar Trip Through the '70s** by Tom Doyle

**Young Soul Rebels: The Dexys Midnight Runners Story** by Richard White
**Yeah Yeah Yeah** by Bob Stanley
**Boogie Man** by Charles Shaar Murray
**Moonage Daydream** by Mick Rock and David Bowie
**The Dark Stuff** by Nick Kent
**Mainlines Blood Feasts and Bad Taste** by Lester Bangs
**Stoned/2 Stoned** by Andrew Loog Oldham
**Nankering with The Stones** by James Phelge
**According to the Rolling Stones** by The Rolling Stones
**Stone Alone** by Bill Wyman
**Life** by Keith Richards
**Nick Drake the biography** by Patrick Humphries
**Freak Out The Squares** by Russell Senior
**Crosstown Traffic. Jimi Hendrix and Post War Pop** by Charles Shaar Murray
**Cher: The Unauthorised Biography** by J Randy Taraborrelli

Rolling Stone article "The Mysterious Case of the White Stripes" by David Fricke
Peter Grant: interview in Raw magazine June 1989
Guardian article "Kyuss: Kings Of the Stoner Age" by Dorian Lynskey 25 March 2011 via Rock's
Back Pages
Pink Floyd Ultimate Music Guide (Uncut)
Uncut article "Mercury Rev: Dream Of a Lifetime" by David Stubbs, Uncut, September 2001 via
Rock's Backpages